1946

A True Story of Wealth,
Extraordinary Success and Great Tragedy

Diana Gillmor

Printed in the United States of America

Library of Congress Control Number: 2020908756
ISBN: Softcover   978-1-64908-184-1
    eBook   978-1-64908-183-4

Republished by: PageTurner Press and Media LLC
Publication Date: 05/27/2020

To order copies of this book, contact:

PageTurner Press and Media
Phone: 1-888-447-9651
order@pageturner.us
www.pageturner.us

CONTENTS

Book 1: 1900–1907

Book 2: 1907–1915

Book 3: 1915–1921

Book 4: 1921–1936

Book 5: 1936–1946

for

EDWINA & REG

thank you

Pam, Gil & Dave

Book 1
1900–1907

1900

I remember my first trip to England as if it were yesterday. Although we had already done a great deal of traveling, it had always been in the United States and never on an ocean liner. Because I have always been an adventurous sort of person, the idea of sailing across the ocean was very exciting. In early November 1900 my family and I had arrived in New York. We were Papa, Mummah and my two sisters, Margot and Ebus. Margot was really Laura Marguerite, Ebus was Mabel Elizabeth, and I was simply Edwina. Margot was named for our great-grandmother Laura Berger Spear, and Ebus was named for Papa's sister Mabel. My name was the feminine of Papa's, Edwin Hudson Spear. Mummah was Elizabeth Plumer.

My family has always had a tradition of commemorating important occasions by having our photographs taken. There was even one of me when I was a baby that was taken in San Francisco where I was born. In the picture, I am sitting on a fancy pillow and wrapped in a blanket. Due to this trip being our first abroad, Papa had arranged for us to have our pictures taken, and Mummah had found the loveliest white dresses for each of us to wear. Margot's and Ebus's were of lace and ruffles, and mine was a crisply pressed pinafore over a dress, also with ruffles. In those days, there were all sorts of rules governing women's hair. As

Margot was thirteen and no longer considered a child, she wore hers piled on top of her head, and Mummah had pinned a lovely rose on her shoulder. Ebus, at eleven, was also required to pin her hair up and she had a big silk bow in her curls. I was only eight, so I was still a child; the hair rules of the day dictated that I was not to wear my hair up—that would have been way too grown-up. The front was pulled up and secured with a huge bow, and the rest of my long curls were loose on my shoulders. Whether one wore her hair up or not, it was taboo to cut it, so all the women in my family actually had long hair. Wearing one's hair down was considered too risqué for a grown woman. As for Papa, I remember he looked so handsome in his stiff white collar with his hair was neatly parted in the middle and his elegant moustache. Papa had such a nice face. He always looked so eager and excited, as though he could hardly wait to see what was next and needed to hurry so he wouldn't miss something.

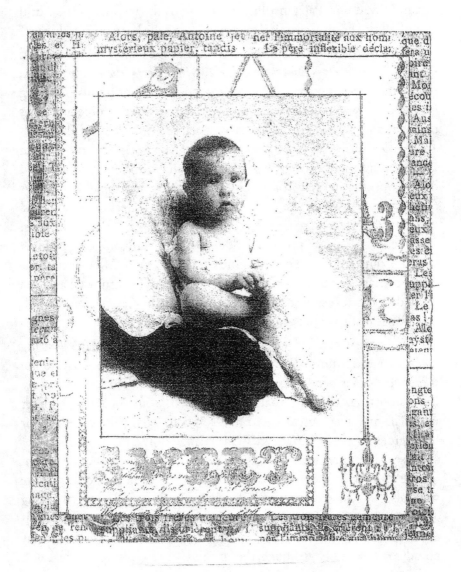

Edwina Spear - SanFrancisco

1893

On the very day of my ninth birthday, Papa hired a carriage to take all of us down to apply for passports. He was so proud as he introduced each of us to the gentleman behind the desk. Papa had told us we were going to start the new century with a great new adventure across the ocean. I loved how Papa instilled in each of us the wonder of the world and of all the exciting possibilities that life might have in store for us.

In those days, the only way to get to Europe was by ship. Papa had secured five first-class tickets on the *Kaiserina Maria Theresa*. It had two masts and three smokestacks and was positively enormous! Arriving on the dock was especially exciting. Great masses of people and piles of boxes and crates were everywhere as large cranes moved things all about. Deliveries seemed to be constantly arriving by horse-drawn vehicles. Papa told us that there were actually two hundred thousand horses working in New York then. There were also a great many dogs on the pier, ship's officers in handsome uniforms checking passengers' tickets and porters carrying mountains of baggage on little handcarts in all directions. Papa said there would be nearly a thousand other people traveling with us, so you can imagine the commotion. After getting out of the carriage, we had to wait for the wagon with our trunks. Papa also needed to locate a steward and find the proper line, so we had to wait a bit. That just gave me more time to look at things and study people.

We were dressed in our best traveling clothes, with Papa wearing his bowler and Mummah in a large, elegant hat with feathers. Although there were other people dressed similarly, most of the passengers were in more casual clothing that seemed worn, constructed of simpler materials and just not as beautiful. I also noticed they carried their belongings in paper boxes tied with string, canvas bags, and smaller suitcases. The burly men who pushed carts around and arranged them for the crane to load onto the ship wore crumpled, baggy clothes. There were also lots of sadly dressed children; they seemed to be working alongside the men. In among the crowd were also a number of well-dressed ladies holding little dogs with fancy collars. They seemed to be afraid for their dogs to touch the ground, as if walking would cause them harm.

Finally Papa handed our tickets to an officer, and he directed us to a dangerous-looking stairway that went up to the top of the ship; our things were taken up behind us. At the top, another officer escorted us to our cabin.

Our suite had a parlor and three bedrooms. Margot and Ebus had a room to themselves, Mummah and I shared another and Papa had his own. There were also two bathrooms. The furniture was dark, heavy, and German-looking, with a patterned carpet in deep colors. There were pictures of what must have been German landscapes on the walls. Each of the beds was against the wall on a sort of paneled platform surrounded by curtains you could close. The windows were small circles, and many of the chairs and chests were secured to the floor. My sisters and I explored every nook and cranny while Mummah and Papa organized our things and put them in drawers and closets.

After Mummah felt we were settled, Papa announced we should take a tour of the ship. It was amazing, especially considering it was on a ship rather than in a house. There was a dark wood grand staircase that led to the public areas of first class, the first of which was a huge dining saloon that had an immense, domed, colored-glass ceiling. It must have added six feet to the height of the room—a very impressive space. The word *saloon* sounded kind of cowboy-like, but that was the term for the dining room of a ship back then. Next we went to the wood-paneled gentlemen's lounge where men smoked. Then we visited the ladies' lounge, where we often had tea in the afternoon. There was also the children's room, where nannies took the little ones, and a burgundy library with leather-paneled walls and a great many gilt-edged books. All that leather made the room smell so wonderful, I wanted to sit right down in one of the comfy velvet chairs and read. You were allowed to borrow the books and take them back to your room, but who wouldn't want to read right there?

Then we all went on deck and stood at the railing to watch all the excitement below. We stayed there as the ship was pushed out into the harbor by tugboats and passed the Statue of Liberty. It was enthralling.

During the voyage, we had almost all our meals in the saloon. At that time, all liners used long tables and chairs bolted to the floor, with seven people on each side, kind of like at a boarding house. It wouldn't be for another ten years that smaller tables and moveable chairs came into fashion. There was also a special grill room in which we sometimes had a meal. It was operated by the Ritz Carlton in Paris. The food there was more exotic. I had my first taste of antelope and roast ox there! Though delicious, it was not all that different from steak and pot roast. Their most interesting entrée was "fresh" seafood accomplished by keeping fish and lobster in tanks onboard that you could actually see as you entered the dining area. I would later learn that our dinner in the grill room cost as much as a single one-way ticket in steerage! After dinner, an orchestra always gave a performance in the music room, during which lots of people danced.

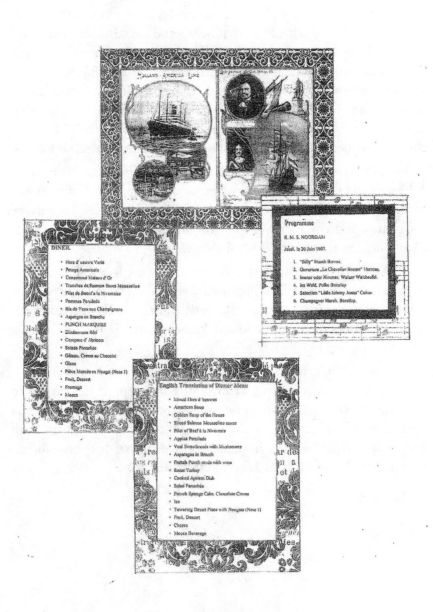

HOLLAND AMERICA LINE

DINER.

- Hors d' oeuvre Varié
- Potage Americain
- Consommé Maison d' Or
- Tranches de Saumon Sauce Mousseline
- Filet de Boeuf à la Nivernaise
- Pommes Persilade
- Ris de Veau aux Champignons
- Asperges en Branche
- PUNCH MARQUISE
- Dindonneau Rôti
- Compote d' Abricots
- Salade Panachée
- Gâteau, Crème au Chocolat
- Glace
- Pièce Montée en Nougat (Note 1)
- Fruit, Dessert
- Fromage
- Mocca

Programme

R. M. S. NOORDAM

Jeudi, le 20 Juin 1907.

1. "Billy" March Borron.
2. Ouverture „La Chevalier Hraton" Herman.
3. Immer oder Nimmer, Walzer Waldteufel.
4. Im Wald, Polka Borstlap.
5. Selection "Little Johnny Jones" Cohan
6. Champagner March. Borstlap.

English Translation of Dinner Menu

- Mixed Hors d' oeuvres
- American Soup
- Golden Soup of the House
- Sliced Salmon Mousseline sauce
- Filet of Beef à la Nivernais
- Apples Persilade
- Veal Sweetbreads with Mushrooms
- Asparagus in Branch
- French Punch made with wine
- Roast Turkey
- Cooked Apricot Dish
- Salad Panachée
- French Sponge Cake, Chocolate Creme
- Ice
- Towering Desert Piece with Nougats (Note 1)
- Fruit, Dessert
- Cheese
- Mocca Beverage

There was a large portrait of Empress Maria Theresa in that room over the fireplace. She had ruled the Holy Roman and Hapsburg Empires in the eighteenth century and her kingdom had included Austria, Hungary and eight other countries. She was a little chubby around the face but had great posture and certainly looked like a formidable woman not to be trifled with. We sometimes had tea in that room too, accompanied by a string quartet. During the voyage, the ship went up and down and side to side a bit, but it didn't seem to bother any of us. We met lots of lovely people during that crossing, many of whom we would encounter on other trips. Actually, traveling the Atlantic became the primary source of my family's dearest friends.

Much later, I learned the passage for the five of us to travel to England represented 45 percent of an average American family's annual income. It was also three times the cost for five to sail in steerage. Of course, as a child I never gave any thought that my life might be different from that of any other little girl.

After arriving in Southampton, we took a carriage to Paddington, St. James, in London where Papa had arranged for us to live in a lovely house on Devonshire Terrace. Mummah hired an English cook and another as housekeeper, and also a French maid. That would be our home for the next two years.

Our first Christmas in England was positively enchanting. I remember Papa arriving with armfuls of gifts wrapped in shiny paper and fancy ribbons. And, of course, we had our first English Christmas, even though the custom of decorating a tree wasn't English at all. Queen Victoria's German husband, Prince Albert, had brought the popular custom of his homeland to Great Britain.

1901

After the Christmas holiday, Papa stayed in London while Mummah took us girls across the English Channel to France. There we boarded a train for Switzerland. We had a lovely compartment all to ourselves, done up in red velvet and polished mahogany with etched glass doors to the corridor. Comfy beds folded out of the wall, and the porter made them up for us at night. We took our meals in a dining car with pretty French chairs, fresh flowers, linen tablecloths and waiters in starched white coats. With beautiful scenery passing constantly by the window, it was spellbinding. I suppose that first magical trip through Europe forever instilled in me a love of the magnificent landscapes of France and Switzerland.

As the school was about three hundred miles east of the French coast, the trip took several days because the train stopped at many little towns along the way. As each station approached, I looked forward to seeing how the village looked and what the people wore. Those we met on the train also added to our adventure as they told us stories about where they were from and the places they'd been. I have always found foreigners interesting because their clothing, mannerisms, and language are often different from our own. I love listening to different accents too. Even when I don't understand a language, I enjoy hearing

11

how the words sound. Actually, I think American English spoken with an accent is so much more beautiful than without. When I was allowed to exit the train at a station, I especially loved the smell of flowers from a nearby field or food cooking in someone's kitchen. The train had to back track a little to reach Geneva, but it hardly mattered if we ever reached school, the trip was so wonderful.

I thought Switzerland was especially romantic. Around every curve was a miniature farm or small village, like its own little kingdom nestled among towering mountains. Now and then, a few black-and-white cows would suddenly pop up in a brilliant green meadow. Sometimes you could even hear the clanging of the bells they wore if the train stopped. Sweeping hillsides also held tiny cabins with wispy smoke streamers drifting from stone chimneys. As the train traveled along the side of a mountain, you could often look out the window on one side of the train and see a deep valley with a sparkling ribbon of river at the bottom, while simultaneously on the other side of the car, towering snowcapped peaks loomed above you. It was like something out of a storybook and would remain wondrous to me as I traveled back and forth to different schools for the next ten years. Mummah enrolled us in so many different schools; I can't remember their names now or even which country they were in. The first was memorable only because it was so different. It was in the little village of Sion in Switzerland, and it was only for girls. Stepping from the train was breathtaking! We were in a valley surrounded by huge snowcapped mountains of gray rock. The deep blue Rhone River was just over the ridge, though I wouldn't know that until later.

All the schools my sisters and I attended were staffed by nuns, so I guess they would be called convents, and were Swiss, French, or Austrian. My parents wanted us to be educated in a broad range of subjects, learn at least one other language and be exposed to the art and culture of Europe. They also wished for us to meet other nice girls and their families and become accustomed to European manners. Margot, as the oldest, would attend school on the continent for only four years, while Ebus and I would spend the majority of the next ten years living outside the United States. All our summers and Christmases were spent at home though, and that was always where Mummah was, most often not in America.

That first year, Mummah stayed a week or so until she felt we were settled and then returned to London. At first it was difficult because all our classes were taught only in French, which we didn't understand. If there is no alternative, one adapts and learns quickly. Our education may seem strict now, but I don't think any of us felt that way.

After five months at school that first year, Mummah came for us, and we returned to England together aboard that lovely train. Though it was only part of the next two years of my life, I really grew to love England. It's so green and lush with the sea all around, though quite damp and foggy for the same reasons. I never minded because the scenery was so beautiful. The cloudy weather actually caused the British to have difficulty keeping flowers in their gardens, which was the very reason they invented those lovely floral "chintz" fabrics, to bring flowers inside those "clouded" rooms. The English are so accustomed to their weather; they never seem to give it a thought. I remember an equestrian friend telling me she had just come in from a ride. When I remarked, "But it's raining!" she countered, "I'm English. If I waited for it to stop raining, I'd never get to ride."

As my sisters and I learned French, we found it fun to babble with our French maid at home and pretend to be discussing very important things that Mummah couldn't understand.

When we returned to England that first summer, the country had a new monarch; Queen Victoria's son King Edward VIII had succeeded her after she died.

1903

By spring we were back in New York. Construction of the city's first underground subway, begun in 1868, was still in progress. We didn't stay long though because Papa wanted to avoid the oppressive summer heat and register several of his inventions in London. They were for money counting machines, like the ones used in turnstiles or in buses. May 1, we sailed back to England. Margot was then fifteen, Ebus thirteen, and I was ten.

After enjoying another English summer, Mummah took the three of us to Dresden, Germany and told us we were going to live in Germany's cultural capital. She rented a charming cottage while we girls headed off to another new school.

Papa had two patents published that October, and we enjoyed our first real German Christmas. No matter where in the world Papa was, he always joined us for Christmas. That holiday is spectacular in Germany. The country is positively magical with thick, soft snow falling all the time, horses wearing bells as they pull sleighs through the white streets of little towns and huge, silent forests all around you. We also greatly enjoyed the German tradition of using real candles on our tree. Papa stood by with a bucket of water just in case things got a little too bright. After the holidays, Papa took the train to the northwestern coast of France and boarded the *Noordam* for New York, while we would live in Dresden for the next two years.

That June, Papa had two more patents published and another in October. He also came home for our second German Christmas.

1905

On October 9, Margot turned eighteen. The following month, Mummah received an invitation from Mrs. Astor to her Winter Ball to be held that December. Mummah immediately decided we would spend Christmas in New York that year.

We took the train to Berlin where Mummah knew the consul general at the American Embassy as we needed passports to leave Germany and cross France. He immediately arranged for our documents, and we boarded another train for Boulogne-sur-Mer and then sailed on the very same ship Papa had just taken to New York.

Although Mrs. Astor was seventy-five, she was still the head of aristocratic society in the city and held elaborate parties for her friends and their families in her Fifth Avenue house. Her Winter Ball was the event of the season and *the* occasion to present your daughter to New York society. Such balls were called cotillions, and the young women were debutantes. To be invited to Mrs. Astor's Winter Ball, you had to have turned eighteen that year and then had to appear in a white evening dress—actually white everything. And unless you received Mrs. Astor's invitation, you were simply not part of upper-crust New York. This was the dividing line between the city's aristocracy and "the others." Principally, it had a lot to do with old money and new money.

Old money was inherited from the hard work of at least three of your family's previous generations. New money was the product of a single generation's labor. The more generations of wealth you had behind you, I suppose the older your money was. Sounds silly, but that was how it worked then. Mrs. Astor had her own rules within those boundaries though, and wealth alone would not get your daughter into her French chateau; she had her list of four hundred. To be part of that list, your family must have demonstrated the desire to preserve traditional New York society, practiced acceptable behavior in public, and should have never done anything to tarnish your family's good name. There were definitely some old-money families of which Mrs. Astor did not approve, however. Uncouth behavior was usually the reason; the original Vanderbilts seemed to have acquired this unfortunate label.

Mrs. Astor had her usual list of four hundred invitees, and there were many theories about how she had arrived at that number. It was said her ballroom couldn't hold more guests. That couldn't be true because the room could actually accommodate two thousand! I also heard she thought there were only four hundred people in New York suitable enough to be included. Though she may have actually said that, the magic number had been decided by her opinionated friend Mr. Ward McAllister. When Mrs. Astor died in 1908, that magic number was abandoned because so many more families had become wealthy. The New York Social Register then came into existence, and everyone's name was printed in the Blue Book. Gradually the qualities Mrs. Astor used to assess acceptability became less discriminating, and today many less than wonderful people appear between those blue covers. Actually, I know a great many very nice people who are not listed. I also find it a little sad when people rush to look up those they have just met to assure themselves that they are from "good" families. It really isn't an assurance of very much anymore, and I feel it is a social standard whose time has passed.

As soon as we returned to New York, we set about shopping for Margot's outfit. That entailed searching for every white dress in the city and finding all those perfect accessories: shoes, gloves, handbag, wrap, and jewelry. It was exhausting, but we had a wonderful time! Margot was a sport and tried on everything we suggested, with some outfits receiving ovations while others received eye rolls and "No, no, no."

Finally we arrived home, quite pleased with ourselves. Margot then put her entire ensemble on and paraded about the parlor. Papa announced he loved everything and declared Margot would certainly be the most beautiful debutante there.

On the appointed evening, Papa appeared in tails, top hat, and a cape as Mummah glided into the parlor in a romantic mauve creation. Mauve is my least favorite color now, but it was very fashionable then. Then my beautiful sister waltzed into the room in her divinely romantic gown, and they all left at seven thirty.

Ebus and I were supposed to be asleep when they returned at nearly two in the morning, but we jumped out of bed and ran to meet them. Papa demonstrated how he escorted my sister down the grand staircase and paraded her around an enormous ballroom before the 397 other guests. Then he put on a very serious face and told us he had personally spoken to every one of them, and they had all agreed…Margot was the most beautiful. Then he announced he was very tired and was going to bed but would grant further interviews in the morning. Mummah and Margot told us about enormous flower arrangements, huge palm trees, thousands of footmen, and a buffet fit for a chateau. Then Mummah said we must all go to bed. That night I dreamed of waltzing in a romantic ball gown with a handsome man … he even had a moustache like Papa's.

At breakfast, Mummah continued with everything she could remember about the evening. She said footmen opened every door, footmen took wraps, and footmen announced your name before you entered a room. Footmen also served champagne from huge silver trays as more of them passed exotic hors d'oeuvres. Then she added that they all wore white powdered wigs and French livery in Mrs. Astor's colors. I immediately thought, *we don't have colors and must choose some.* Of course, I was only thirteen and thought pink would be lovely; they would have looked like officer pigs! Mummah also said a full orchestra played throughout the evening, and after the presentations, everyone danced in the huge ballroom. Everything Gibson Girl was the rage then, and she noted that the prettiest dresses seemed to be in that style. At midnight, there was   a huge buffet served in another enormous room and more champagne. Margot told us she danced with many nice, good-looking young men, some of whom she had met previously.

As I listened, it sounded to me like the evening was a sort of shopping expedition for the bachelors and seemed unfair to the less gorgeous girls—a beauty pageant masquerading as a very expensive party. I would later learn the realities were not at all as I imagined. It was far more important that a young man choose a bride whose father had a great deal of money. Seven years later, Margot would tie the knot with a man she met that very evening, and I'm sure that's exactly what he had in mind.

Sometime after Margot's debut, I learned an amusing story about Mrs. Astor. Until 1887 she had been known as Mrs. William Backhouse Astor Jr. When her husband's mother died that year, she shortened her name to Mrs. Astor. Her nephew thought, as the oldest of the Astor sons, his wife should have the honor of being *the* Mrs. Astor and attempted to persuade his aunt to return to her previous moniker. She flatly refused, however. Even after his grandmother died and he inherited his grandfather's estate and became the titular head of the Astor family, Mrs. Astor continued to pose as the female head of the family. In frustration, he moved his entire household to Great Britain and tore down his father's mansion. In its place he built the thirteen-story German, Romanesque-style Waldorf Hotel. He also made it known that he did so specifically to dwarf his aunt's mansion next door. Mrs. Astor was apparently not pleased to be beside a huge hotel, and a German one at that, and she began calling it a glorified tavern. Then she had her own house torn down and built the larger Astor Hotel in its place. The two hotels eventually merged to create the Waldorf Astoria, but in 1928, the hotel and land were sold to make way for the Empire State Building.

After Christmas, Mummah took us all back to Dresden for another year. Now that Margot was eighteen, Ebus and I would be the only ones attending school while she stayed at home with Mummah.

1907

That was the year my family moved from Chicago to Evanston, Illinois, while I was away at school.

During the ten years I lived at school in Europe, I was not able to go home as often as most of the girls who lived on the continent. As I had no choice, I had to adapt as best I could. I think that experience served to remove me a little from involvement in my own children's lives after I married, even though child rearing of the first half of the twentieth century was more hands-off for wealthy parents anyway. In 1907, for the first time I was the only one in my family in Europe, and at fifteen, I did feel quite distant from them. That feeling would be especially pronounced after October.

One morning in early November, a nun came to my room and said the head mistress would like to see me in her office after I dressed. That was something that had never happened before. I immediately began imagining what awful thing I'd done as I rushed to get my clothes on and hurried down the hall. Finally I was standing at her door. She asked me to come in and sit down; the sit-down part made me even more nervous. But any punishment would have been better than what she had to tell me. She said a letter had arrived from my mother and it contained some upsetting news. I must be brave. Brave?

Then she got a sort of distressed look on her face and said there had been an accident and my father had been seriously injured. The doctor came at once, but there was little he could do because my father was so badly hurt. Then she told me he had died! Papa was dead! How could that be? There must be a mistake! Of course, I didn't say any of that; I was too stunned to say anything. I don't remember very much of what happened in the next few days. I did go home with my friend after her mother came for the two of us.

At her house, I received a letter from Mummah. She wrote that Papa had been at the theatre in Chicago that night. He must have been very tired because he fell asleep on the train home and failed to wake up when it stopped at Evanston. By the time the conductor noticed and woke him, the train had just begun to move. She supposed Papa thought it was going slowly enough that he could still get off. Somehow he got his arm caught in the car handle though and was dragged a little before the train could be stopped. A doctor came immediately, but he was badly injured. She wrote that Papa died before they could get him to the hospital. That was October 26. They took Papa back to Toledo and after the funeral he was buried in the Spear family plot. They were all heartbroken that I wasn't able to be with them, and everyone asked for me, but it couldn't be helped. She said she would come for me early and we'd all be together for Christmas. I couldn't stop trying to remember the last time I'd seen Papa or what we'd said, and now he was gone forever. It was an especially difficult time for me, particularly as my mother and sisters were so far away. I could never have imagined that three decades later Mummah would again be the one to tell me of an even more devastating tragedy.

1907

Book 2
1907–1915

1907

That was the year Ebus would have had her debut. Mrs. Astor did send Mummah an invitation, but it was too soon after Papa's death, and she sent her regrets.

The year 1907 was also important for a man I had not then met and wouldn't for another eight years. Our chance encounter would have a profound effect on my life for thirty-one years. That year, he graduated from the United States Naval Academy in Annapolis, Maryland, with an engineering degree; he was apparently a math wizard as well. He had entered at sixteen and is still the youngest man to ever attend. Later I would learn he had actually failed the entrance physical because of an enlarged heart and supposedly poor physical condition. In spite of that, he was among only 37 percent of his class to graduate. Some of his classmates would die in a diphtheria epidemic that swept through the area, while others succumbed to severe hazing practices at the hands of their fellow cadets. During his four years there, he would also endure many lonely years away from his family, just as I had.

During the Christmas holiday in Evanston, Mummah suggested we should move someplace else and make a new life away from where we had lost Papa. As she already had a great many friends living there, she thought New York might be a good place. It had a lot of cultural things to see and do and traveling abroad would be much easier. After talking it over, we all agreed it was a great idea and even decided Papa would have approved. Mummah began writing to her friends asking where we might set up house. Glowing reports began arriving about a new hotel that had just opened October 1. It was on the south side of Central Park at the corner of Fifth Avenue. They said it was a residential hotel catering to people who often stayed in the city but didn't want the responsibilities associated with owning a house. The hotel provided butlers, maids, and housekeeping as well as personal secretaries and laundry service. Residents could also avail themselves of French-trained chefs for private functions in their apartment, and transportation was always available at the front door. A few royal guests had apparently already taken up residence! My sisters and I thought how wonderful it would be to encounter a king in the elevator. But as we thought more about that, we decided identifying them might be difficult, as most probably they wouldn't be wearing a crown or a sash. Other letters told of a well-appointed lobby, restaurant, lovely furnishings in the apartments and public rooms, as well as lots of well-trained staff and beautiful floral arrangements everywhere.

REGINALD EVERETT GILLMOR

United States Naval Academy

1907

These descriptions only served to encourage us to pack faster until at last we boarded the train for our new life at the Plaza Hotel!

Once in New York, Mummah hired a carriage, and we all excitedly proceeded north to our new address. As we got closer, we couldn't help but see the Plaza's nineteen-story French chateau looming above the surrounding buildings.

Our driver stopped at the entrance, and a uniformed footman helped us down. We found ourselves standing in front of a set of gleaming brass doors flanked by more footmen. Our new home certainly made an outstanding first impression.

Inside, everything was decidedly posh. High ceilings were adorned with gilded squares, and huge marble columns framed the walls. The upholstery was in elegant, deep shades of burgundy, navy, and green. The room was quite large, but small groupings of furniture made the atmosphere very inviting. A number of large chandeliers also gave the space a glittering lightness, and huge Persian rugs nearly covered the marble floors. A number of gigantic flower arrangements and huge palm trees completed the elegant setting. As Mummah spoke with the front desk, Margot, Ebus, and I looked at the hotel's brochures spread out on tables. It appeared that sixteen hundred crystal chandeliers were hanging in the Plaza's rooms, and the hotel's dinner service was "the largest order of gilt china the manufacturer had ever produced." Later, I heard that the first guest to register was wealthy sportsman Alfred Gwynne Vanderbilt. Upon signing the register, he left the checkout date blank. I was hoping our stay would be just as long.

When we first came to the Plaza, the surrounding area was primarily residential and decidedly upper class, centered around the large home of Cornelius Vanderbilt just around the corner on Fifty-Eighth Street. Gradually over the following decades, exclusive retail stores began to displace the large homes.

In very short order, we all decided the Palm Court was our very favorite place in the entire city. We loved having tea among the overhanging trees, the pretty tea sandwiches and pastries that arrived at your table on a little silver cart, and, of course, the divinely romantic violinists that strolled among the tables. The hotel also had a beautiful dining room called the Oak Room and there was also the Oak Bar, reserved for men only.

After we had settled in, we went downstairs one afternoon intending to visit the famous 770-acre Central Park, just across the street. On the train from Evanston, we had imagined little boys in sailor suits guiding their model boats about the lake, afternoons strolling among the trees, explorations of the park's many castles, and even riding on the bridle paths. It was the first public park in America and contained an astonishing thirty- two bridges and even a man-made lake. Four million trees and bushes had also been brought in and arranged to look as if they'd always been there, when it had been only thirty-five years since the park was officially opened. Sheep had even brought in to graze on the meadow for a pastoral effect. Finally, when we were able to ask at the front desk about visiting, we were told all that loveliness had fallen into disrepair. It seemed Central Park was no longer the beautiful place we'd read about and it was strongly suggested that young ladies should seek amusement elsewhere. Looking back now, I remember it wouldn't be restored to its former beauty until the mid-1930s. During the Great Depression, the sheep even had to be removed for fear they might be slaughtered for food. We quickly decided there were so many wonderful things to do and see in New York; Central Park just wouldn't be one of them.

The Plaza Hotel - New York

Mrs. Astor's "Chateau"

1910

The American Museum of Natural History was a place we certainly grew to love. At that time, the public was very interested in the discoveries being made of new animal species and distant cultures. The museum's exhibits displayed things ordinary people could never hope to see otherwise. Many kinds of stuffed wild animals could be viewed in the museum's dioramas, and these were always my favorite things to visit. These room- sized exhibits had amazing backdrops with expertly painted skies, cliffs, prairies and arctic landscapes. They provided the viewer with a glimpse of the displayed animal's natural habitat. Extraordinary lighting effects in these cases contributed greatly to the creation of some breathtaking natural landscapes. The viewer stood at the glass end and could experience the sweeping vista of a desert, deep canyon or frozen snow-covered land from some faraway place. My favorite window featured a pack of wolves running through a snowbound forest. They were gasping for breath, with the leader just inches from the glass. Every time I stood in front of that scene, I was transfixed by the beauty of those animals. There were also a large group of elephants striding down a hall, and because you could stand right next to them, you really felt their size. Dinosaur skeletons that had just recently been discovered were being assembled and regularly added to their own exhibition space. It has always fascinated me how it is possible to assemble a skeleton of an unfamiliar animal from a pile of bones, most likely from many different species, with many fragments even missing. They also might not even know what it was supposed to look like. Years later, I learned people had to be protected from the radioactivity in dinosaur bones. That's why they are painted gray, rather than left as they appeared when they were first cleaned.

The Metropolitan Museum of Art was another place we loved. It was on the west side of the park. We always went to the Furniture and Decorative Arts Galleries. You really learn to appreciate beautiful things when you have the opportunity to see fine examples of superior craftsmanship. Another section we enjoyed was the Medieval Gallery with its great array of armor. I always wondered how men managed to get about in those stiff suits or sit down. If you were knocked off your horse in battle, there would certainly be no hope of standing without assistance, and remounting must have been out of the question; I suppose it was then time to play dead, even if you weren't. Horses wore those heavy suits too. They must have been considerably more muscular than those we are accustomed to seeing now. Waging war seems like a silly wasteful pastime, but history tells us a nobleman's principal activity was attempting to take his neighbor's land.

New York has also always been brimming with all sorts of shops selling beautiful antiques, exquisite jewelry and lovely paintings too. Even if one cannot afford to buy them, it's always fun to look.

In 1907 it was remarkable to see so many automobiles on the streets of New York, even as they were far outnumbered by horse-drawn vehicles. Early cars seemed to mimic the style of an open carriage without the horses in front, rather than focusing very much on the comfort of passengers.

My sisters and I were thrilled with the adventure of New York, but in no time at all, Mummah had us all off to France again. I still had another three years of school, but Margot and Ebus would return to the Plaza with Mummah after delivering me to the nuns. As I watched them leave me that day in Switzerland, I remember feeling especially alone. I suppose those experiences instilled in me an independent spirit; either that or one could choose to be frightfully insecure. I followed in Papa's footsteps and decided to embrace new adventures.

During those years in Europe, I spent some holidays with school friends from several different countries. These visits gave me an appreciation of the food and cultures of other countries in a way I might never have been afforded. I especially remember an Italian friend whose large family welcomed me into their home as if I were another daughter. I still have warm memories of them as my school family. We often enjoyed cooking lessons in their big friendly kitchen. Though that was not the sort of thing usually allowed in upper-class families, we managed to persuade her mother to agree to our proposal by going on about, "What if cook got sick with the plague! Shouldn't we know how to make some basic things?" Cook was lovely and patient and taught us how to make such "survival" foodstuffs as chocolate soufflé and crème brulee. We always enjoyed eating our creations too even though sometimes a soufflé looked more like a misshapen mushroom, they always tasted delicious! Actually, except for those fun afternoons as a young girl, I have never cooked anything. I don't think I could follow even the simplest recipe. In my fifties, I did learn to make coffee though!

It wasn't until my last years at school that I really began to understand what a privileged life I had lived. When it's all you've ever known, it takes awhile for you to look outside your world. Only then did I realize that a great many children didn't have beautiful clothes to wear, a lovely family to look after them, nourishing food, and warm shelter. But privilege doesn't keep tragedy away.

1910

By spring I had finished school for good. I went to Italy with my friend before I was to sail home. Mummah wrote that I could buy a few new things to travel in and celebrate my graduation. It was also the first time I'd be traveling alone. When my friend's family heard that I had been given the opportunity to buy a new outfit, all the women began talking about their favorite shops. Over the next few days, we must have visited dozens of them and even squeezed in some lovely afternoons in the Italian sunshine, laughing and sharing several bottles of wine. I have never forgotten those dear people and cherish the time they allowed me to enjoy in their warm embrace.

With the help of those wonderful women, I bought an elegant tweed suit with a velvet collar and a gorgeous lace blouse. I also had my heart set on a hat to finish my new outfit, and they also helped me choose one. It was a gorgeous velvet creation with a large cabochon rose pinned on the side. It was called a "merry widow", and I adored it! Of course, to commemorate the occasion, I asked them to find me a photographer. I still love that picture of myself as a young woman, just setting out into the world. I must admit though, that hat was probably the largest one in all of Italy.

On May 12, we all piled in the cars and set out for Genoa. I remember standing on the pier in front of the *Princess Anne* as we hugged and kissed a thousand times and I told them how much I loved them all. We promised to keep in touch, but sometimes life gets in the way, and time passes too quickly. I watched from the first-class deck as the ship pulled away and waved until I could no longer see them. It was sad, but my heart was filled with the promise of the future. At that age, lack of experience blinds us to the possibility that misfortune could be just over the horizon.

In 1910, ten years after my first trip abroad, the income of the average American family had only increased $124, just 14 percent of the all US homes had a bathtub, most births occurred at home, only 6 percent of the population even had a high school diploma, and two out of ten adults couldn't read or write! It's startling to see now how far we've come. Furthermore, if you had access to a doctor, there was only a 5 percent chance he'd had any sort of college education! Strangely, 80 percent of American families had at least one full-time household servant though. Most astonishingly of all was that just 230 people were murdered that year, in the entire country.

Edwina

1910

My first Christmas in New York, without the weight of having to return to school, was positively enchanting ... even as it was our first without dear Papa. Living at the Plaza was definitely a huge part of that pleasure, though Christmas in New York is magical anyway. I remember walking around the city noticing everything as if I'd never seen it before. Actually, I decided then and there that is the perfect way to go through life that each experience will never occur again. I also try to treat everyone I meet as special person too. Such an approach ultimately makes one happier and more grateful too.

Shopping in the city during Christmas is especially wonderful as well. Even the anticipation of what you'll see in each new store window is delicious! As you crunch along in the snow, all bundled up in warm clothes, with snow falling against the backdrop of dark buildings, every shop seems like a parade of interesting people you might like to meet. Boughs of evergreens and red ribbons adorn doorways and lampposts, and people are hurrying along, wrapped in wooly scarves and fur hats. Occasionally, carriage horses also pass by wearing bells that jingle, the air is filled with the distinct smell of chestnuts roasting and people are toting treasures they've purchased for loved ones, all wrapped in red and green. Sometimes you can even hear carolers singing the traditional melodies you remember from childhood. It's a fabulous time to be in New York!

To add to the festive atmosphere that year I was to be presented at Mrs. Astor's Winter Ball. Though she had actually died two years earlier, her family was carrying on the tradition as if nothing had changed. This year's mothers and daughters were looking forward to being the stars of the grand ball, even if their hostess had expired. Society must go on! I was also now among the young women of New York looking forward to parading about in white in Mrs. Astor's two-thousand-person ballroom!

Mummah organized a tour of the best shops to ferret out every white evening gown in the city and, yes, it was exhausting. We loved each other's company so and enjoyed every minute. Of course, as I had expected, Margot and Mummah were considerably more into ruffles than Ebus and I, but I tried on everything any of them thought might be even remotely divine. We also got to go to the Palm Court now and then to rest our eyes and feet, and refresh with our minds with a little tea and a few cucumber sandwiches; the violins always made one feel less exhausted. The search seemed interminable, but we finally we agreed on *the one*. We took note of a runner-up in case it was needed; perish the thought of appearing in the same dress in a season! After all that effort, I must admit I don't remember much about my perfect dress. When I finally put everything on together, I did look lovely, delicate, and very white. The right clothes can make almost anyone look wonderful, at least from a distance. Those long white kid gloves that came past your elbow certainly added a tremendous amount of elegance, even if they took all afternoon to get on with all those ten buttons.

As Papa wasn't there, Mrs. Astor arranged for an escort to come for us at the appointed hour. Mr. Harry Winslow arrived precisely at 7:30 and looked quite fetching in tails and a top hat. After brief introductions, we gathered our wraps and headed to the lobby. As we wove our way to the front doors, I noticed people whispering about how lovely Mummah and I looked; I felt like a princess!

As our carriage pulled up to Mrs. Astor's chateau, the scene was like a fairy tale. The night looked especially dark against the golden glow from the chateau's tall, elegant windows and it cast a special sparkle on the snow-covered sidewalks. Two footmen helped us down and escorted us up the front stairs to a pair of gilt French doors. They were held open by two more liveried footmen, all wearing those ridiculous wigs.

Inside, I drank in every detail as if it were a dream I might not remember in the morning. The foyer was a great expanse of white stone, two stories high, with the second floor looking down over balustrades, flanked by life-sized female nudes of marble. The walls were divided by a series of flat columns with very large tapestries hanging between them, and the ceiling held a gigantic colored-glass skylight surrounded by sculptured garlands of fruit and flowers—definitely over the top! It was a room I couldn't possibly have imagined living in. A marble staircase with an elaborate iron railing ornamented with gilt leaves and deep red carpet led to the second floor where an acre of drawing room with more white walls and columns topped with gilded, mirrored panels greeted us. Apparently Mrs. Astor didn't believe in too much of anything as all about this room were a great many pieces of gilt French furniture surmounted with a huge collection of very large porcelains.

An enormous portrait of Mrs. Astor loomed over the fireplace, and though she certainly wasn't beautiful, she did appear proud and powerful. Before going into the ballroom, we strolled into a black and gold dining room filled with more tapestries, columns, and the biggest crystal chandelier I had ever seen, possibly twelve feet across. The ceiling in there was elaborately painted with very, wildly colored flowers. Way too much for my taste. Most astonishing of all were the three hundred chairs precisely placed around an endlessly long, carved dining table. I didn't think I could possibly have remembered the names of that many people in one evening. Meanwhile, the air was perfumed with the scent of millions of flowers; there must have been enough to fill an entire train.

I had barely become accustomed to the visual effects of Mrs. Astor's home when I noticed the lilting music of an orchestra, and Harry and I were ushered into a room where the other couples were gathered, while Mummah was escorted to the ballroom. Hardly any time passed before we were lined up, and the first debutante and her escort were standing in an archway above the grand staircase. When our turn came, we stood in the same doorway, and I remember hearing, "Miss Edwina Spear, daughter of late Edwin Hudson Spear and Mrs. Spear, escorted by Mr. Harry Worthington Winslow." I remember thinking that was an especially nice name Harry's parents had given him as I gathered myself, held my head high, and concentrated on negotiating a huge cascade of steps without some awful mishap. The orchestra must have played suitable presenting music, though I don't remember hearing it. At the bottom of the staircase, Harry led me around the room as though he loved me dearly and wanted everyone to see how beautiful I was; apparently Harry was an old hand at this sort of thing. When all the debs had made their entrance, a lovely waltz was played, and Harry whirled me around the room with the other couples. Then we were free to dance with whomever we wished, look for our friends, or stand around and people watch.

I met many very nice men that evening but never made any attempt to beguile any into considering me as a bride. When Margot was presented five years earlier, I remembered thinking the whole thing was rather silly. But now that I'd had my turn, it seemed to make more sense; turning eighteen was something special. If no young man ever said another word to me that night, it didn't matter. I was officially Miss Edwina Spear, and everything was going to work out fine, no matter what was next.

The huge New York mansions of America's early industrialists were built to mimic the Old World aristocracy of Europe, to create such a class in our new world. The primary function of these Fifth Avenue castles was to impress, and as such, usefulness was subordinated to splendor. In time, the generations that followed these first families found these monuments cold and unsuitable for the task of actual living, a quality for which they had never been designed. Most would eventually be torn down when they no longer attracted even the wealthy.

1911

That year, the young naval officer was twenty-three and had served his country as an Academy instructor and spent four years on several ships. August 9, he was the chief electrical engineer on the pride of the US Navy, its first dreadnaught class battleship, the *Delaware*. She was docked in Boston Harbor, and a special guest was on board supervising the installation of a new navigational device. The visitor was fifty-one- year-old inventor Elmer Ambrose Sperry, and the instrument was his newest invention, the gyrocompass. The device was to undergo a three- hundred-hour test at sea, but as Mr. Sperry was a civilian, he would not be allowed to sail with it. The lieutenant would be responsible for recording the machine's performance. During the trial, he noted how the instrument behaved, made adjustments and suggested possible changes that would improve the instrument's performance. Reading those notes, Mr. Sperry was very impressed with the officer's knowledge of electrical engineering and used the lieutenant's observations to improve his invention. He would also remember the young man when he showed up at Sperry's office the following year. Twenty-seven years apart in age, their meeting that day would be a major event in the lives of both of them. In time, Mr. Sperry would come to believe the young officer would be his successor.

After the sea trials of the gyrocompass, the US Navy ordered six.

During the previous two thousand years, most navigation had been done with the compass, which pointed to Earth's magnetic north. That location can be as much as twenty-two degrees from true north and at sea can mean a difference of hundreds of miles. With the advent of metal ships, magnetism became even more unreliable. When metal gun turrets on the deck of a naval vessel were swung around, their movement tended to encourage the compass needle to swing as well, and the advent of longer- range guns made sighting them accurately very difficult. The introduction of electricity aboard ships further compromised the capability of the compass and using the compass as a navigational aid in submarines was sheer guesswork. Mr. Sperry's gyrocompass didn't rely on magnetism but used electricity to set in motion and maintain a gyroscope. Additionally, Mr. Sperry's invention gave automatic course corrections and latitudes based on the speed of the ship.

By 1911, Mr. Sperry had been working on his invention for fifteen years, though the gyroscope itself was a by-product of an 1852 experiment by Frenchman Jean Foucault used to demonstrate the Earth's rotation. After its discovery, no practical purpose could be found for the gyroscope and for the next sixty years, it languished as merely a child's top. Mr. Sperry's gyrocompass gave Foucault's discovery practical commercial value. In just a few short years, his steamer trunk-sized invention revolutionized the navigation of everything in and under the water and eventually in the air. His genius would also influence how war was waged, transform industries around the world, lead to the development of multitudes of other products, drastically alter transportation, and provide employment for hundreds of thousands of people.

To truly appreciative the inventive mind of Elmer Sperry, it is worth returning to his humble beginnings. He was born in a small Upstate New York community to a mother who died giving birth to him. As his father's job required him to travel, he gave the newborn to his unmarried sister to look after; she would become a kind and loving mother to young Elmer for most of his childhood. As he grew, it quickly became apparent that the child had an insatiable curiosity about how things worked. He studied every piece of machinery he find and then turned to books in his local library. He would spend all his free time studying mechanical diagrams to understand how machinery worked and was assembled, essentially teaching himself engineering. Though he eventually attended Cornell to study engineering, he left after only a year. That day on the *Delaware*, was just sixteen months before he had founded his Sperry Gyroscope Company, but by then Mr. Sperry had already invented many improvements to trains and electric cars. Because he had been unable to obtain financing for his new enterprise, he used his own money. At its founding, his company had no employees and no products. Its only asset was Mr. Sperry's insatiable enthusiasm for inventing products that addressed practical commercial needs and concentrated on problems that, if solved with a new invention, would likely result in financial rewards.

Considering this meager beginning, it is still astonishing to consider that Mr. Sperry would hold over 350 patents during his lifetime. These would include the gyrocompass, firing controls for naval weaponry, the marine stabilizer, the pitch and roll recorder, depth charges, the ballistic compass, the repeater compass, the autopilot, antiaircraft firing controls, night-flying instruments, searchlights for both defense and landing, devices to allow firing through a moving propeller, instruments that allowed a weapon to automatically led a target, the aerial torpedo, the artificial horizon, and the atitude indicator. He also developed new technologies for trolleys, dynamos, and mining equipment. The secretary of the navy would say of Elmer Sperry, "No other American has contributed so much to the progress of the United States Navy." He would also be recognized by his peers with numerous awards long before Thomas Edison received similar honors.

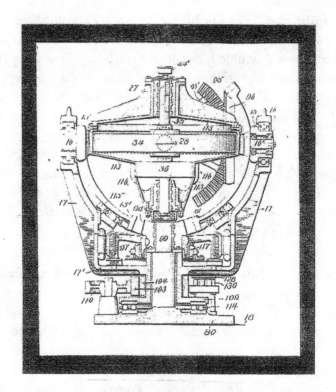

Gyrocompass Patent 1915

First Gyrcompass Test Model

The year 1911 was the same year Glen Curtiss began producing his first "flying boat" in San Diego; it would become the largest-selling aircraft in the country. The US Navy saw the potential of air power, ordered two of these planes, and sent three officers to learn how they worked and to fly them. One of these first navy pilots, Lt. John H. Towers, was a friend of the lieutenant's brother. Later Lt. Towers' own son would meet my son in flight school and they would become lifelong friends. Their sons in turn would also enjoy a close friendship throughout their lives, and live near one another.

In December, Mummah and I received an invitation from Mrs. Alexander Thaw to a New Year's Eve dinner dance in honor of her daughter Katherine. It was to be at her home around the corner from Mrs. Astor. Mummah decided Ebus needed a little more social exposure and requested that my sister attend as my chaperone in her place; chaperones were de rigueur then, at least for proper young ladies. I was then nineteen, and Ebus twenty-two. As Katherine was still seventeen, I supposed this was a practice debut for her.

Though Mrs. Thaw's house was certainly smaller than Mrs. Astor's, I much preferred the more intimate setting. During the evening, I found myself standing with some friends when I happened to hear a conversation about Katherine's uncle having shot the famous architect Stanford White.

When we returned home, I asked Mummah if that could be true, and she immediately responded, "Yes. Five years ago, Mr. Thaw actually killed Mr. White." Then, to my great surprise, she added that he had done so in full view of hundreds of people attending a play at the Roof Garden of Madison Square Garden.

Though I had never met Mr. White, I was quite familiar with his work; he seemed extraordinarily gifted and designed the sort of buildings that used classical proportions and timeless design elements. In New York City alone, he had done the Washington Square Arch in the village, the Metropolitan Club, and the Colony Club, and in Newport, Rhode Island, Rosecliff. I had heard he was very outgoing and had a large circle of friends, but later I also learned he was a connoisseur of teenage girls! His death had actually been the result of one of these liaisons with the then fifteen-year-old model Evelyn Nesbit. Mr. White was forty-six; a three-decade difference of age is still rather unseemly. Miss Nesbit had originally come to New York with her widowed mother to better their financial circumstances. Then she met Mr. White, he fell madly in love with her, at least temporarily, and they spent a year together before parting on friendly terms. I suppose at sixteen, Miss Nesbit was getting too old?

It was then that Katherine's Uncle Harry came into the picture. Mr. White's notoriety and well-known relationship with Miss Nesbit had brought her to Uncle Harry's attention, and he began pursuing her. Eventually, he lured her to a romantic holiday in Europe with her mother as chaperone. Her holiday did not go quite as she'd hoped though. He became enraged after persuading Miss Nesbit to reveal intimate details of her time with Mr. White and then declared he was going to defend her honor. Somehow these chivalrous intentions led him to separate Miss Nesbit from her mother and whisk her off to a secluded castle in Austria. There she was forced to endure several weeks in his company before finally escaping to New York where she immediately sought the comfort of her former lover, Mr. White. Mr. White was apparently not pleased with what she told him and decided to sue Mr. Thaw for violating the teenager; he conveniently forgot about having done so himself three years earlier. Oh well, the past is past!

Ah, but before long, sensible young woman that she was, Miss Nesbit decided to accept Mr. Thaw's proposal of marriage. Then her new husband set out to ruin Mr. White, on the grounds that he had destroyed his wife's reputation. It didn't make all this up, I swear.

The trial of the century began in 1907 with the press capitalizing on every tidbit of information they could get their hands on. Photographers were even allowed to take pictures of Mr. Thaw in his tiny jail cell enjoying an evening meal sent over by his wealthy mother. The table is draped with linen, set with family china, silver and a lovely glass of wine, most probably chosen especially to complement the meal. Immediately behind him is a brass bed outfitted with a down comforter and fluffy pillows. Uncle Harry was even appropriately dressed for the occasion in a starched shirt and snappy bow tie. His trial lasted two months even before the jury began deliberations. Eventually, they were deadlocked with seven believing he was guilty and five not guilty by reason of insanity. Two years later, Mr. Thaw was retried, found guilty, and sent to an asylum and seven years after that, his "devoted" wife divorced him. In 1918, he was finally released but was almost immediately rearrested for kidnapping and assault, and returned to another mental institution.

The morning after Mrs. Thaw's party, we were downstairs having breakfast in the Oak Room. Ebus and I were going on about the previous evening, though she actually seemed much more interested in talking about one Monty Stafford. Margot, meanwhile, kept asking about a Herbert Soames. Mummah wasn't really participating, because she was reading the morning's *New York Times*. Suddenly I noticed something had caught her eye on the society page and she quietly folded the page and handed it to me. I could hardly believe my eyes! With all the people at last night's party, the reporter had chosen to write about Ebus and me. It certainly wasn't in bold print, but I had never seen my name in any newspaper, much less one so important. Two sentences read, "A number of the year's debutantes were present, among them Miss Edwina Spear and her sister Miss Elizabeth Spear, as chaperone."

Wow, I was famous; for a very, very brief moment.

1912

I t had been just nine years since the Wright brothers managed to get a plane aloft for fifty-five seconds, but in early 1912, an aircraft was able to fly from Florida to California and utilized Mr. Sperry's gyrocompass for the first time.

It was also the year Japan gave the United States three thousand cherry trees to symbolize their close friendship. They were planted along the banks of the Potomac River in Washington, DC. Time sometimes radically alters these connections.

In May of that year, Margot became engaged to Herbert Jerome Soames; he was twenty-five and she twenty-four. His father was a graduate of West Point and a decorated colonel in the army. Herbert was born in North Dakota, where his father was stationed at the time. His family was from Sag Harbor on the far eastern end of Long Island, but his parents had moved to Fox Lane in Flushing, Queens, by then. The announcement received huge coverage in the *New York Times*, most probably because of our family's connection with Mrs. Astor.

They were married at St. Mary the Virgin on Forty-Sixth Street Wednesday, April 3. Nowadays people don't usually have weddings on weekdays, but it was quite common then. My sister was given away by Mummah's friend Mr. Peter van Norden and wore a beautiful ivory satin and lace dress with a long veil and train. Mummah pinned orange blossoms on the hem of her dress and train. She wore a small crown of the same flowers on her head as well. During the Victorian era, each flower had a specific meaning, and orange blossoms were a symbol of fertility. Margot also carried a huge bouquet of orchids and lilies of the valley. My sister was beautiful anyway, but she looked breathtaking that day. Ebus and I were her only attendants and wore pale pink and blue dresses with matching hats. Mummah decorated us with flowers too, on our dresses, hats, and on the Directoire canes we carried—yes, canes. Must have been quite the fashion then, but it does seem a little strange now. The church was festooned with white roses and palm trees and smelled like heaven itself. Ebus and I walked up the aisle behind seven small acolytes carrying candles and wearing red robes. As Margot made her entrance up the center aisle, she stopped at the first pew, and Mummah stepped forward to give her away. She wore a gray chiffon dress trimmed with cream lace and a cream and black hat. She looked very elegant.

Just before we entered the church, I prayed Herbert would love and appreciate my dear sister throughout a long and happy life together. I don't think God heard me.

After the ceremony, Mummah hosted a small reception at the Plaza. Herbert had arranged for a four-month honeymoon in Europe and reserved a large suite on the *Carpathia*, which was to sail April 11. At the time, it seemed extravagant, but most probably was arranged to impress Mummah. It would be the most expensive thing my sister ever received from Herbert. Thereafter, what generosity he may have possessed appeared to completely evaporate.

That same year, the British White Star Line announced the maiden voyage of its newest liner, *Titanic*, the largest passenger ship ever built. It was also reportedly the most luxurious, with an indoor squash court, a barbershop, heat, elevators, several libraries, four promenade decks, separate rooms for reading and writing, and electric baths; those actually sounded like something to be avoided. The vessel also boasted four first- class dining rooms and six palatial staterooms with their own promenades. First class accoutrements included lavish paneling and furniture of the Victorian, Renaissance, and Empire periods.

A huge amount of publicity announced that first sailing on both sides of the Atlantic, but only half the tickets ended up being sold. To encourage sales, White Star even resorted to publishing the names of the wealthiest people who had booked staterooms for the voyage. Mrs. Astor's son John Jacob IV and his pregnant wife appeared to be at the top of the list. That struck me as bad form, but maybe he just liked to see his name in print.

During *Titanic*'s sea trials, the period when everything is tested without passengers aboard, the huge ship required 150 feet and over three minutes to come to a complete stop. That would be way too long for what was coming up.

The day finally arrived, and *Titanic* sailed for New York April 10 from Southampton; without the 220 passengers that might have been on the ship's maiden voyage had she been fully booked. Though the ship had more lifeboats than British law required, they could only accommodate half those on board. Prevailing English lifeboat theory of the day dictated that because the *Titanic* was unsinkable, only enough lifeboats would be needed to ferry her passengers to another ship. To further add to the tragedy that was rapidly approaching, the crew had not received any training in evacuation procedures or even how many people to put in each lifeboat.

Four days after leaving Southampton, the ship's captain began receiving warnings about a large field of icebergs that lay ahead off the coast of Newfoundland—seven in all. The nearby *California* even radioed *Titanic* that they had stopped to avoid striking one. The *Titanic*'s captain chose to ignore these warnings, however, and continued on at full speed, not unusual then. This decision might have been influenced by the fact that the owner of the White Star Line, Mr. Ismay, was making the historic crossing, and also that a new record would have brought both the ship and the captain numerous accolades.

The night of April 14, it was cozy and warm inside *Titanic*, and though many people had gone to bed, others were still drinking and playing cards. Outside it was clear, calm, and very cold. As the ship came within 370 miles of Halifax, Nova Scotia, the night watchman saw the barely visible blue mountain and shouted, "Iceberg dead ahead!" The captain immediately ordered the ship to reverse her ninety-eight-ton propellers in an attempt to avoid colliding with the rapidly approaching iceberg. The decision was not only too late, but it also resulted in the loss of all the ship's forward propulsion and rendered her unable to change direction. At 11:30 p.m. she gracefully glided into the iceberg on her starboard side. Many passengers noticed when the engines were shut down, and a few even heard the screech of the iceberg as it scrapped along the side of the hull. Immediately the first five forward "watertight" compartments began to fill with water and within ten minutes, fourteen feet of frigid North Atlantic began to weigh down the front of the ship, even though the doors connecting those spaces were immediately shut to prevent further flooding; *Titanic* had a fatale design flaw that would prove catastrophic though. The architect who had designed the ship was on this maiden voyage and he immediately ran to investigate. Then he rushed to find the captain. He unrolled his construction drawings and showed him that none of the compartments now filling with seawater were sealed at the top; as the ship listed forward, water would continue to spill over the walls and into the next compartment until the weight would draw the ship under… and there was no way to stop this.

Knowing there were not enough lifeboats, perhaps the captain decided not to announce the inevitable, for fear of mass panic and an even uglier situation. He did, however, decide to lock the gates leading below first class. This condemned most of the second- and third-class passengers to almost certain death. Then he ordered the crew to get everyone in the lifeboats. Of course, he didn't really mean everyone. As he gave no order to abandon ship, even those passengers who had arrived on deck wearing their life vests were reluctant to board lifeboats. They might have been thinking, *It's way too cold to practice drills, especially since Titanic is unsinkable.*

Once *Titanic* collided with the iceberg, she had two hours and forty minutes before she would begin the descent to her watery North Atlantic grave, but it was nearly an hour before the first lifeboat was even launched and the sixty-five seats in it, only twenty-eight were occupied. It was also only then that the crew began sending the first of eight distress rockets aloft. In the last hour and forty minutes before she sank, 697 people made it into the remaining lifeboats, with the last leaving just fifteen minutes before the front half of the ship groaned, broke away, and began the plunge to the bottom two miles below.

What terror those clinging to the remaining half of the mammoth liner must have felt as they watched such an unreal thing happen. They themselves had only moments before they met the same horrible fate though.

Those in the lifeboats must have been transfixed as the huge ship disappeared. Then they were alone with the pleas for help from 1,500 of their fellow passengers struggling in the twenty-eight-degree water. When the screams finally ended, there was only silence and the blackness of ocean and sky stretching to the horizon. It is difficult to explain why, with plenty of room in the lifeboats, only thirteen people were pulled to relative safety but the punishment for those seated in the boats was having to watch all those frozen bodies, twice the number huddled in the lifeboats, floating around them for four hours, and so near. I don't suppose you could ever erase memories like that.

Titanic's radio operator sent distress signals until the very last moment, and though the liner *California* was only a few miles away, she wouldn't be coming to help. Just five minutes before the collision, *California* had shut down her radio for the night, standard practice then. Some of those on board California had noticed *Titanic*'s distress flares but assumed they were celebratory fireworks.

The next closest ship was *Carpathia*, fifty-six miles away. Without hesitation, her captain immediately ordered his ship to steam for *Titanic*'s reported position. Everyone onboard must have been hurriedly preparing to welcome and care for a large number of survivors and see a huge disabled vessel, dead in the water. What they would actually see in the early morning darkness must have been a tremendous shock. Though all seven hundred passengers on *Carpathia* were traveling first class, they rose to the challenge and willingly shared their clothes, food, blankets, and beds. Some even gave up their staterooms.

When *Carpathia* finally arrived at *Titanic*'s last known position, it must have been stunning to see just twenty lifeboats with a few hundred survivors and no sign of the famed liner. After taking aboard those they could help, *Carpathia* headed back to New York through rough seas, thunder, lightning, dense fog, and more icebergs.

When we heard *Carpathia* was nearing the city, the three of us set out for the pier. We soon found a great many others had the same idea. Even though it was raining heavily, forty thousand people quietly waited for *Carpathia*'s arrival at 9:30 the night of the eighteenth. We finally spotted Margot and Herbert and all went back to the Plaza. Margot told us how shocking it was to discover *Titanic* gone, so few people in the lifeboats, and the vast field of frozen bodies. She gave away all her warmer clothes to the women and tried to comfort them. She quietly said she saw no reason not to share their large cabin but Herbert wouldn't hear of it and spoke of two little boys whose parents couldn't be found among the rescued. Mr. Ismay was also helped from a lifeboat, but she never saw him again on the trip back to New York. I later learned he tried not to disembark in order to avoid legal action once on America soil.

Over fifteen hundred people died in the sinking; 92 percent were second- and third-class passengers and crewmen. Only 8 percent of those who perished had been in first-class.

After *Carpathia* was restocked, Margot and Herbert set out again, but I couldn't help but think the sinking was a bad omen.

As with many such tragedies, the sinking of *Titanic* produced some major improvements in maritime safety; ship wireless communications were required to operate twenty-four hours a day, an international Morse Code distress signal was instituted, enough lifeboats to accommodate everyone on board were required and crew training in both the loading of passengers and the lowering of lifeboats became mandatory.

That year, the lieutenant studied advanced engineering and naval management at the US Navy's Postgraduate School in California. While there, he also developed an interest in international relations. In the fall, he resigned his commission, joined the Reserves, and went to work in the tiny workshop of Sperry Gyroscope at 18-20 Rose Street in Brooklyn as the company's second employee. After several months of study, he formulated a marketing plan for the company that centered on taking Sperry products abroad. For that reason, he also decided Sperry needed a London office. He and Mr. Sperry both believed it was critical to maintain strict quality standards, so all manufacturing would remain in New York while sales, product demonstration, and servicing would be transferred to London. Mr. Sperry also offered his new director 2 percent of all sales as well as a salary.

1913

In New York, Grand Central Terminal officially opened that
February. The station had taken ten years to build and replaced
Grand Central Station. Four railway companies converged at the
location. In spite of its new name, however, New Yorkers continued
to call it just Grand Central. With later additions, the building would
eventually cover forty-eight acres. In the building's pediment over the
entrance, there were three enormous forty-eight-foot sculptures of the
gods of transportation, travel, and trade. Inside, the 3,400 square foot
lobby was an architectural gem. Tall, elegant windows flooded the
space with sunlight, and a blue, domed ceiling replicated a medieval
map of the stars. The press called it the largest and most beautiful train
station in the world.

February 3, 1913, the United States passed the Sixteenth
Amendment to the Constitution and for the first time in our history,
the federal government was authorized to collect taxes to pay for things
the country needed. The lowest tax rate was 1 percent, but you had to
earn at least

$3,000 a year ($6,600 in 2010 dollars) before that applied. The
highest rate was 7 percent, but that was only for those who made
more than $500,000 ($11,010,700 in 2010 dollars). Over the next

ten years, this tax structure was gradually changed, with those making the least amount of money increasingly paying larger percentages of their income. I suppose that was because those making the laws were our wealthier citizens and they were often in a position to decrease their tax liability and did so. Besides being unfair, I didn't think it made good economic sense. Poorer people pay their taxes from basic-needs money and have nothing left over after buying necessities. The more financially well off pay theirs from money they would have used for luxuries. Often, the more money you acquire, the more you want though. When asked how much more money he wanted, Mr. Rockefeller replied, "Just a little more."

I think the new tax law worried Mummah, and she began saying how much she had loved living in England. Then that changed to announcing we'd lived in New York long enough and it was time to return to the more civilized ways of England. Ebus politely countered that she preferred America, but I think Monty Stafford had a great deal to do with that.

After their lengthy honeymoon, Margot and Herbert went to live in his parents' house. When Margot heard we were moving back to England and that Ebus didn't want to go, she said Ebus could come live with them. Ebus was delighted and immediately accepted. I'm sure her presence was a great comfort to Margot, but it wouldn't be for long.

After six wonderful years at the Plaza, we kissed Margot and Ebus good-bye and sailed for Southampton in late February. Once in London, we settled in at the Stafford Hotel in St. James.

Fate was drawing the then twenty-five-year-old lieutenant closer and on March 29, 1913, he crossed the Atlantic to establish Sperry's new London office on Victoria Street, just a mile and a half from our hotel.

As I would later learn, the director's marketing strategy made use of the long-established European tradition of royals marrying other royals. His first mission was to contact the British officials responsible for defense and make them aware of Sperry products. This was then followed by demonstrations. After establishing personal connections with these men, often members of the royal family, he would ask them for letters of introduction to similarly placed officials in other countries. This often led him to family members of those he had met in England. He would then travel to those countries, present his credentials, and begin the whole process again. But there he would also ask for recommendations of men who might represent Sperry in those countries. These contacts became local representatives for Sperry and were tasked with monitoring their country's military needs and reporting back to the London office. They also received articles about Sperry products written in London that they were to submit to their local trade publications. This strategy proved so successful that within a few months it became necessary to establish a production facility in England. In little more than a decade, Sperry Gyroscope would be the ninth largest company in America with offices in fourteen countries. By November, a little more than seven months after setting up Sperry Gyroscope London, the young director had traveled to and hired representatives in St. Petersburg, Russia, Constantinople in the Ottoman Empire, Milan, Italy, and Paris, France. When I eventually heard about all this, I was astonished that such a young man could accomplish such an amazing feat in so short a time.

Prince Louis of Battenberg

Louis & Edwina Mountbatten

1922

Winston Churchill

In his work the director became friends with many important people in England. They would include First Lord of the Admiralty Winston Churchill. Although Churchill was thirteen years older, they shared a similar interest in naval science and the newly developing field of aviation. Churchill would be the driving force behind the aerial defense of Britain during both the First and Second World Wars, though it did take some years before the country realized the need for such an air corps. Aviation was only in its infancy in 1913 and quite a dangerous activity. Consequently, that must have made it difficult to imagine their usefulness in the face of bullets from the ground and bombs from dirigibles. Churchill's enthusiasm for the future of aviation also led him to take his first flying lessons that year.

Sperry's director also met and befriended fifty-eight-year-old First Sea Lord Prince Louis of Battenberg. Though Austrian by birth, he had become an English citizen at fourteen and would eventually serve forty years in the Royal Navy. Later in 1917 while Germany was bombing England during the First World War, anti-German sentiment among the British public grew so widespread that the king felt compelled to change his family name from the German "Saxe-Coburg and Gotha" to the more English-sounding "Windsor." All the royal family seemed happy to follow suit, but King George V also insisted Prince Battenberg do so. Eventually, he was not only forced to change his hereditary title to marquee and his family name to Mountbatten but also resign his position as first sea lord, which suddenly left him without a job. I thought the king might have done better to remind his people that the prince had been both the commander of the British Atlantic fleet and their director of intelligence. One of the prince's brothers had also married Queen Victoria's daughter, and another brother had married her granddaughter. I was living in England then, and I remember some official outrage about how badly the prince was being treated.

August 13 marked the first time an aircraft used both a Sperry gyrocompass and gyrostabilizer.

During the early part of the twentieth century, New York seemed to be hosting a race to build the tallest building in the city. In 1913, the Woolworth Building set the bar at 792 feet. The rapid pace of construction was constantly changing the title holder though.

During Christmas that year, Ebus became engaged to Monty, officially F. Montague A. Stafford. It was not announced in the *New York Times* because Ebus didn't want all that fuss. My dear sister was twenty-four, and Monty twenty-five. Monty ran a newspaper in Montreal, and though he didn't seem to have much money, Ebus adored him. Mummah and I came from England to help her find a wedding dress and trousseau, and to arrange the wedding and reception.

1914

They were married February 7 at Margot's home; she was seven months pregnant and protocol of the time didn't allow her to be in a wedding; I was my sister's only attendant.

During their life together, Ebus certainly never again enjoyed the luxuries of her childhood. That didn't seem to have any effect on their happiness though. She never gave any indication that living with less was a hardship. My dear sister had always been up to challenging circumstances anyway. I sometimes even thought she might be the most happily married of us all but it was a little sad that they would never have children. As the years passed, it seemed that Monty was becoming increasingly dependent on my sister for even the smallest things. On one of their visits to us, I was talking to Ebus in their room when I noticed a large piece of paper taped inside the lid of his suitcase. She explained that because Monty traveled so often, she had made a list of what he should take, so he wouldn't forget anything.

Though I wouldn't have ever considered doing such a thing for my husband, Ebus seemed pleased she could help him and felt needed. As his dependence increased, I even began to wonder how Monty got on at the office. Perhaps it was Ebus who actually ran the paper? Everyone has good qualities though and a good marriage is based to some extent on appreciating them in your partner. It was truly heartwarming to see how happy Ebus was. She seemed thrilled that she'd found such a wonderful man who wanted to spend the rest of his life with her. That's really what each of us should want in a partner.

March 1, Margot had her only child, John Jerome Soames, while she and Herbert were in Lakewood, New Jersey. Actually, I forget why they were there at that particular time. The area had attracted a number of wealthy, socially connected families and perhaps he was scouting for business opportunities; he could also have simply wanted to keep Margot away from us at the time. Herbert always seemed to have hidden agendas that no one else would have ever thought of.

Sperry's London director received permission from the German government to demonstrate the company's gyrocompass. The Germans, however, wanted to make it a competition with one of their own design. They also insisted on making all the arrangements for the trial themselves. The director agreed and then returned to London. When the local Sperry representative arrived to set up for the test that May, he found the mounting the Germans had provided was unstable and he asked that it be replaced. The German officials in charge refused and demanded the competition proceed as scheduled. The first test damaged both the German and Sperry machines but the Germans promptly replaced theirs. Sperry could not. Then the Germans prevented their gyroscope from spinning as fast as Sperry's. Not surprisingly, the Germans declared themselves the winner. When the London office was notified of the situation, the director immediately returned to Germany to ask for another trial but was told that wouldn't be necessary; their model had clearly proven to be superior. That sort of fear of failure and the resulting wrath of one's leader might very well be a trait that could be problematic for Germany.

The following month, the director arranged another demonstration in France; this one would be in the air. First he wrote a sophisticated, twenty- page paper detailing the problems inherit in controlling an aircraft. Then he detailed an explanation of how Sperry's gyrostabilizer addressed these difficulties.

Today we take for granted that if a pilot takes his hands off the controls, his plane won't immediately plummet to the ground. That's because all aircraft are now equipped with a myriad of Sperry-designed products to maintain their stability. That was not the case in 1914. Early aircraft required the constant attention of the pilot as they were highly susceptible to the ups and downs of air currents. Crashing was always pending, even as the pilot kept his eyes and hands on the controls. In fact, seventy-six pilots died in 1911 trying to master early flight in those fragile constructions of wood and fabric. The treacherous characteristics of early flight would all but be eliminated by Sperry's gyrostabilizer and the many other instruments the company would develop in the coming decades.

For that June demonstration, designed by Mr. Sperry himself, Glenn Curtiss shipped one of his hydro-biplanes to France. Sperry's twenty-one year old son, Lawrence, was to be the pilot of the aircraft and Lawrence's French mechanic Emile Cachin would be beside him in the cockpit as his assistant.

Gyrostabilizer Test - France

1914

The director drove the invited American, British, French, and German attaches to the airfield on the North Bank of the Seine several miles northwest of Paris in Bezons. Representatives from other foreign embassies were already on the field when he arrived, as were delegations from the Aero Club of France, the Pathe and Gaumont news services, and various representatives of the press. Mr. Sperry and his entire family were there as well.

At four in the afternoon, Lawrence and Emile took off and headed for Paris. When they reached the city, Lawrence turned the plane back toward the crowd. Then he stood up in his seat and put his heads over his head as Emile climbed out onto the plane's lower wing six feet. With clearly no one at the controls, the aircraft maintained the position in which Lawrence had left it. The crowd gathered below could also clearly see the trailing edge of each wing automatically adjusting up and down. Both men then returned to their seats, and Lawrence headed back to Paris. When he turned toward the airfield again, he stood up and put his hands above his head, and this time Emile crawled out toward the propeller as far as possible. The plane again maintained its position. The next day, the demonstration was repeated, but this time the aircraft was set at a forty- five-degree angle. There were no problems because the gyrostabilizer did all the flying. This single invention represented a major leap forward in the quest to master flight.

Just ten days later in the streets of Sarajevo, Serbia, the Archduke Franz Ferdinand and his wife were shot and killed by a disgruntled Serbian assassin as they passed through the streets in an open carriage. The archduke was the Austrian administrator of the country that was then composed of Bosnians, Croats, Slavs, and a small minority of Serbians. The Serbs resented Austrian control of their land. The perpetrator was promptly arrested, but the Austro-Hungarian government demanded that Serbia apologize. As they had no part in the plot, they refused. The Austro-Hungarians then began mobilizing their army to attack Serbia, who responded by assembling their own troops. These were the opening actions that precipitated the start of the First World War on July 28, 1914. Other countries had signed treaties to defend their allies in the event that they might be attacked. Russia declared war to protect Serbia, and Germany joined in to defend the Austro-Hungarians. Then Germany also declared war on Russia and invaded Luxembourg. Germans need only minor slights to join a fight or start one. While their army was marching in that direction, they decided to attack France and then, why not take Belgium "while we're here." Britain had sworn to defend Belgium, so they felt forced to declare war on Germany and send troops to aid their French allies. Then tiny five-thousand-square-mile Montenegro declared war on the huge Austro-Hungarian Empire, and Germany decided it also wanted to fight the Austro-Hungarians, even though they had just recently been on their side. Meanwhile, England announced they were against the Austro-Hungarians too. What a mess. But wait, over in the Pacific, Japan declared war on both the Germans and the Austro-Hungarians. Granted this is extremely simplified but all the same, still true. It does make war look like a bunch of boys declaring. "I'll show you!" Irresponsible leadership, unwise foreign policy decisions, and the desire for more land and power are usually the reasons nations engage in war. And it ends when everybody gets tired or defeat is in the headlights.

During the beginning months of the Great War, Germany seemed to have the upper hand, but by fall Britain had captured a German codebook used between their warships, U-boats, merchant vessels and Zeppelins; it's not good when you don't realize your enemy knows your codes. Then Britain set up a naval blockade to starve Germany of supplies. Germany responded by announcing it would torpedo any ship flying a British flag or the flag of an ally, warship or not. Apparently, up until this time, the rules of sea battles stated that an attacking ship must allow those on board its target to escape into lifeboats before it blew up the offending vessel; difficult today to believe things actually happened that way. After this declaration by Germany, Churchill instituted his Ram Rules. They mandated that if a U-boat surfaced to allow British seamen to escape death by torpedo, the British ship was required to ram the U-boat. Newspapers quoted him as saying, "The submerged U-boat had to then rely on underwater attack, and risk sinking neutral ships, drowning neutral people and embroiling Germany with other powers." This certainly made it seem like Churchill was not familiar with the very reason submarines were invented in the first place. He also announced that all merchant ships and liners entering British waters would henceforth receive escorts to thwart these U-boat attacks.

He would, however, make special exceptions, including a famous one the following year.

Among the warring nations involved in what is now called the First World War, each had its strengths and weaknesses. Germany had a large professional army always at the ready, and as an industrial nation, it was able to provide them with arms. The Austro-Hungarians had a sad history of military ineptitude, but that didn't seem to impede their desire to wage war. France had few able-bodied men from which to muster an army, and though Russia had a limitless supply of men, the vast majority of them had no military training. Furthermore, the country was not industrialized and needed an ally to provide supplies. The country's land mass was also huge, including both inhospitable terrain and weather, and their rail system was woefully erratic. Consequently, the transport of men and equipment would be arduous and extremely problematic—a considerable number of negatives. Great Britain had traditionally been a world sea power, but as a small nation, it was limited in the number of men from which to draw an army. The country's strict class system also gave them a distinct disadvantage, though I don't think they anticipated that as a problem at the outset. Because Britain had no middle class, troops had to come from the lower class. Though willing, these men had subsisted on such meager foodstuffs for such a long period of time, fully 40 percent of those who volunteered were found physically unfit. Great Britain could initially only muster 160,000 men at the start of World War I while simultaneously Germany had a million soldiers on the front lines alone.

Sperry's demonstrations in France that June proved very effective. By early December, the London office received seventy-five orders for gyrocompass systems, totaling 84 percent of the total value of the company itself!

As Mummah and I read the war reports in the newspapers, our presence in London began to seem a little too close to the fighting on the continent. The English Channel is just twenty miles wide, and London is a mere seventy-five miles further inland. December 16, the Germans bombed England from a huge fleet of ships sitting just off the coast. Eleven hundred shells were dispatched and over 130 people were killed.

1915

January 20, two German Zeppelins bombed an area just a hundred miles from London. After Mummah heard this, she announced we were leaving for the States, and the next morning we went to the American embassy for emergency passports. Two days later, we left for New York on the *Baltic*.

Once the ship got underway, I noticed two attractive men who seemed to be traveling together. One had a moustache, and the other an interesting accent; I later learned it was Spanish. As is often the case on board a liner, the captain asked us to join him for dinner one night and we met him at the entrance to the dining room. Just as he was telling us that he had also invited some other passengers to join him, those same two men appeared beside the captain and he introduced our dinner companions; the two men I had noticed previously. Count Leonardo Casanova was traveling with his friend Reginald Gillmor, the man with the moustache and the director of Sperry Gyroscope London! During dinner, the count told us he had a lot of other names but to please call him Leonardo. Mr. Gillmor said he had always been Reg. The captain kindly seated one on either side of me. Reg told us he was from Menomonee, Wisconsin, though his parents then lived in Red Oak, Iowa. Leonardo was a Castilian from Northern Spain near

Madrid but had immigrated with his older brother, Telesforo, and both of them now lived in England. Their parents had also left Spain and were then living in Argentina. During the voyage I would also learn that Leonardo was just seventeen. That really surprised me, as he seemed so polished and at ease. Eventually, he would join Sperry as director of public relations.

Well, what a most fortunate evening! Though, then I couldn't possibly have known the parts these two men would play in my life, they would be enormous. We had a wonderful time talking about interesting things and our travels, and we got on famously! During the voyage, we would often encounter them on deck and always asked them to join us. Their company felt so natural and relaxed, as if we'd all known each other   a long time. January 27, we even had a party to celebrate Leonardo's eighteenth birthday, and shared toasts to the future, good things, and   a long friendship. Our meeting on the *Baltic* that year would have far- reaching happy consequences for our lives, but eventually lead to great sadness.

Once we were settled in at the Plaza again, Mummah and I began entertaining and happily, Reg and Leonardo were often among our guests. Though one or the other of them was often away in London, we were always delighted to see either. Over time, I noticed that though Leonardo didn't have a job, he always wore beautiful, well-tailored clothes, dined at expensive restaurants, and often went to the theatre. He also had a natural, uncontrived way of making a woman, any woman, feel beautiful. I suppose he didn't have the name Casanova for nothing.

That February, Germany declared the seas around the British Isles a war zone and began attacking merchant ships without warning.

The business of flying an airplane was so rudimentary then that they were not being used in Britain for bombing. The Germans, however, had mobilized an air corps of dirigibles for that very purpose. They called them Zeppelins with a capital Z to honor their countryman Count von Zeppelin who had become famous operating a fleet of Zeppelins that carried mail and passengers all over Germany from 1900 to 1910. During the company's first three years, he had made an astonishing 1,900 flights and had transported 35,000 passengers, so I suppose he was a sort of celebrity.

In March, Great Britain obtained the luggage of a German spy in which was found yet another German codebook to add to the country's growing library.

By 1915, the British passenger ship *Lusitania* had been sailing between New York and England for eight years. When Churchill issued his Ram Rules, the then captain of the vessel resigned, saying he was no longer willing "to carry the responsibility of mixing passengers with munitions and contraband." Two replacements followed him, and by May 1915, *Lusitania*'s fourth captain had only been at his post six weeks. May 1, his ship was docked in New York and taking on cargo.

Some time prior to that crossing, Churchill had requested a report on "the consequences of a passenger liner being sunk by Germany that resulted in the loss of American lives." Certainly an odd exercise if you were not contemplating such a thing? At that point in the war, Churchill was convinced that Germany would soon control all of Europe, and England, if the United States didn't join the Allies. Sometime after he received his report, he met with President Wilson and discussed England's desperate need for war materials. He must have been very convincing because the president agreed to allow the *Lusitania* to carry such needed cargo on this very voyage, a clear violation of US law.

Among the longshoremen on the dock loading *Lusitania* were German sympathizers on the lookout for contraband heading to Britain. It was inevitable that they would discover an "irregular" shipment; some heavy crates labeled as butter that was not traveling under refrigeration. Further investigation revealed the crates contained ordinance and weapons. The cargo manifest was brought to the attention of the German ambassador, who decided the public needed to be reminded that a war was going on. He placed advertisements in every East Coast newspaper stating the danger in crossing the Atlantic at that time, but someone alerted the State Department to their pending publication, and they were blocked. When the German embassy learned of this, the ambassador met with Secretary of State William Jennings Bryant and showed him the manifest; Bryant then authorized the release of these communiques. Someone even higher up, however, overruled him. Just a single banner slipped through and was printed in the Des Moines, Iowa, *Register*:

NOTICE! TRAVELERS intending to embark on the Atlantic voyage are reminded that a state of war exists between Germany and her allies and Great Britain and her allies; that the zone of war includes the waters adjacent to the British Isles; that, in accordance with formal notice given by the Imperial German Government, vessels flying the flag of Great Britain, or her allies, are liable to destruction in those waters and that travelers sailing in the war zone on ships of Great Britain or her allies do so at their own risk. IMPERIAL GERMAN EMBASSY WASHINGTON, D.C. April 22, 1915.

The *Lusitania* sailed as scheduled, and five days later, well before she was scheduled to arrive in Great Britain, King George V held a meeting with British High Command during which he asked, "Suppose they sink the *Lusitania* with Americans on board?" Because England possessed all the relevant German codebooks, everyone in the room not only knew that German U-boats were in that area, but they even knew which ones were closest to *Lusitania*.

When the liner reached British territorial waters, the captain slowed his ship to wait for his British escort. It was nowhere in sight; that was because Churchill had ordered it back to port. At 2:30 on the afternoon of May 7, a German U-boat fired a single torpedo directly at *Lusitania*. She was a virtual sitting duck. In his log, the captain described the explosion as "like a heavy door was being slammed shut." Then he wrote that a second explosion was "much larger and rocked the ship ... an unusually heavy detonation." I guess ninety tons of "butter" would make for a very big explosion. The ship sank in just eighteen minutes with the loss of eleven hundred lives.

The sinking of *Lusitania* was thought to be a pivotal moment that turned the world against Germany. It did not, however, convince the United States to join the war. That would take another two years.

Many years after the sinking, Churchill was interviewed about Britain's role in the event, and he was quoted as saying, "There are many maneuvers in war ... the maneuver which brings an ally into the field is as serviceable as that which wins a battle."

I was really shocked!

In late May, Reg had a private meeting with Mummah of which I was not aware. He had wanted her blessing to ask me to marry him.

70

Afterward, she told me she could barely keep silent. One afternoon sometime later, I was reading in the drawing room when I heard someone at the front door. Then suddenly Reg was standing in the doorway. I was delighted to see him but also surprised. He asked if he might come in and proceeded to pull a chair to sit across from me. Then he began talking about how very pleased he was to have met me and my family and how much he had grown to care about me in particular. He proceeded to take a small black box from his pocket and, without opening it, told me how much he'd grown to love me very much and couldn't imagine a life without me. Then he said it would make him very happy if I would agree to be his wife, and opened the little box. Inside was a beautiful ring made of diamonds and sapphires! I dropped my book as I stood up, looked into his beautiful blue eyes, and said, "Yes, yes!"

Book 3
1915–1921

1915

Of course, that immediately launched Mummah into wedding mode!

Now, brides and their mothers spending a considerable amount of time making the perfect arrangements and attending to every detail, but then, it was just a couple of weeks. The first thing was the dress, but Mummah insisted I also needed appropriate clothes for every English occasion, as well. She said it was especially important because I would be representing my husband's company, and an American one at that. That meant everything to complement each ensemble; shoes, gloves, handbags and, of course, hats! You cannot imagine how many shops we visited. It was great fun but definitely exhausting. Our excursions always ended at the Palm Court with those lovely relaxing violins.

I tried on several beautiful wedding dresses and rather quickly settled on one we both loved. It was a very ethereal, white tulle creation with a small train. I chose a simple veil of the same material which was held on my head by a thin circle of small pearl orange blossoms. It was very elegant and romantic without being sugary—perfect for who I was. We also selected a shower bouquet of white roses, with orchids and lilies of the valley for me to carry. As my attendants, Margot and Ebus would wear tea-length dresses of pale pink and light blue; those were very fashionable colors then. May 23, my engagement was announced in the *New York Times*: "Mrs. Edwin Hudson Spear of New York announces the engagement of her daughter Miss Edwina Spear to Reginald Everett Gillmor of London, England and formerly of the U.S. Navy."

The war in Europe had suddenly taken on a more personal dimension and it seemed the Germans were stepping up their bombing campaign on Britain. Alarmingly, the English didn't seem to have any sort of defense plan in place either. German Zeppelins were cruising all about the countryside with impunity and the public was apparently getting very upset. The government finally decided to address the problem though oddly their solution was to limit all statements about the raids to only those provided by them! I suppose they thought, with the proper wording, their countrymen could be convinced the situation wasn't really that bad. Some people were not persuaded, however, and anti-German mobs even began attacking shops believed to be owned by people of German descent. Back in New York, two weeks after our engagement announcement, we were again featured on the society page June 6:

> The wedding of Miss Edwina Spear, daughter of Mrs. Edwin Hudson Spear of New York to Reginald Everett Gillmor, formerly of the United States Navy, will be celebrated at four thirty o'clock on Wednesday afternoon in St. George's Church, Flushing, L.I. The Rev. Dr. Winthrop Peabody will officiate. The bride will be attended by her sisters, Mrs. H. Jerome Soames Jr. and Mrs. F. Montague A. Stafford, who will be matrons of honor. Lieutenant Aubrey W. Finch, Commander of the Yankton, will act as best man, and ushers are: Lieutenant Charles Pousland, U.S.N., Lieutenant Renssalar W. Clark, U.S.N., Lieutenant Frank Crosby, U.S.N., Lieutenant Andrew Fletcher, U.S.N., Lieutenant George McCourts, U.S.N. and Lieutenant Allan S. Farquhar, U.S.N. Following the ceremony a small reception will be held at the home of Mrs. Soames, the bride's sister, in Flushing.

Aubrey had graduated from the Naval Academy the year before Reg and would eventually be appointed superintendent there in 1945. Later he became an admiral. Allan had graduated a year after Reg.

It was a small, intimate ceremony in a lovely church built in 1702. We had a beautiful small reception with a light buffet afterward, also at Margot's. It was especially wonderful to have all the Spear women together again. Leonardo was also among our guests.

Albert Einstein published his famous theory of relativity that year. He would receive the Nobel Prize for this work six years later in 1921.

Back in England, soon to be our home, bombings by German airship continued. The only deterrent appeared to be the famous English fog.

Five days after our marriage, I applied for a new passport as Mrs. Reginald E. Gillmor. In those days, a proper married woman would never have used her given name in print; that would change but very slowly. It was sad that we were only recognized as our husband's wife.

Mrs. Reginald Everett Gillmor

1915

Two weeks later, even though it had only been a month since the sinking of *Lusitania*, and England had endured eleven bombing raids by then, we eagerly boarded the *St. Louis* for the trip to our new home. In an attempt to avoid a U-boat attack, the ship constantly changed direction, so the voyage took eighteen days. But it was our honeymoon, so we just enjoyed the time together. It was during the trip that Reg told me about the house he had found us. It was in a lovely out-of-the-way village called Cobham in Surrey, twenty miles southwest of London; the house was actually called Heddingly. He said on first seeing the property, he immediately decided it was perfect because the house was surrounded by rose bushes, and he remembered how much I loved flowers. Further descriptions made it sound like something out of a storybook.

We arrived in Liverpool on July 8, and Leonardo was there with a car to take us to Cobham. As we drove toward our new life, the landscape that swept by the window grew more and more beautiful. When we finally turned up the drive and the house appeared around a bend, I could hardly believe my eyes. It was right out of an English country novel with roses blooming all around a clipped lawn and carefully manicured borders. Actually, both the style of the house and its setting greatly reminded me of Long Island and its weathered cedar buildings trimmed in white. A huge covered porch spanned nearly the entire back and looked out on a velvety, emerald lawn surrounded by more rose bushes. Leonardo walked about the grounds with us a bit, then excused himself and returned to London. Inside, the house was furnished with old British things in just the sort of style I loved and would have chosen myself. My new husband was turning out to be a genius in ways I would never have imagined. Conscious that I was quite unaccustomed to keeping house, he had also thoughtfully engaged a cook, housekeeper, and maid to look after us.

In a very short time, we were happily settled in our beautiful new home and had established a regular routine. Reg's driver would come for him in the morning and return him in the evening. If we had an evening engagement, the car would come for me later in the day and return us home together. Occasionally I would also go up to London to visit friends, have lunch, shop, or stop by Sperry. We often entertained, and I enjoyed meeting Reg's friends and their wives. Having lived in

England before, I was more familiar with British customs than Reg so I was delighted when one of my suggestions led to tea being served in the afternoon at Sperry. Mr. Sperry was visiting one day and seemed delighted with the new arrangement. We mingled easily with Reg's business associates and were invited to stay at some lovely country estates. We began to forge a wonderful life together, and thanks to Mummah, I had just the right outfit and hat for every occasion!

Heddingley - Cobham - England

1915

After attending a number of social functions with Reg, I became aware of some attitudes among a few aristocrats that I found disturbing. I was hearing things like "the many years of peace and prosperity England had enjoyed had led to a certain national decay", and to put things right, England needed "the adventure in terror and danger of war", even "the splendor" of it! I also discovered that many upper-class men believed war would "shake the country awake and induce some much-needed discipline, sacrifice, and endurance," and "bring the country together." I found one remark especially upsetting: "fighting in a war would disinfect the stagnant pool with its red stream of blood!" Of course, I kept quiet, but I wanted to say, "Are you kidding!" Strangely, I never heard these same men mention kill, slaughter, or maim when they were holding forth on these war pronouncements. My overall impression was that they thought war would get ordinary citizenry "back in line." These ideas were not only espoused by the landed gentry but also appeared in print from a few writers like H. G. Wells. After seeing firsthand the extremely demanding and relentless lives of British servants, I felt certain they'd be outraged to hear how their employers viewed their endless hours, poor diets, and lack of normal freedoms. As these former servants returned home from war though, they brought with them very different ideas about how they wanted to spend their lives, and most often that did not include working on a large estate. Instead, they had dreams of owning their own business, marrying, and having children, things not possible as servants of the wealthy. The new ambitions of these people, more than anything else, led to the collapse of many country estates as there were simply not enough servants to run them. England would be forever changed by the Great War but in ways it had probably not anticipated.

During the three years we lived in England, I met many of the friends Reg had made before our marriage; some might have familiar names. It was at a formal dinner party that I was first introduced to Winston Churchill and his wife, Clementine but by then, he'd been replaced as First Lord of the Admiralty. From Reg, I knew Churchill was very keen on the use of aircraft for defense, but as I listened to him talking with Reg, I began to see the nature of the British government's objections to investing in the development of a flying corp. They viewed the usefulness of aircraft as primarily for reconnaissance and the monitoring of ship traffic. Some officers were even hostile about using them at all. Prevailing views among the public centered on them being only for acrobatic displays or as the hobby of rich men. The English are very traditional and quite stubborn about accepting new things. German Zeppelin bombing would force them to reconsider some of those notions.

When I first met Clementine, she and Winston had been married seven years and had four children. I liked her very much even before I learned she spoke French and had attended some of the same schools I had. From then on, we always used French with one another. I found Clementine both intelligent and strong, but I suppose one had to be, married to a politician. I remember a story she told me about traveling on a private yacht without her husband. A group of ladies, including her hostess, were listening to a radio broadcast in the salon when the commentator made some derogatory remarks about Winston. This was followed by loud agreement from the hostess. When the woman didn't apologize, Clementine said she promptly went to her cabin, packed her things, and left the ship. I admired her determination, though I don't think I could have mustered the courage to do such a thing. During the years we lived in England, I often met her oldest child, Diana. I had such lovely memories of her that when my son would have a daughter, I convinced them to name her Diana.

On another occasion, I met First Sea Lord Prince Louis of Battenberg and his beautiful wife, Princess Victoria. We had been invited for a weekend stay at their Isle of Wight home Kent House. He was very handsome even at sixty-one and I was delighted to find he spoke beautiful French as well. He said it was the language he and his mother had spoken together, even though she was from Poland. During that same visit, Reg and I also met their lovely twenty-six-year-old daughter, Princess Louise. She was quite charming, but you had to be sure to face her during a conversation, as she was very hard of hearing. The prince's two sons also joined their parents that weekend. Prince George was only three days older than I, and Prince Louis then just fifteen. Reg especially enjoyed George, as he was quite the mathematician and read calculus books for pleasure! The following year when he married the Countess Nadejda de Torby, granddaughter of Czar Nicholas I, he graciously invited us to the wedding. In 1922, the younger Prince

Louis, by then Lord Louis Mountbatten, married Miss Edwina Ashley, and he also invited us to his wedding at St. Margaret's in Westminster. Before their marriage, she had inherited her financier grandfather's large estate. Most fortunate, as young Louis was practically penniless by then. Louis's childhood friend, the future King Edward VIII, was his best man, and many of the royal family attended the wedding. It was all quite spectacular. The newlyweds took an extended honeymoon in America, and we spent some time with them when they were in New York. She was very young at that time and seemed rather frivolous. She also had a habit of lavishing a little too much attention on the men present and positively set upon Leonardo. Many years after first meeting her, my son happened to be in England and stopped by their home to say hello. Though they hadn't seen each other since he was four, Louis and Edwina very graciously insisted he stay with them. Lord Louis's sister Princess Louise ultimately married Prince Gustaf of Sweden at St. James Palace the year after her brother was married. I especially remember all the festivities in their honor, as it was just six days before my thirty-first birthday. We had a wonderful time, made some new friends, and were able to catch up with old ones. The charming couple would later become the king and queen of Sweden.

I also met Edward the Prince of Wales during that stay at Kent House. He had just turned twenty-one. I remember him as fun and witty but slightly eccentric. He often appeared in rather flamboyant outfits featuring a great many different patterns. There was something about him that seemed feminine, but perhaps I was just unaccustomed to British men. Rumors did circulate that when he contracted mumps, it had left him sterile and could have possibly feminized him, but who would really know that? It seemed a stretch to me. At the beginning of the First World War, Edward joined the Grenadier Guards and was also very interested in flying. As first in line to the English throne, it seemed slightly irresponsible of him to pursue a pilot's license in 1918, but he managed to get it. When his younger brother Albert married Elizabeth Bowes-Lyons, it was said that he began teasing her by calling her Queen Elizabeth. That, of course, would turn out to be her real title later. The prince apparently wasn't shy either about telling his friends he intended to renounce the throne after his father died. Edward did seem to enjoy being the Prince of Wales, however, and was quite popular with the public, especially the married ladies. He wasn't all that serious about applying himself at school though and failed to receive any academic qualifications after eight terms. One's ancestry is the only deciding factor when selecting a king; academic achievement is far down the list, if at all. When his father died in 1936, Edward did become King Edward VIII, but only for 326 days and was never actually crowned in a ceremony. A certain divorced-and-still-married American woman was his official reason for abdicating, though I really think Mrs. Wallis Simpson was a woman of convenience. Her presence enabled him to avoid the obligations associated with being king and look heroic abdicating "for the women I love."

His younger brother Albert then became King George VI. I have never quite understood why kings and queens don't use his given name. As king, he gave the couple the titles Duke and Duchess of Windsor. Lovely, but I don't think the duke and duchess were prepared for being barred from returning to England by his brother. As time passed, the duke's behavior seemed more and more like that of an insolent child, bent on getting back at his family by publicly embarrassing them. In 1937, the couple visited Hitler, not a good thing for a member of the royal family to be doing just then as he was already promising to kill all the Jews in Germany. After they returned to England, the duke was heard to remark that he didn't think Hitler was "a bad chap." When sent to Australia on a diplomatic mission, Edward referred to the indigenous people as "revolting" and as the governor of Bermuda he publicly declared the island "a third-rate colony." During a tour of America, the president found the couple's German friendships so disturbing that he assigned them twenty-four-hour surveillance. The FBI even discovered the duchess had a continuing amorous relationship with the German ambassador in London and before the war ended, British intelligence was needed to retrieve some sensitive correspondence between the two. Edward seemed singularly unsuited to be king, no matter who his father was.

August 15, after ten horrible years of backbreaking work, exposure to the dense mosquito infested jungle, numerous deaths from tropical diseases and the expenditure of $375 million, the Panama Canal was finally finished. Astonishingly 27,500 workers had lost their lives during the long and arduous construction process.

Just a month after we'd come to live in Cobham, two German Zeppelins came in over the northeast coast. One bombed some small villages while the other made for London. Though searchlights found it and antiaircraft guns blasted away, it was cruising at ten thousand feet and was essentially untouchable. It managed to damage twenty-four buildings, broke all the windows in over a hundred more, destroyed a church, and killed ten people. Then it sailed off into the night without so much as a dent. Two British planes had taken off in pursuit, but neither could even find the two zeppelins and both crashed and were destroyed during landing. Before the month was out, more airships bombed a village eighty miles from the coast, but again, the four aircraft sent aloft to defend the nation failed to intercept any of them.

September 1, Germany quietly suspended its U-boat attacks in the Atlantic. Reg said that meant they were running low on men at the front. The following week, three more Zeppelins came across the North Sea intending to reach London. Heavy fog forced one to settle for some villages a hundred miles east of the city while another sailed right over the center of the city without dropping any bombs, then hit the Cattle Market. I never thought cows could be considered strategic bombing targets? It also hit a small house and tragically killed a family of four. As antiaircraft guns fired at one airship that was totally out of range, another dirigible bombed some nurseries and hit a few large homes, flew right over the Tower of London and began dropping bombs as if the guns on the ground firing madly at it weren't even there then gracefully drifted out of sight undamaged.

The raid did kill eighteen people, but it seemed a ridiculous expense to send Zeppelins to attack such relatively insignificant targets and kill a few non-combatants. Another Zeppelin came over the next night and managed to hit a chemical factory, an ironworks, three houses, a bank, a pub and an inn, shattered hundreds of windows, and barely missed a hospital. Some people standing in the street staring up at the thing were also killed. It went on to attack London's financial district and drop a single six-hundred- pound bomb that created an eight-foot hole in the street and created fires everywhere. A great many bombs then landed around Guildhall and hit a bus. Though all the passengers and the conductor were killed the driver only suffered the loss of a few fingers. More bombs landed on the bus station and killed everyone inside. One bomb penetrated an underground rail tunnel and left gas and water mains in disarray with huge holes in the surrounding streets. At that point, electric lines were also knocked out. During the entire raid, antiaircraft artillery was blasting away, and three airplanes had taken off to defend the city. None of them saw a single Zeppelin, and one pilot died trying to land.

By the end of September, Reg and I were expecting our first child. We were both very excited though the bombings were a constant worry.

From conversations with Reg, it appeared that because Britain had neglected to support Winston's plan to develop an air corps, the country was, for all practical purposes, defenseless. I also learned that the only way to down a Zeppelin was to hit the gas cells in the back. Because English aircraft were so underpowered, they were unable to fly high enough to get in such a position so downing one would be sheer luck. British searchlights weren't strong enough to illuminate airships at the heights at which they bombed either and because of the extreme altitudes at which they usually traveled those on the ground had little warning of an impending attack and little time to take cover. Actually, the idea of seeking shelter even seemed slightly ridiculous. Reg said Sperry was working on more powerful lights and he expected them to be ready soon. We lived well away from areas likely to be targeted, but this was still not comforting. He also thought the concept of a dirigible as a war machine was severely flawed. Because it was filled with highly flammable gas, it was forced to fly out of antiaircraft range, and because it was so large, in order to avoid detection, it could only bomb at night. Navigating in the dark at such high altitudes made it impossible to both maneuver and bomb with any accuracy. With better searchlights and more suitable aircraft, he thought airship bombing would eventually be abandoned.

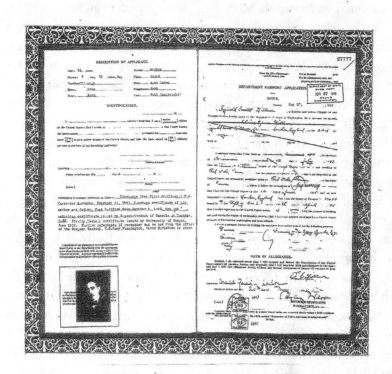

Reginald Everett Gillmor Passport

1916

Sadly, it wouldn't be until the fall of 1916 that Great Britain was able to mount any real defense against these raids.

Meanwhile, Sperry was doing famously. Recent sales figures were positively unbelievable; those from 1912 sales had increased over the previous year's by 573 percent, and 1914 figures had jumped another 790 percent, with 90 percent of those sales originating in London. These astonishing increases were all most probably the result of Reg's work. I couldn't have been prouder of him.

After six months of Germany's bombing campaign, public criticism of Britain's lack of a defense strategy was at a fever pitch. The public also complained about all the deaths caused by falling antiaircraft shells from the country's own guns. It was even more disturbing that as their targets were out-of-range, they shouldn't have been fired anyway. I guess the military needed to pretend they were doing something to defend the country? Finally, public outcry forced the RFC into action. New airfields were built northeast of London with observer positions around them. They also were provided with direct communication links to the War Office. New aircraft were also ordered, as was a new cannon. The latter would quickly prove useless, so it was fortunate only one was in the works. Mobile antiaircraft gun units were formed, and new fixed-gun positions were equipped with searchlights. All these things seemed so obvious it was difficult to understand why they hadn't been initiated from the outset.

The first test of all these improvements came rather quickly that October when five Zeppelins came over the North Sea and several lightships in the area radioed ahead to put four airfields on alert. Two British planes got aloft and immediately began climbing to ten thousand feet. Unbelievably, that would take an hour as several of the incoming airships managed to surround London and a single gun position fired at one of them. The targeted dirigible answered by knocking the position out. A searchlight position and gunnery emplacements targeted another Zeppelin, but it was too high and went on to bomb the city's theatre district. At the Lyceum Theatre, it was intermission, and many people had gone out into the street to buy refreshments; seventeen were killed. A single bomb also made a huge hole in the street and broke a gas main. Though a significant amount of antiaircraft fire attacked the airship, it sailed on unscathed to bomb the Royal Courts, three more streets, an inn, and some buildings in the jewelry district. All of this destruction was just two miles from Reg's office and a mile from the hospital where I was to have our baby! As the same Zeppelin approached the center of London, the new cannon was frantically moved into position. Sounds promising! It fired a single shot … that fell considerably short of the target. The huge airship continued dropping bombs and destroyed a bank, a hotel, a restaurant, and numerous other structures. Then it climbed, hit the Royal Mint, and drifted off undamaged as if on a sightseeing tour. During the ten-minute raid, thirteen gun batteries had fired everything they had, to no effect. British air defense was even less effective; not a single plane was even launched. Outside of London, one airship bombed Surrey, and another managed to kill twelve soldiers and sixteen of their horses. That raid was just nine miles from our house! Sitting in the dark listening to the explosions, made me feel as if the Germans were stalking us. Mercifully, that was the last raid of the year.

1916

January 27, Great Britain introduced conscription, a year and a half after they declared war; a little late? That year also saw the most intense Zeppelin bombing of World War I. The first raid appeared February 1. Though I understood nine airships were originally launched for Liverpool, weather conditions forced them to settle for targets in the north of England. Twenty-two British pilots bravely took to the air, but the fog that hampered the dirigibles also forced all of them to land. New takeoff and landing procedures proved to be so riddled with danger that six of them crashed and tragically all those pilots were killed. One of the Zeppelins also crashed in the North Sea as it tried to return home to its base on the continent and there were no survivors.

In early January, Russians in Petrograd revolted against three hundred years of Romanoff rule. I think the lavish, secluded lifestyle of the Czars served to disconnect them from the sufferings of ordinary Russians. Romanoff incompetence, the aristocracy's generally cruel treatment of generations of peasants, as well as poor working conditions in the country's factories, very low wages, and long hours all combined to create a desperate populace. Russia's participation in World War I had also dealt a disastrous blow to the country's economy, as it had blocked the country's exchange of goods with the rest of the world. This resulted in closed factories, food shortages and many hungry Russians.

By January 17, 1916, six million Russian men had been killed in the war, and these deaths had left many families without financial support. To further stir up an angry population, the military rank and file generally considered their leaders incompetent, and morale was extremely low. It was estimated thirty-four thousand men deserted every month. Thinking his presence would encourage the troops, Czar Nicholas went to the front to lead his army. Unfortunately, at no time had he ever received any leadership training, and his presence just created more problems. During his absence, he had authorized his unpopular English wife to manage the affairs of state. Though the granddaughter of England's Queen Victoria, she also lacked the necessary managerial skills, and things didn't go well on that front either.

This array of adverse conditions justifiably made for a great many angry Russians and they were easy prey for radical leaders. Communists, in particular, encouraged their rebellion and told them "their way" would solve all the problems that were making their lives miserable. Three days after the revolution started, all Russian industrial and commercial private enterprise was shut down. To control the resulting rioting, 180,000 Russian soldiers were put on the streets of Petrograd. With no police training, these men thought "control" meant using their weapons. Because many women were among the protestors, some of the soldiers refused to fire their weapons, while others mutinied and even shot their leaders. This turned the crowd even more hostile and private citizens suddenly appeared toting their own weapons.

The chaos went on for a week. Then the czar abdicated and a provisional government was democratically elected. Meanwhile Russian Communists stayed quiet and waited for the right moment to take control of the situation. Though the new government created a great deal of optimism, democracy was a very new concept for the average Russian to understand. When land reform didn't immediately come and food shortages continued, Vladimir Lenin and his Bolsheviks stepped and encouraged the overthrow of everything. The country certainly seemed on the verge of collapse, but much more terrible things were just a season or two over the horizon.

February 10, Mummah disembarked in Plymouth after crossing from New York. This port was used to imply the ship wasn't actually headed for England. I went to fetch her in the car, and was thrilled to see her. She would be staying with us for a while, as Reg was often away on Sperry business and he wanted to make sure I was in good hands should something unforeseen happen. Truthfully, it had also gotten a little lonely. Once in the car, we immediately began chattering away like two schoolgirls.

During the ride I also learned about a truly antiquated idiom used to describe a pregnancy. On her passport, she had noted that she was traveling to be with her daughter during "her confinement." What a ridiculous idea! It sounded as if I'd been bad and must stay out of sight until evidence of my crime had disappeared. Now, it seems almost funny … but also really sad. Before we headed home, Mummah had the driver stop at the Mayfair Hotel in London just a few blocks from the hospital where I was to deliver the baby. She wanted to be sure we had a place to stay that was closer to the hospital, in case there was an emergency. Ah, Mummah the ultimate planner. Then we headed to Cobham.

On first seeing the house, Mummah had the same reaction I did. She loved everything!

March 1, Germany resumed its Atlantic U-boat campaign. It was almost as if Hitler knew Mrs. Edwin Spear was crossing that April and didn't want to inconvenience her ship by sinking her ship.

Shortly after her arrival, three more Zeppelins came over the north coast of England. Though strong winds and snow blanketed the area, they managed to cause considerable damage and the same weather conditions prevented any British planes from getting aloft to mount an attack. The next raid was enormous; seventeen airships bombed some small villages, killed thirty-two soldiers living in a church, and hit an explosives factory. One antiaircraft gun battery scored a direct hit on one of them though, and it began to lose altitude. A British pilot stayed with the wounded airship and eventually dropped three bombs on the giant balloon but each one missed! In his defense, during that particular time in aviation a pilot had to fly his airplane and keep track of his intended target and the activity of other aircraft in his immediate vicinity with the bombs in his lap and at just the right moment, drop them over the side by hand. Just keeping the plane aloft was difficult enough. The damaged Zeppelin and made it to the English Channel but eventually broke in half and plunged into the chilly March water below. The survivors waited five hours in the dark before a British destroyer picked them up; the Germans would have never have been that merciful. The next night, two more Zeppelins made it across the North Sea and dropped ninety bombs that successfully killed a few chickens and broke some windows! Mercifully, there wouldn't be any more raids for a month. That May, the Germans used chlorine gas against enemy troops for the first time on enemy troops in trenches on the continent; over 1,200 British soldiers were killed. The wind suddenly changed direction though and 1,500 German troops lost their lives as well.

The third week of March, Mummah decided we should move to the Mayfair. In those days, babies were delivered by appointment, with the doctor telling you the date, as soon as he confirmed you were pregnant. Expectant mothers also delivered their babies under total anesthetic. Reg made all the arrangements, and Mummah accompanied me to St. George's Hospital on March 25. I had a lovely room and a beautiful bouquet of flowers greeted my arrival. Reg stopped in the evening. The next day, we were the parents of a beautiful little boy; I wouldn't know that until I finally woke up though.

When I returned to my room, Reg was there with more flowers, this time my favorites, peonies. Each of these beautiful flowers is composed of many petals that remind me of the tissue surrounding a gift. Gradually, as they unfold, they give up the most divine fragrance. They only bloom in spring and come in the three shades of deep red, strawberry pink, and white. This delicate but large and very showy flower has always reminded me of the stages of life. The white ones, often with red center petals, evoke youth, naiveté, and early heartbreak. The pink bring to mind the thrill and excitement of young adulthood, love, and marriage, and the red ones remind me that tragedy and the sadness of death is ever present.

Reg has always been a reserved man, but after our baby was born, he seemed openly thrilled and amazed that he suddenly had a son. We named him Reginald Everett Gillmor II and would call him Reggie. He would be the shining light of my husband's life.

It wasn't until then that I truly understood how many friends Reg had made in England before our marriage. Within hours, my room began to look like a flower shop and I felt as if I'd suddenly acquired a whole address book of new friends.

As it was definitely a special moment, Mummah arranged for a photographer to come to my room and commemorate the event. The resulting picture was a beautiful hand-colored portrait I have always treasured it, especially later in my life. Reggie is lying in my arms, with his little hands in front of his face. He is wearing a lavish christening dress, and the two of us are on a chaise, surrounded by all those flowers. I have on a lovely silk dressing gown and jacket, and Mummah insisted I wear an old-fashioned lace nightcap she'd found, to add the perfect touch. I guess no outfit is complete without a hat, even in bed. I have always kept this photograph in an exquisite frame that Winston and Clementine gave us on the occasion of Reggie's birth. It is decorated with delicate gilt roses and cherubs flying about with floral swags on a pale blue, silk background. I stayed in the hospital several weeks with a nurse constantly fluttering about me as if I were the queen. I guess the upper classes thought women were very delicate though I was definitely aware that many new mothers are expected to get right back to work.

Edwina Gillmor - Reginald Everett Gillmor II

1916

When I finally returned to Cobham with our son, my ever-efficient Mummah had hired a nurse for Reggie as was usual for those in the upper classes. Actually, the lovely woman would stay on as Reggie nurse until we left England to return to the states. At that time, everyone I knew arranged for other people to look after their children; first there was a nurse, then a nanny and a lastly a governess. Later, I came to believe that doing this didn't make for much of a relationship with your children. It also afforded parents little opportunity to teach their children important things that they should know before they reached adulthood. They did learn good manners though.

After I returned to Cobham, I read that Turkey was actually killing the Armenian Christians who lived in their country, not just men and women but also children. I couldn't understand why this was happening but finally it came out that it was simply because they were Christian. By the time the slaughter was stopped 1,500,000 people had been killed. Apparently, the government must have been ashamed of their treatment of these citizens, because the massacres would be hidden from ordinary Turkish people and never mentioned in their history books for decades. Eventually, word got around about what the government had done, but it was brushed it off as a "civil" war; difficult to consider it a war when one side has no weapons? In June, there was a tremendous explosion in New York City. Actually,

it was on the New Jersey dock where three million tons of munitions were being readied for shipment to Britain and France. The Black Tom Explosion occurred just across the water from the Statue of Liberty. Apparently, around midnight, a few guards noticed some small fires on the dock. Fearing an explosion, some of them fled while others tried to put them out. Two hours after they were first discovered a single detonation sent shrapnel everywhere. Forty people were killed as smaller explosions continued for several more hours.

The blast measured 5.5 on the Richter scale and was felt as far away as Philadelphia, Maryland, and Connecticut. Thousands of windows shattered in Lower Manhattan, including every stained-glass panel in St. Patrick's Cathedral uptown. The Statue of Liberty was so damaged her torch had to be closed and immigrants waiting to be processed on Ellis Island had to be evacuated. The total property damage was estimated at $429 million (2013), with repair to Lady Liberty costing an additional $145,000 (also 2013). A German-American commission later formed to investigate later found that two German guards had set the fires, and the United States was awarded $50 million in damages.

Across the English Channel, another world reigned in France. The Battle of the Somme, named after a nearby river, began July 1. I guess because it was so close we were able to follow it a little more in the newspapers. The initial devastation certainly had a great deal to do with Germany's newest weapon, the Maxim.

In 1883, the American Hiram Maxim had presented his newest invention to a committee at the British War Department—a gun that could fire six hundred shells a minute. The distinguished gentlemen listened politely but eventually decided they weren't interested; it seemed too dangerous. The Germans, however, thought it was a splendid idea, and having no problem with stealing intellectual property, immediately began producing their own version. They even used the inventor's name and called it the Maxim; the world's first machine gun. At the start of World War I, Germany had twelve thousand, and Britain had two!

During the first hour of the Battle of the Somme, 30,000 British soldiers were killed by the Maxim; that's 500 every minute. By the end of the day, that number had doubled. To add to the devastation, that was half the number of men Britain had allotted for the entire battle. Furthermore, as Britain had not anticipated such a huge number of casualties, they were unprepared to care for them in the field or transport them to base hospitals. British commanders in charge compounded these losses by deciding they simply couldn't allow Germany such a quick victory and the battle dragged on for nearly five more months, with neither side gaining much territory. Halfway through the ordeal, the British decided to introduce their own secret weapon; forty-nine tanks. This was their first appearance on a battlefield. Things didn't go quite as planned though. When it came time for their grand entrance, seventeen wouldn't start, and of the remaining thirty-two, another seventeen were almost immediately immobilized in the ever deepening mud; I guess they'd only tried them in the parking lot. When the winter rains arrived on schedule and thick mud nearly covered the entire battlefield, the warring troops on both sides simply dispersed. In the end the British and French together lost 600,000 men with

Germany incurring another 440,000; a horrible, tragic waste of lives, but also really stupid.

One evening, Reg told us some stories about things he'd been hearing from the battlefield. Apparently British officers and enlisted men had very different living arrangements. While the troops lived in tents, officers and their staff were allowed to "commandeer" local housing regardless of the occupant's cooperation. This gave them access to real beds and sometimes even bathrooms. When wounded, each group was taken to different hospitals. Most interesting, however, was that officers and their staff were drawn entirely from the upper class, no matter how incompetent; class distinctions adhered to even in war?

Officers were also permitted to have fancy food like wine, game, and homemade pies delivered to the battlefield from their country estates. They could even orders for cigars, caviar, and chocolates delivered from their favorite London stores. Reg pointed out that while enlisted men were indeed given far superior and more nutritious food than they were accustomed to at home, each meal was controlled to the ounce! Shouldn't maintaining a healthy, robust army be more important than controlling the cost of rations? Perhaps the officers thought that would spoil their men and this would lead to complaints after they returned home to their estate lives? Reg also said he'd seen and heard officers being rude to their men and treating them as if they were incompetent. He even told us a story about a group of generals enjoying a lovely outdoor picnic with several bottles of family wine from their private cellars as they watched their men being slaughtered in battle. Even in death, the British maintained their class structure with separate cemeteries for officers and enlisted men. But I was most astonished by the separate brothel tents; blue lights for officers, and red for the troops. I suppose it was important not to find oneself accidentally with the wrong sort of woman.

Three weeks after Reggie was born, Reg arrived home and asked me to come into the drawing room and close the doors. He said the United States needed a skilled observer to report how the war was really going on the continent, and they had asked him. I had a sudden feeling of danger but as he continued, I heard him say they wanted the two of us to go! What? Toward the war! He calmly began discussing the particulars of this adventure, as if he was telling me where we were go to dinner the next evening! He said the government would provide us with diplomatic papers and a "traveling couple" for protection, as well as a new residential address in London and we were to "visit" Paris and Rome. What a lovely holiday amongst the machine guns and tanks! He finished his little desertion with, "This is very important to the United States government and your going with me will arouse less suspicion." After a little more discussion and convincing I decided yes, I guess I could do this; maybe it would even be exciting, if we didn't end up in a German death camp? Then he slipped in that after our little European holiday, we'd go to New York, deliver his report and be able to make the dedication of Sperry's new building in Brooklyn. It was only then that I convinced myself that it might be a "fun" adventure; maybe fun wasn't the exact word I thought of?

Well, we had new pictures taken for our faux documents. For Reg's, he shaved his moustache and wore a fedora. He also uncharacteristically lowered his chin a little for the photograph and managed to look like your typical I-don't-know-anything kind of guy. Actually, he looked so clueless I almost didn't recognize him. Our new address was an attractive-looking townhouse on John Street in London, but Sperry had its real address. After a while, I got used to the idea and thought it could really be an interesting "new" adventure, if we didn't die in the process. We were living under the constant threat of bombing raids anyway. I'll come back to our November "holiday aboard" later though.

Germany launched more raids on Britain in late July and early August. The first one included one of their newest models, a huge 650-foot-long Super Zeppelin. It had nineteen gas cells and was designed to fly at altitudes above seventeen thousand feet. I can't imagine how one could see a thing on the ground from that height; it might have even been difficult to spot a country. The new airship contained two million cubic feet of highly explosive hydrogen and represented a 75 percent increase over their largest previous model. I thought the designers must be crazy, as it was very cold at those altitudes, and there was very little oxygen. Maybe the crews were supplied with fur coats and whiskey to stay warm. They would also suffer from altitude sickness though, so probably wouldn't want to drink. None of the July raids caused any significant damage, but I'm sure things were pretty miserable in the air. One of those raids came across the northeast, but it only damaged a single village and not very much. Before July was out, another huge fleet also managed to cause some minor damage in the north. Later in August, a single Super Zeppelin made it to London in spite of strong winds and in just ten minutes destroyed a few houses, an engineering plant, the Army Reserve Headquarters, a dry dock, London Electric, a railway station, a shop, and the Army Horse Reserve Stables. Low cloud cover also prevented British searchlights from locating the airship, and no planes could be launched. It was then that some wealthy industrialists and newspapers began offering rewards for bringing down a Zeppelin.

By the end of August, England had Sperry's more powerful searchlights, but their aircraft were still severely underpowered.

In September, sixteen airships crossed over the North Sea in heavy rain and snow. Only six of them were able to slog through and finally reach London though. British Command had been alerted, and six aircraft had taken to the air with one immediately beginning the long climb to ten thousand feet. Searchlights also illuminated one of the dirigibles, and numerous antiaircraft positions began firing as it began bombing. One airborne British pilot suddenly discovered a Zeppelin within bombing range and closed in for a kill but just as suddenly it disappeared in the clouds. Then another one drifted out of a cloud but before he could change course, it too vanished. By then, six British planes were circling a single Zeppelin, and a crowd had gathered on the ground to watch. As the mosquito-sized planes buzzed around the giant, metallic goliath, the fans below cheered as if they were at a local soccer match. Before long, several searchlight positions had locked onto the Zeppelin as it continued bombing. Then he climbed to get away from the lights, and another pilot found himself in a position to strike. After a little maneuvering he managed to get behind the massive thing and emptied an entire drum of ammunition into the back end. Slowly he saw a faint glow appear and then a tremendous explosion and the flaming carcass began a roaring descent to the ground. The spectators went wild! In nearby villages church bells rang, people danced in the streets, and trains blew their whistles. "Zepp Sunday" was declared, and the pilot immediately became a hero and was awarded the Victoria Cross.

CERTIFICATE OF REGISTRATION OF AMERICAN CITIZEN.

I, **Robert P. Skinner**, Consul-General of the United States of
America at **London, England**, hereby certify that **Reginald Everett Gillmor**
is registered as an American citizen in this consulate. He was born **July 13, 1887**
at **Menomonee, Wisconsin**, and is a citizen of the United States by birth.
He left his residence in the United States on **March 20, 1913**,
and arrived in **London, England** on **March 30, 1913**, where he
is now residing for the purpose of **Managing the Sperry Gyroscope Co., Of New York.** He is married
to **Edwina Spear Gillmor**, who was born in **San Francisco, Cal.**,
and resides at **2, John Street, London. W.**

He has the following children:

Reginald Everett Gillmor born in **London, England**
on **23rd May, 1916.** and residing at **2, John Street, London. W.;**

and,

on .... and residing at ....

and,

on .... residing at ....

Asked **OCT 9 1916** File

His local address is **Office, 15, Victoria Street, London. W.**
Private, 2, John Street, London. W.
The person to be informed in case of death or accident is **Mrs. Gillmor, 2, John Street, London. W.**

His citizenship of the United States is established by **Passport No. 64658 issued by**
the Department of State, **Washington, April 10, 1915.**

This certificate is not a passport and its validity expires on **May 25, 1917.**
The following is the signature of ....

In testimony whereof I have hereunto signed my name and affixed
my seal of office.

[L.S.]

Robert P. Skinner,
American Consul General
per ....
American Consul.

(NO FEE.)

See reverse instructions concerning expiration.

Reginald Everett Gillmor & Edwina Spear Gillmor

Certificate of Registration of American Citizen

1917

At the end of September, twelve more Zeppelins sailed in with four of them being Super ones. They bombed some small villages and destroyed a lot of houses, a church, a pub, a few industrial buildings, a match factory, and an oil depot, all in and around London. A great many guns had blasted away on the ground, and though one Zeppelin had been hit, the crew was so busy bombing they hadn't noticed. Only when their craft began losing altitude did they finally panic and began frantically throwing things over the side to lighten their ship, including all their guns and ammunition. The huge thing eventually came down in a country field, and all aboard survived. They promptly set their dead Zeppelin on fire, then with their commander leading, began marching in formation toward the coast; so very German. Along the way, they encountered a constable on a bicycle who was coming to investigate the fire. Mind you, all of the men were in German uniforms. The group continued on marching as the policeman rolled along beside them chatting. The commander even asked directions. As they approached a village, a second constable rode up on a bicycle. Only then did the two locals decide everyone should visit the nearest police station.

The very next night, three of those really big airships came in from the north and one made it to London. Even though it immediately attracted several searchlights, it dropped over fifty bombs and hit Kensington Park, a few houses, and a bridge. Another airship released a great many other bombs that only broke a few windows. All the while, ground artillery was blasting away to no avail. Finally, three British pilots zoomed in to defend the nation and one scored a hit. This ignited one of the Zeppelins and it made a dramatic, fiery descent to the ground.

Germans are a determined lot, and by October 1 they were back again. I understood four Zeppelins had to turn back because of strong wind, snow, ice, heavy rain, hail, and thick fog but one made it to London. There, six searchlights locked on the huge dirigible and lit it up like a giant star on a Christmas tree. Two gun batteries also gave it their all, though the monster kept right on bombing and destroyed four houses and all the windows in over three hundred others. It also wiped out forty "enemy" commercial nurseries. Four pilots managed to lock onto its tail though and one managed a volley into the back. Within seconds, the Zeppelin exploded and went down in a fiery mass.

The pilot was very close to the explosion, barely escaped with his life and was so upset he crashed his plane on landing.

November 21, the hospital ship *Britannic* was sailing off the coast of Greece with over a thousand wounded British soldiers on board. She was the largest of White Star Line's Olympic liners and one of *Titanic's* two sisters. *Britannic* had been launched before the war as a passenger liner, but by 1915 had been refitted as a hospital ship to operate between the Mediterranean and Britain. After *Titanic* sank, she'd been modified to make her safer; a partial double hull was added, half of those famous "watertight" compartments were made taller, and the engine's horsepower was increased. More lifeboats and stronger launching devices were also added. Though the ship sank in just fifty-five minutes and most of those on board were disabled, only thirty people died. By contrast, *Titanic* had stayed afloat two hours and thirty-five minutes.

More Zeppelins bombed during October and into November and the British managed to shoot down one from the ground, but two aircraft pilots died in the process.

That November, Reg and I made our little Christmas shopping/ spy mission. We were accompanied by our "dear friends" Mable and Elliot. I'm sure those weren't their real names, but as long as we stayed alive, I didn't care if they were Clyde Barrow and Bonnie Parker. They were actually very nice and quite interesting, though I was never sure if anything they said was really true. It was a little stressful and often exciting, but looking back now, it does seem like a really crazy thing do. We eventually made it safely to New York and Reg handed off his report to someone I never saw. Then we headed to Brooklyn. It had been just five years since the company had been founded and Sperry's meteoric success was astonishing. From that small shop on Rose Street and an equally small office at 40 Wall Street, Sperry was now moving into a huge 320,000-square-foot, eleven-story building. This would also signal the rise of company assets from $1 million to $5 million. December 8, we joined the Sperry family and a group of employees on the building's roof for a dedication. Reg was just twenty-nine then and very young to have had such an important role in the success of the company; I was so proud of him. We enjoyed a wonderful celebration downstairs too with a special guided tour by Mr. Sperry himself! What an amazing day.

Then we were off to rejoin Germany's bombing campaign again!

Happily, they didn't return for four months.

1917

That year, Reg told me a wonderful story about how one of Sperry's important inventions had come about. It also illustrates the confidence Mr. Sperry had in his sons. Prior to the United States entering the war, Mr. Sperry received a call from Rear Admiral Ralph Earle, chief of Naval Ordinance. By then, German U-boats had been causing havoc in the Atlantic for some time, and Britain had developed depth charges to combat these attacks. Because the United States had not entered the war then, they were not privy to how these devices were made. Admiral Earle felt the navy might shortly be in need of such defenses, so he called Mr. Sperry for help and told him to come to Washington. Mr. Sperry sent his twenty-three-year-old son Elmer Jr. During the meeting, Admiral Earle blustered at Elmer, "Build some of these depth charges and in a hell of a hurry!" When Elmer asked, "What do they look like?" the admiral tersely replied, "I don't know!" Before returning to Brooklyn, young Sperry asked around for anyone who had heard about them or seen them used. On the train back to New York, he made some preliminary sketches, and within a few days, Sperry had made three prototypes. Elmer took two of the large explosive barrels to Penn Station, rented a Pullman sleeping car and loaded them in the upper berths. After delivering them to Admiral Earle's headquarters in

Washington for testing the design was approved. Because the company was so small then, Elmer had to walk up and down Canal Street in Brooklyn, searching for fabricators who could make the non-precision parts. Three months later, when Admiral Sims sailed for England to command the Atlantic Fleet, five hundred of them were ready.

It would be only another sixty days before the United States declared war on Germany, and Sperry eventually produced ten thousand.

Reg also told me that Mr. Sperry's son Lawrence was an accomplished inventor in his own right and actually owned twenty-three of the company's patents. He ran Sperry's aviation department, where he developed and manufactured gyrostabilizers. In 1918, he would form his own company, Lawrence Sperry Aircraft, and branched out to invent and produce other aircraft instruments as well. Even now when I recall the creative and spirited young man, I feel very sad. His life would be tragically short.

In mid-January back in London, one hundred thousand pounds of TNT exploded at the Silvertone Munitions factory; 75 people were killed, nine hundred buildings were destroyed, and over seventy thousand others were damaged. The blast devastated the city as far as the Victoria Docks and was reportedly heard all the way to the coast. Sadly, it would not be the only such event in England during the war. Another in the Midlands at National Shell Filling would take 137 lives.

First Sperry Gyroscope Building

Flatbush Avenue - Brooklyn - New York

Elmer Ambrose Sperry

1917

That March, Reg received a patent for a voltage regulator.

On April 6, President Roosevelt seized over a hundred German ships docked at US ports and declared war on Germany. For the first time in US history, all immigrants would be required to pass a literacy test in their own language.

Because of the nature of Sperry products, the company immediately implemented strict security measures. All entrances were controlled by armed guards, and all employees had to prove they were American citizens. As a direct result of our entry into World War I, Sperry's workforce would increase dramatically to two thousand at first and continue to rapidly expand from then on.

When Reg resigned his commission in the navy in 1911, he became part of the Naval Reserves. With the United States now at war, he immediately volunteered for active duty and was made the flag secretary for Rear Admiral William Sims. After the war, Admiral Sims wrote *Victory at Sea*, which detailed his experiences. It would win him a Pulitzer Prize.

May 26, the German Kaiser sent twenty-six bombers to attack London but it was so shrouded in fog they couldn't find the city and left without dropping any bombs. Three weeks later, six Zeppelins made the first raid of 1917 but only dropped one bomb between them. One of them apparently developed engine trouble and was forced to descend to try to catch a prevailing tail wind to push it home. The summer sky was much lighter then, and the crippled dirigible immediately attracted the attention of four British planes. Three pilots scored direct hits, and the dirigible burst into flames killing everyone on board.

A British plane made the first successful takeoff from a moving ship, an amazing feat for 1917. Landing on one would be altogether a different matter though.

By October 1, I was pregnant again. Reggie was almost a year and a half old and Mummah was still living with us. I had always enjoyed her company, and neither of my sisters was in a position to welcome her into their homes. Reg and I were both delighted to have her with us. By then, she had been a widow for eleven years and was fifty-three; she would have had a lonely life living alone, and we felt lucky to have both her companionship and assistance. She was an invaluable organizer!

In the middle of October, I read a report about a woman being executed by a French firing squad for being a spy! She was found guilty of causing the deaths of 50,000 French soldiers! She was actually a Dutch citizen, and before settling on a career in espionage, she had been a kindergarten teacher and a mail order bride in Java. When arrested though, she was actually a very famous exotic dancer in Europe and, amazingly, is also considered one of the founders of modern dance along with Isadora Duncan. She is much more famous as a spy, however, and reportedly worked for both Britain and Germany, simultaneously! Her German code name was H-21, and her real name was Margarethe Zelle, but everyone knows her stage name, Mata Hari!

In late October, thirteen Zeppelins crossed the North Sea intending to attack London. Fierce winds, however, kept all but one from even crossing the coastline. The lone airship successfully bombed an aerodrome and destroyed several cottages as it crawled toward London. It was so high and cloud cover so thick that no one knew it was there, so no defense was mounted. Suddenly a single six-hundred-pound bomb appeared out of nowhere and destroyed part of the fashionable Swan & Edgar department store, a number of houses, a doctor's office, a fish 'n' chips shop, and left a twelve foot hole in the street. It continued dropping smaller bombs, then attempted to return home. The same winds were still intense so it was forced to descend and was immediately spotted by an already airborne British pilot. The Zeppelin climbed again to avoid him but was swept uncontrollably to the south, rather than northeast to its base. Panic must have surely overtaken the crew, as the prevailing air current would eventually send the airship over France or Spain where it would be in much greater danger from ground artillery.

In early November, Lenin and his Bolsheviks overran the Russian Winter Palace and took control of the government. They nationalized all banks, seized all their private accounts, and declared the country's foreign debts null and void. They also confiscated all church property, took control of all factories, limited workdays to eight hours, and froze wages at record highs. This immediately transformed Russia into the very first communist country in the world.

Admiral William Sims - Congratulatory Note

1917

1918

In early January, the new Russia surrendered to Germany. They had enough trouble at home to occupy them for decades.

Reg resigned his position with Admiral Sims that January. The US government thought he'd be more valuable to the US war effort stateside at Sperry. He would be awarded the Silver Star for his service in England during World War I. That February, we returned to the states; first Reg and I with little Reggie, then Mummah. She kindly stayed behind to pack our things and arrange for their shipment to New York. We took up temporary residence at the Plaza until Mummah returned and bought a house in Forest Hills, Queens, on the same street where Margot was living. It was also conveniently just a short drive from Sperry headquarters in Brooklyn. We hired a cook, a maid, and a nanny for Reggie. My goodness, what a huge relief to be away from the bombing; England is a lovely place but not during a war.

By January 25, it was possible make a call from New York to San Francisco, 3,400 miles away; amazing!

Reg was thirty that year, and he became the vice president and general manager of Sperry. At the request of the US Navy, he also reorganized the company into four divisions: Finance, Engineering, Factory, and Contracts. Company sales between 1915 and 1918 had risen tremendously but after the United States entered the war, only 25 percent of them were of foreign origin.

March 15, the British launched the world's first aircraft carrier. It wasn't very successful though and wouldn't really be for another decade. Meanwhile back on the continent, the Germans had a new weapon, the Paris Gun. It would be the largest artillery piece used in World War I.

The barrel was 112 feet long and could fire a 250-pound shell over eighty miles. In doing so, the shell was supposed to travel at 5,400 feet per second and reach an altitude of twenty-six miles; slightly unbelievable? If true, it would be the first man-made object to enter the Earth's stratosphere. Impressive, but it didn't seem very efficient; its poor accuracy meant it could only hit a city-sized target; it needed a crew of eighty-one to operate and required frequent barrel changes. But the Germans seemed to love it and fired twenty-one shells a day at Paris for four and a half months! Because the gun was so far away, Parisians had little warning a missile was on its way and 250 people were killed during this shelling campaign. Any other country would have abandoned it, if only because the payload was so small.

The famous German flying ace Manfred von Richthofen was shot down over France during a dogfight that spring. Later, it was determined the fatal shot had actually come from an artillery position on the ground. Though mortally wounded, the Red Baron landed his plane and died in his seat. He was believed to be the most successful fighter pilot of the Great War, and supposedly having shot down eighty Allied aircraft.

Regularly scheduled airmail service began that May between New York, Washington, DC, and Philadelphia.

On June 11, our second son was born. We named him William Sims Gillmor after our friend. Bill was a darling and had the same blond hair as his two-year-old brother, except it wasn't curly. We received many lovely gifts from our friends in America and abroad celebrating his birth. We also chose the Sims to be Bill's godparents, but because the war was still raging, they were unable to leave Britain until the following year. When scheduling permitted, we held Bill's christening at the same church where Margot was married in order to be more convenient for the admiral and his wife. Mummah arranged a lovely luncheon afterward at the beautiful apartment of a friend on East Sixty-Sixth Street.

In England, I read that twenty-two German bombers had suddenly appeared in the skies over London; what a terrifying roar they must have made. No less than a hundred aircraft took to the air to defend the   city but between them they only managed to damage one and three pilots crashed on landing. British defense during World War I seemed almost embarrassing. In my view, that responsibility lay primarily with the country's leadership, not the brave men who took enemy fire and flew dangerous missions to protect their homeland.

President Roosevelt's youngest son, Quentin, was shot down over France and died in July; he was just twenty-one.

In 1918, Leonardo was also twenty-one, and he became Sperry's director of public relations. He still spent most of his time in London though.

The Bolsheviks were hiding Czar Nicholas II, his wife, and their five children in a house in the small Russian town of Ekaterinburg. The Czechoslovakian army was advancing on the area, and Lenin feared they were coming to rescue the family. July 16, he ordered their captors to kill them and they were taken to the basement and shot. In reality, the Czechs knew nothing about the prisoners. It would be a long time before the world even heard rumors about the family's demise.

Five Zeppelins came across the northeast coast on August 5; one carried the commander of the entire dirigible fleet. He had been convinced the Kaiser to use them in the first place. Advance warnings of the approaching armada allowed two British planes to get aloft and the fleet was immediately spotted. Both pilots decided to concentrate their fire on the largest one airship and it was only minutes before it exploded in a huge fireball and plunged to the sea below. Everyone on board including the commander was killed. The crash marked the end of Germany's World War I Zeppelin campaign as well. I felt such relief for Britain.

The English death toll during those four years and thirty raids was 557 with 1,350 wounded. Most of the casualties were not soldiers, and the majority of damage was inflicted on relatively low-value targets in the countryside. Germany had spent a great deal of money to kill children, horses, and chickens, break windows, destroy tenements, and make huge holes in vacant land. In the final analysis, the country's cloudy, foggy weather had played as important a role in the country's defense as its military.

Reg's patent for improvements to the construction of an aircraft tail section was published in 1918.

In 1917, a highly contagious respiratory disease had developed in the birds and pigs that were kept in pens as fresh food for the troops in Europe. Eventually the infection spread to the soldiers themselves and it wasn't long before the numbers of the infected reached epidemic proportions. Wartime censorship of the press in Great Britain and Germany kept the epidemic from being publicized in those countries. But Spain, as a neutral nation, and had no such controls on reporting, so news of the virus spreading was freely reported in Spanish newspapers. That gave the public the impression that Spain was the only country affected, and the illness became known as the Spanish flu.

The epidemiology of the disease was quite different from the usual virus that normally attacks those with weaker immune systems, specifically the old and the very young. Though the Spanish flu affected all age groups, it was most deadly in the healthiest people because their immune systems were able to mount a more robust defense. It was the very strength of that response that killed them.

On August 11, 1918, a Norwegian ship docked in New York. Uncharacteristically, ambulances and medical personnel were waiting on the pier for its arrival and twenty-one of her crew and passengers were evacuated to a hospital. The Spanish flu had arrived on the East Coast. Five days later, another ship brought twenty-two more people infected by the virus, and September 4, twenty-two more, including two who had died at sea. By the twelfth, the docks were quarantined and no ships were allowed in or out. A few days later, the US Navy also sent twenty-three sailors to the hospital and by the end of September 424 victims were being treated in Brooklyn, quite near Reg's office. In an attempt to identify the infected before they joined the general population, examination rooms were set up in Pennsylvania and Grand Central Stations. The statistics quickly became frightening; October

4 there were 1000 cases, and five days later, the number jumped to 3,100. The next day it was 4,300 and then just as quickly 4,800.

The enormous number of patients also caused nursing shortages. Ordinary people began volunteering to care for the sick, collect food and transport people to the hospital; some even donated their cars. Nurseries had to be set up in schools to care for all the children who couldn't go home because there was no one there to look after them. By the end of October, three thousand children were living in schools. Sanitation workers, the police, and ordinary pedestrians began wearing protective masks in the streets and so many people had died that local gravediggers were unable to keep up; two thousand bodies were being stored in Queens.

Mercifully, after three months the number of new cases began to diminish and by mid-November the epidemic was declared over. In the New York area alone, 147,000 people had been infected, and 20,000 had died. The death toll throughout the United States reached five hundred thousand, and worldwide it was thought to be one hundred million—5 percent of everyone living around the globe. It was difficult to think that so many people had died because of something that sounded so minor.

In September, the war's aggressors seemed to be getting tired of the conflict. First Bulgaria surrendered to the Allies then the Ottoman Empire and the Austro-Hungarians gave up. Germany's Kaiser Wilhelm II abdicated in early November, and Germany conceded defeat the following day. World War I was officially over November 11, 1918, at eleven o'clock in the morning, nearly four and a half years after it began. Reportedly sixteen million people had lost their lives with another twenty million were injured. Tragically, six million of those deaths were noncombatants, 38 percent and 30 percent were the result of the Spanish flu. There most probably wouldn't have even been an epidemic if it hadn't been for the war. Of all the Allies, Russia suffered the most losses with 9,150,000 dead, wounded or missing, fully 75 percent of their men. France lost 73 percent of its fighting force, or 6,160,000. The United States fought the least amount of time but still lost 323,000. Among the Central Powers, Germany counted 6,100,500 killed or wounded; a 65 percent loss of their army. But Austria who started it all lost 7,020,000 men; 90 percent of its soldiers.

The statistics dramatically illustrate the devastation of war and must also include the untold numbers of families that lost those they loved and held dear. War also wastes enormous resources that could be put to better use and destroys centuries of human accomplishment—all so one group of people can stop another group from taking control of others. All participants suffer terribly though, even the winners.

The next global conflict will be far more devastating, as each succeeding war always is, and its primary aggressor will again be Germany.

As a result of Germany's surrender, an impound lot was created at a Royal Naval base in Scotland. On November 20, Germany's remaining fleet of ships was to be held there until the Treaty of Versailles was signed.

Twenty thousand Germans sailed 178 submarines, battleships, cruisers, and destroyers into the base's harbor. They were met and would be guarded by 370 Allied ships.

Seven months would pass before the treaty was signed though, and the sailors living aboard those German ships gradually dwindled to just 440. Though their government sent them rations, they weren't of very good quality. Lots of brandy was also sent, but only three hundred cigarettes a month had to be shared; for a smoker, one and a half a day was probably challenging, especially with nothing to do. The British didn't help the situation by not allowing these men to go ashore or visit the other impounded ships, and though they had doctors on board, there were no dentists.

By the middle of June, the German admiral in charge was making plans to sink all his ships, a violation of the terms of their surrender. The Allied commander at the base had been thinking this might happen and was making preparations to seize control of the German fleet the very second after midnight the day the treaty was to be signed, June 22. The German admiral also knew the date because he'd read it in the newspaper so he decided scuttling would begin twenty minutes before midnight the day before June 21. At the last minute, the signing ceremony was postponed to the 23, but it wasn't reported in the paper so the German commander wasn't aware of the change.

On the 21ˢᵗ, the Germans opened all the portholes, flood valves, and watertight doors on every ship. They also smashed internal pipes and even drilled holes in the hulls. Unfortunately, the bulk of the British ships guarding the harbor had been ordered out to sea that very day for a training exercise…a really silly idea!

The effects of the sabotage went unnoticed for twelve hours, but about noon on the 22ⁿᵈ, the strange tilt of the impounded fleet became alarmingly evident. Every available British seaman scrambled aboard the sinking vessels and attempted to beach them first; twenty-three were saved, but fifteen battleships, five cruisers, and eight destroyers went down. Nine Germans were also killed as they attempted to escape in lifeboats. Eventually, sixty of the scuttled vessels were salvaged, but 118 others were lost.

1919

In early January, an enormous accident occurred in Boston when 2,300,000 gallons of molasses broke free from a ninety-foot-wide tank at a rum distillery. This caused a fifteen-foot wave of thick syrup to creep through the surrounding streets. It was slow but buildings were pushed off their foundations, trains lifted off their tracks, and a bridge was knocked down. Several blocks around the factory were eventually encased in three feet of goo. The rush of air the tank's collapse created also hurled trucks into the harbor, killed twenty-one people and numerous horses, dogs, and cattle. At first it sounded sort of funny, but it certainly wasn't if you were "stuck" in it.

February 19, Cunard's nine-hundred-foot luxury liner *Aquitania*, in service between Liverpool and New York, became the first passenger ship to sail with Sperry's gyrocompass.

That April, a series of letter bombs were sent to some prominent Americans around the US. Among them were the police commissioner of New York, J.P. Morgan Jr., John D. Rockefeller, a Supreme Court justice, and the US attorney general; two were injured. The entire country was on edge because no one knew who might be next. A two-month lull ensued, and the nation thought the attacks were over. Sadly, another more powerful batch of eight went out in June, and two people were killed. The US attorney general's house in Washington was also completely destroyed and Secretary of the Navy Franklin Roosevelt and his wife were injured while taking a walk. In an attempt to prevent more attacks, ten thousand people were arrested, and five hundred deported. Anarchists were again believed to be responsible.

Two Englishmen made the first transatlantic flight from Newfoundland, Canada, to Ireland in the middle of June. They traveled the 1,890 miles in just under sixteen hours, then promptly found a nearby pub and celebrated. The Axis Powers finally signed the Versailles Treaty on June 28. It required Germany to accept full responsibility for causing all the damage and losses incurred by World War I. This was referred to as the War Guilt Clause. They were also forced to disarm and concede a substantial amount of land they had taken by force and were prohibited from maintaining an army of more than a hundred thousand men. Germany was also required to pay $442 billion in war reparations. While some historians thought the fines were excessive, others felt they were lenient. In reality, they had little impact on Germany's economy, regardless of what Hitler would later claim in his speeches. Germany would also be neither shamed nor weakened, as the world would soon find out. It would be just a little over two and a half years before the country's first violation of the treaty, though the world wouldn't discover this until it was too late to intervene and the conflict that ensued would be a far more aggressive and devastating.

In July, Winston was practicing his flying skills when he and his instructor crashed. Though he was only bruised, the other gentleman required many surgeries. Winston never tried again.

We had a lovely, peaceful Christmas that year, our first without the constant threat of bombs. Margot and Herbert joined us for dinner Christmas Eve, and we all went to their house the next day. As I watched my sister playing hostess, I felt an overwhelming sense of sadness; she seemed transformed. She didn't talk very much and appeared sort of detached from things happening around her. I felt certain her cold, demanding husband was the reason. Papa would have been devastated by the direction her life had taken. It would get much worse though.

New Year's Eve, Leonardo joined us to celebrate the start of what would eventually be called the Roaring Twenties.

During the holiday, I noticed Reg looked rather pale and seemed quiet and withdrawn, not at all like him. It was concerning. I suggested he take some time off and that perhaps we could go somewhere with the children for a little holiday. His work for Sperry had demanded near constant attention for the last six years. Not only was he in charge of supervising and expanding the company's markets but also the development of new products and oversight of new production facilities, so say nothing of the constant traveling in the US and abroad. His position with Admiral Sims, though relatively short, was equally intense. I pointed out that Mr. Sperry greatly depended on him and in order to meet these challenges, he must take care of his health. As a perfectionist, I knew it wasn't possible for him to leave anything undone, so it was especially important that he always be prepared. Taking a little time away from his work would keep things in balance and enable him to be at his best. Somehow, I reached him and he decided we would take a trip and include the boys.

Reginald Everett Gillmor - Passport for Edwina - Two Sons

1920

1920

January 23, Reg and I boarded the *Jacinto* with Reggie and Bill for a six-month stay in Nassau, the Bahamas. Mummah joined us a week later. We rented a lovely villa overlooking a sparkling, crystal-blue bay. The house had plenty of rooms, even for visitors to join us. A retinue of attentive servants cooked for us and took care of the house and gardens. We went to the beach, out boating, and enjoyed a fabulously relaxing holiday in the sunshine. Both Reggie and Bill celebrated their birthdays there that year. It was really the first time I had had the opportunity to enjoy my husband's company for such an extended period as he was always working. In hardly any time, he looked tanned and rested.

On January 18, Prohibition went into effect and made it illegal to make, transport, export, or import alcohol. It also seemed like an invasion of one's private life. Ultimately, it was a misguided law that led to some dangerous, unforeseen consequences.

It had been passed as a result of the protests of a very vocal minority that believed liquor caused a whole host of evils that not only included not only drunkenness but crime, poverty, and mental illness. They also resorted to some outrageous tactics to promote their position. Some rewrote the Bible to eliminate all references to alcoholic beverages, while others suggested the government distribute poison alcohol to bootleggers, send drinkers to concentration camps, forbid them to marry, put them on public display in stocks, sterilize those who imbibed, even stage public whippings. The Ku Klux Klan came out in favor of it, which seemed reason enough alone to table all discussion of passing the law.

In reality, Prohibition actually increased some of the very behaviors it sought to reduce; child neglect and disrespect for the law among them.

It also had far-reaching consequences that affected the country in very negative ways that would not be anticipated. Americans seemed to enjoy drinking, and the backlash was enormous. Furthermore, the mafia began to notice this and saw a golden opportunity to make a lot of money. They would go on to develop a huge underground network supplying liquor to anyone who could pay for it. Under the management of organized crime, bootlegging became a major American industry and generated a huge amount of wealth for the bosses. Worst of all, Prohibition gave the mafia a foothold in the United States that would never have been possible without the law's passage. Al Capone reportedly made $60 million during each of the fourteen years the law was in effect, and it was tax exempt. During those same years, the average factory worker made $1,000 a year and paid his taxes. The "cruise to nowhere" was invented during this period to take parties to international waters where everyone was free to drink all they wanted. New industries also developed to accommodate illegal drinking. In New York City alone, an estimated 100,000 speakeasies sprang up to satisfy thirsty Americans.

An article in the newspaper concerning a trial in Los Angeles illustrated how deprived some Americans felt during Prohibition. A bootlegger was acquitted because during deliberations the jury had drunk all the evidence! Trying to enforce Prohibition also cost the country $40 million while doing nothing to stop distribution or consumption. The loss of $860 million in tax revenue was also pretty amazing and put a strain on state and local government operations.

John D. Rockefeller, a lifelong nondrinker, eventually even supported the repeal of Prohibition, but by the time that happened, it was too late to oust the mob; their presence would never be eliminated.

When the law was finally repealed President Roosevelt declared, "What America needs now is a drink."

The decade of the twenties was also known as the Jazz Age and ushered in streamlined, angular design for everything from jewelry to architecture and clothing. The social fabric of America also changed dramatically, especially for women. During the war, while men had been away at the front, huge numbers of women had joined the workforce in their places. For many, it was the first time they worked outside their homes, but it was also the first time they were paid for their work. This experience gave them a different sense of their worth and independence. With their men away, they were also able to make their own decisions, and Pandora's Box would never be closed again. In their new working roles, restrictive clothing was impractical; long skirts were in the way and time-consuming hairstyles were a bother. Because they spent their days out in public rather than at home, they also developed a keener interest in their appearance and began to see how makeup could improve on nature. It was only a matter of time before they sought to participate in activities previously enjoyed by only men. Smoking and drinking in public were followed by dancing and partying in nightclubs. The Roaring Twenties quickly became an apt description of this new liberation. It was an exhilarating time to be a young woman. I was twenty-eight when the decade began.

Coincidently, it was also a time when many Americans were enjoying more economic prosperity. Compared with the average family of 1910, annual income rose 250 percent. Suddenly a broader percentage of the population could afford nicer clothes or a meal in a restaurant now   and then. Thanks to Mr. Ford, cars also were more affordable and they flooded the streets of New York. The telephone and radio soon became indispensable and the rich, as they always do, became richer. Some of their parties became wilder and more extravagant, even notoriously so. Thanks to newspaper and magazine reporting, the public also became fascinated with them.

In an attempt to prevent another world war, the League of Nations was formed in 1920. Its stated purpose was to achieve "world peace through collective arbitration." The United States funded the mission but refused to join. I never quite understood this stance. At its peak in 1934, thirty- eight nations were members. It was certainly a noble cause but depended on the Great Powers to enforce the rules. It ultimately failed because the more powerful countries were reluctant to intervene in disagreements for fear of hurting the smaller nations. This became abundantly clear when the league failed to prevent Hitler from overrunning its neighbors.

Italian businessman Charles Ponzi was arrested that April and charged with eighty-six counts of mail fraud. As it turned out, his real calling was as a con artist. Those who invested with him were promised a 50 percent return on their money, in ninety days no less! Anyone who believed that was possible was extremely naïve. Mr. Ponzi's investing strategy did not actually involve investing. He simply paid his first clients the profits he'd promised them from money he collected from his next marks. His business model had actually been tried before, twenty-one years earlier by a Brooklyn bookkeeper. Mr. Ponzi's business did quite well at first; in the first seven months he made $420,000 ($453 million in 2010). Just a month later, however, cash flow caught up with him and he was $7 million in debt. Eventually he went to prison for five years, but when additional charges were filed his sentence was extended to nine and when released he was immediately deported.

During our stay in Nassau, Reg and I discussed buying a house of our own now that we planned to live permanently in the States. We had heard about a community in Connecticut called Shippan Point. It was on a peninsula overlooking Long Island Sound and had originally been a four-hundred-acre farm until a developer purchased it in the late1800's. In order to sell lots, the company began running a steamship to and from New York City and later even built a hotel to accommodate overnight stays; a lovely weekend away from the foul air of New York City might be just the thing to convince prospective buyers to settle in such a beautiful place. Eventually homes were built, and a few families decided to live there permanently. It became so popular that several swimming resorts were built, as well as a carousel, a public stable, and a casino. Then a yacht club was formed with tennis courts and a golf course. The peninsula also had a number of lovely small beaches. At one time you could even take an airplane ride to select your piece of paradise. Finally, a rail line was established to connect the area to jobs in Manhattan. Reg and I both thought it sounded like a perfect place to raise our boys.

When we returned from Nassau, Reg's driver took us up. I remember stepping out of the car and being quite amazed to see the New York skyline so close. After a guided tour, we decided to look at a few properties, and in no time, had settled on a modest house on Ocean Drive just across from the yacht club. It had an unobstructed view of the sound too! We were very excited about moving in.

After we returned to Fox Lane and Mummah listened to our enthusiastic descriptions, she said she'd like to visit the area too. Later, she asked if it would be all right if she also bought a place there. Of course, we encouraged her and thought it would be wonderful to have her living close by. Actually, I would have worried about her so far away in Queens without us. My poor sister seemed unable to cope with her own life, much less help Mummah as she got older. I also thought Mummah would be happier watching her grandsons grow up. The following week, Mummah and I went back and took Margot with us. Ostensibly, it was to give her an afternoon away from Herbert, but after she saw our house, she thought she'd like to live in Shippan Point too. So, the three of us went back to the agent. Mummah found a lovely Georgian house just down the street from us, and Margot fell in love with one right next door to ours. I'm sure the gentleman couldn't believe his good fortune. We had a wonderful day and couldn't wait to tell Reg our news. I wasn't sure Herbert would be so happy though and worried about Margot even suggesting such an idea to him.

Count Leonardo Casanova

Chef "Extraordinaire"

Beginning that July, our lives were a constant stream of buying, moving, and arranging. Herbert had actually agreed to buy the house Margot wanted and my dear sister was positively gleeful. Perhaps his mother had suggested it was time he had a place of his own? Of course, Leonardo visited during all the commotion and enthusiastically gave his approval. During the years we lived in Connecticut, he loved coming out to "the country," enjoying the beach and playing tennis. He even tried his hand at golf. It was at our house in Shippan Point that he first introduced us to cooking outside and eating al fresco. I will always remember him grilling a steak on a little box thing, wearing his apron while holding a cigarette in one hand and a martini in the other. We would have so many wonderful days sitting in the sunshine, laughing and enjoying the salt air. In August, the newly signed Treaty of Sevres divided the Ottoman Empire into separate countries: Mesopotamia, Yemen, Hejaz, Asir, and five colonies. I bet hardly anyone remembers the last two now. The French were also given control of Lebanon and Syria while the British were to administer Iraq, Palestine, and Turkey. Britain would encounter a few difficulties managing their new "children" and things actually seemed to go from bad to worst over time.

The Nineteenth Amendment was passed on August 18 and after forty years of trying, American women were finally allowed to vote! Looking back, it's really amazing that men thought women weren't capable of making decisions about anything beyond arranging meals, doing laundry, and raising children. I would vote in my first presidential election the following November and help elect Republican Warren Harding. He received 60 percent of the vote, the largest in history. He would also turn out to be a very strange man. Interestingly, Franklin Roosevelt was running on the Democratic ticket that year and Calvin Coolidge was Harding's vice president. Mr. Coolidge would become the president unexpectedly and, in the next election, be voted president. Mr. Roosevelt was voted president in the following election. It was President Harding's behavior while in office that led me to never again vote for a party rather than the candidate.

Regularly scheduled airmail service began between Long Island and San Francisco that September. Flying one way took over thirty hours because navigation had to be done only during daylight hours using regular road maps and huge cement arrows on the ground.

The last US troops returned from World War I that month, and the country's first Armistice Day was officially celebrated September 10. A huge parade of General Pershing and twenty-five thousand of his men wearing all their equipment marched down Fifth Avenue 117 blocks. Even though they were a small proportion of the 2,000,000 men who'd served, enormous crowds and thunderous applause greeted them all along the route. It was certainly very stirring and made one proud of our country. It also made me wonder why we don't do that sort of thing anymore. We should show more appreciation for those who risked and lost their lives and not take their heroism for granted.

In mid-September, a horse-drawn delivery wagon pulled up to the front of J.P. Morgan's office at 23 Wall Street. The driver immediately abandoned the vehicle and, moments later, a hundred pounds of dynamite exploded. It was lunchtime, and a great many people were outside. Sadly most of them were young messengers, stenographers, and clerks. Thirty- eight were killed, and the interior of the Morgan building was destroyed. Though never conclusively proven, it was again rumored to have been the work of anarchists.

In Germany, thirty-one-year-old Adolf Hitler formed his Worker's Party, but couldn't get anyone to join. Later the same year, he changed the name to National Socialist German Workers' Party whose initials would soon become known around the world. Real trouble was brewing, but no one would notice.

Back in New York, Enrico Caruso sang his last public concert at the Metropolitan Opera on Christmas Eve. We had three tickets, but Mummah kindly gave hers to Leonardo. It was a most memorable evening during which he sang many of his most beloved pieces. A standing-room- only audience enthusiastically applauded, cheered, and whistled after every song. He also graciously gave many encores. It was sad to think we might never hear his wonderful voice again, but even sadder when he died seven months later.

The 1920 US Census revealed a few surprising facts; more people lived in Brooklyn than New York City, and thanks largely to Prohibition, the city was now the crime capital of the world.

1921

I would have my last child that year, but some decidedly unsettling circumstances surrounded the event; they would linger for the rest of my life.

In early January, a twenty-three-year-old woman took her first flying lesson. The experience must have been transformative and before long the world would know the name Amelia Earhart.

One evening, Leonardo was having cocktails with us in Connecticut when the telephone rang. Reg took it in the front hall. When he returned, he said he had to go out unexpectedly, apologized, and insisted he wouldn't be long and would be back for dinner. As it was not at all out of the ordinary, Leonardo and I continued chatting. Our conversation turned to what made life interesting. I especially remember it because he expressed views that definitely characterized his European upbringing and seemed rather at odds with some conventional American thinking of the time. He thought each of us, often without realizing it, had the life we chose even if we opted to stand on the sidelines and just watch. It was still a personal decision. He also pointed out that one's environment actually encouraged those choices; it could cause us to explore less expected life choices or limit us to familiar ones based on our particular social conventions. Then

I remember him saying these social expectations didn't really exist, we just believed they did. Furthermore, adhering to them acted as sort of self-imposed fences that restricted our behavior. I understood his philosophy but still felt that societal conventions often brought us comfort and provided a degree of self-preservation. I have never forgotten that discussion and would remember it often. Whenever I did, it would always induce in me an extremely disquieting feeling.

Most of the time, the atmosphere and values in which I'd been brought up served to protect and comfort me. It was reassuring to know "the plan." But gradually I began to think I should try some new ways of doing things, like so many women of the twenties were doing. This led me to consider applying for a job. I was well educated and spoke French and German, even a little Italian. Certainly such assets could be of value to the right company. Of course, my knowledge of companies was limited, so the "right" company soon became Sperry.

I didn't discuss any of this with Reg though, as I thought he wouldn't take me seriously and immediately dismiss my thinking. One morning after he'd left for Sperry, I put on a suit and called for the car. When the driver pulled up at the main entrance to Sperry headquarters and came around to open the door, I asked him to please wait for me. Then I walked around to the employee entrance. Apparently there were other people with the same idea, and I had to wait my turn. I had only been there about twenty minutes when I heard a familiar voice just behind me quietly say my name. When I turned around, it was Leonardo. Without saying anything else, he gently ushered me toward the door. Once outside, he said, "Edwina, what are you doing?" When I told him, he quietly said, "You can't do this." As I had not imagined this scenario, I was caught completely off guard and couldn't think of a response. After determining I had a driver, he walked me back to the car, told me to wait and went back into Sperry. When he returned, he got in and gave the driver some directions. He also silently indicated that we shouldn't talk. After a short time we reached a small restaurant and went inside. By then, it was past the usual lunch hour, and we were seated at a corner table, with hardly anyone else in the room. He ordered a bottle of wine. He was very kind and said this wasn't the way to change my life. Though his arguments were persuasive, I did feel defeated in my first attempt at independence. I even confessed that

Reg and I rarely interacted the way we had when we first met and that I thought it was my fault; I wasn't interesting. I thought a job would get me out in the world and broaden my thinking; I'd have more to talk about. I insisted I was only trying to improve myself and be a better person.

Looking back, I have decided I was a little too revealing, though I certainly wasn't thinking that at the time; it also may have looked like I was pleading for attention. After lunch, we returned to the car. Then suddenly we were in a small hotel where Leonardo had often stayed.

It was just a few hours, and though lovely, I immediately regretted them. That brief afternoon would have enormous consequences I wouldn't begin to see for decades. I was twenty-eight, and Leonardo twenty-four.

Book 4
1921–1936

1921

By February, I was pregnant again. Though it was definitely a traumatic discovery, I could only push the unthinkable out of my mind. Besides, I loved my husband dearly and was happy about having another child.

Sometime that month, Winston also became Secretary of State of the Colonies; such silly, overly laborious wording. Reg began going on about British policies in Mesopotamia. Winston's first task seemed to be dealing with the Kurds and Arabs in the region. Reg felt Winston wasn't handling things very well. He had decided to make one nation of the Sunni Kurds and the Shiite and Sunni Muslims; three ethnic groups traditionally hostile to one another. From this unlikely union, modern Iraq was created from Basra, Mosul, and Bagdad. Then he made the situation even worse by choosing the Turkish Prince Feisel as the country's new regent. At that time, there were strong feelings that rulers should be of the same ethnicity as those they governed. Winston's choices left the Arabs in this arrangement particularly unhappy, but he had made up his mind that their protests were unimportant and charged ahead. As might have been expected, everyone living in those places vocally rebelled in the streets. Winston responded by using gas on them! This seemed highly inappropriate. Not the way to make friends or influence their thinking. Reg and I watched as the situation escalated. Then we heard that Winston had decided to severely limit financial aid to the new colony. His cost-cutting measures included no monetary appropriations to build hospitals. These decisions would lead to a great deal of animosity and violent rebellion in the region for decades. It had been three years since Reg and I had returned to the United States, and though he visited often, Leonardo had chosen to still live in London. April 6, he and his brother Telesforo left Le Havre, France, to permanently settle in America. He bought an apartment in Brooklyn but spent his first weekend with us in Shippan Point. During a moment when we were alone, he quietly told me he wanted to be in New York when I had my baby, even though I had never discussed my pregnancy with him and never would. When you have no alternative, you just do the best you can. I had decided avoiding the issue was my only choice.

That June, I remember Reg telling me about a struggling aircraft company that had managed to stay in business by manufacturing furniture. Their future was looking much brighter though. They had won a $1,448,000 contract to build two hundred fighter planes for the US Army. He thought Boeing was going to do very well.

On July 14, Ferdinando Sacco and Bartolemeo Vanzetti were found guilty of the armed robbery of a shoe factory in Massachusetts. Sounds like an ordinary trial, but it certainly wasn't. After the verdict, witnesses for the prosecution recanted their testimony, an alleged accomplice confessed he had done the whole thing by himself, and ballistic evidence pointed in several different directions. To add to the confusion, both Sacco and Vanzetti were avowed anarchists, at a time when anarchists were blowing up things everywhere and killing people in the process. The public was understandably frightened and came out against the two burglars solely because they believed in anarchy. Though one's political beliefs don't usually play much of a role in a trial, this would not be the case in this one. During questioning of the defendants, they were forced to explain these beliefs. Most probably the jury was swayed by this testimony and, consequently, the evidence and facts took a backseat. After they were found guilty, their attorney appealed the verdict several times, even before the Massachusetts Supreme Court. On each occasion, the motion was denied. During the appeal process, however, the case drew worldwide attention and huge vocal, outdoor protests against the verdict were staged in many major western cities. Noted Harvard law professor Mr. Felix Frankfurter, later a US Supreme Court justice, even came out publicly against the verdict. Sadly, it seemed to be a time in history when US judges seldom reconsidered their decisions. Undeterred by the protests, both men were executed six years after the verdict, and they hadn't even killed anybody. The execution resulted in more rioting, especially in Paris and London.

September 11, our dear friend Prince Louis Battenberg died. He was just sixty-six and by then had been demoted to the Marques of Milford Haven. The loss of his job had been driven him and his family into such reduced financial circumstances that both he and his lovely wife, daughter of England's Queen Victoria, were forced live at the Naval and Military Club in London. While there, he had contracted influenza. Reg went to the funeral at Westminster Abbey and the burial near his beloved former home on the Isle of Wight.

On November 1, I had a beautiful son. We named him David Spear Gillmor, after my great-grandfather Reverend David Burger born in 1814. All my boys were beautiful babies and handsome men, but David was different; his features were more delicate and refined than those of his brothers. Though he had the same blond hair when he was young, by the time he was seventeen his curls had actually turned black. That did seem unusual but I knew nothing about inherited hair color. As he grew older, his face also seemed to become more beautiful, if that can be a word to describe a man. I remember being at a party with him some years later and on being introduced as his mother, a woman remarked that David was the best-looking man she'd ever seen.

Reginald Everett Gillmor

1922

1922

In February, an international treaty was signed to limit the size of a country's navy and its armaments. It also outlawed the use of poison gas and submarine attacks on merchant shipping. The United States, Italy, France, the United Kingdom, and Japan signed it; Germany's Hancock was absent. Historically nations have paid no attention to the treaties they sign when they don't suit their policies anymore. It probably wouldn't have mattered as Germany would soon decide to begin violating of all the things prohibited in the Versailles. Time will prove those nations that did sign won't abide by the terms either. Again it was a noble idea, but policing an uncooperative and belligerent country seems almost impossible. History has also proven that treaties really cannot be relied upon; succeeding generations ignore covenants when it doesn't suit them. This is especially true of a dictator, as absolute power guarantees them the right to do as they please.

Nineteen twenty-two was also the year that Margot's husband filed for bankruptcy. It had been two years since they'd moved next door to us and I imagined Herbert was not accustomed to paying his own bills. Perhaps his mother wasn't sending enough money as well. My family was quite embarrassed about the suit, but Herbert certainly didn't seem to be. Two years elapsed before the judge ruled against him.

Losing was even more disturbing as it meant Herbert had lied about his financial circumstances. We hoped the verdict might induce some humility in him, but his opinion of himself remained unchanged; to do otherwise would have been out of character really.

September 2, Jimmy Doolittle made the first transcontinental flight from Florida to California, stopping only once in Texas to refuel.

Mr. Sperry paid a return visit to Japan that September. He was the guest of honor at the twenty-fifth anniversary of the Japanese Societies of Mechanical Engineers and Naval Architecture. He and his wife were so warmly received they extended their stay two more months and met top officials in the War Department, the Admiralty, the Mitui family's enterprises, and noted professors at Imperial Tokyo University. He returned with glowing reports of their technical ability though Reg, who'd joined him briefly, thought they were better at copying things, less so at inventing original products.

Sometime in October, Fascist Benito Mussolini convinced the king of Italy to appoint him prime minister. That single decision would bring three years of death and destruction to the country. Eventually, Mussolini became the country's "dictator" though later he decided it would sound better if he were "elected" dictator. After his infamous Secret Police was formed, all opposition disappeared and he ruled a one-party system and controlled all aspects of Italian life with an iron fist for the next twenty- five years.

1923

T*ime* magazine was first published that March.

Russian immigrant Igor Sikorsky founded his Sikorsky Aero Engineering on a former Long Island chicken farm and began developing multiengine aircraft. Only when sales lagged did he decide to concentrate on the helicopters for which he would become famous. It would take nineteen years before he was finally able to master the unusual flying characteristics of this inherently unstable flying machine though.

The first "talkie" movie was shown in New York and Harry Houdini was escaping from things while hanging upside down or underwater.

A 650-foot dirigible flew over the Woolworth Tower. The ZR-1 was built in New Jersey as part of Germany's war reparations to the United States. Watching it cruise overhead certainly brought back some unpleasant memories.

President Harding unexpectedly died that August. Before long some disturbing rumors began to circulate about his character that indicated he was definitely not the man the country believed it had elected. Rumors began to circulate suggesting his wife had poisoned him and some of them might certainly have given her reason to do so.

They involved at least four mistresses and two daughters he'd fathered by one of them, while in office! Furthermore, after his death and President Coolidge moved into the White House, Mrs. Harding refused to leave for a month. It was said she was busy burning his personal papers. I heard that he'd been a member of the Ku Klux Klan and was the direct descendant of a West Indian native. There was also talk of orgies being held in a house on K Street! Thankfully, President Coolidge was a fine man and quickly restored the public's confidence in the government.

In Germany, evil was on the march as Adolf Hitler made his first attempt to take control of the government. He failed and was arrested instead.

Two days before Christmas that year, thirty-one-year-old Lawrence Sperry took off from Rye, England, and headed for France in an aircraft of his own design. The famous English fog quickly enveloped him, however, and he was never seen alive again. Tragically, it took eighteen days before his body was found. We went to his very sad interment in nearby Brookville. His aircraft company was absorbed into his father's, and the family established the Lawrence Sperry Award for Aeronautical Achievement in his memory.

1924

Vladimir Lenin died that January and Joseph Stalin promptly set in motion his plans to take control of all things Russian. First he systematically murdered all his rivals. These included Bolsheviks, Poles, Jews, Latvians, and dissention within the secret police. If they weren't shot, they were imprisoned in remote Russian labor camps. This behavior toward his countrymen eventually troubled his wife so much she later killed herself.

We all went to Carnegie Hall to hear George Gershwin's newest work,

Rhapsody in Blue. We loved it, and the audience enthusiastically agreed. Twenty-four-year-old J. Edgar Hoover was appointed head of the Bureau of Investigation, later known as the FBI. Actually, he would turn the agency into his own secret police and managed to hold his position and misuse it for an astonishing forty years. Mr. Hoover eventually became so powerful, even the president of the United States was afraid of him. He did this by collecting highly personal information on all manner of public figures. Everyone feared that if they challenged his authority, he'd ruin their reputation. President Harry Truman even accused Mr. Hoover of running his own private police force.

A new immigration law went into effect in the spring of 1924. It limited the number of people from a single country who were allowed to immigrate to the United States to 2% of the number that had done so in 1890. Those from Southern and Eastern Europe seemed to be the target ethnicity but that region would change from time to time. The goal of the law was said to be the "preservation of American homogeneity." It seemed to me the very nature and strength of American lay in its diversity. It enabled us to benefit from the talents of many different peoples and the success we draw from this heritage sets us completely apart from all other nations in the world. We should be proud that all of us are from somewhere else, that our joining together is the very reason that we prosper as no other country has ever done. This new immigration policy had the unintended effect of ending the American Gilded Age of the Robber Barons by limiting the supply of new labor and halting industrial expansion.

June saw the first radio broadcast of a national political party convention. The Democrats were selecting their presidential candidate in the city's Madison Square Garden. For a while, it was fascinating, but rather quickly the event turned chaotic and uncivilized. Nearly eleven hundred delegates representing various factions battled for control of the process, including Northerners, Southerners, Urbanites, Catholics, and Anti-Prohibitionists. A particularly aggressive group from the Ku Klux Klan earned the convention the nickname the Klan Bake. A New York governor and an attorney from California were the early favorites, but as a two-thirds of the majority was required to win, they got lost in the endless reshuffling. After sixteen days and 103 vote counts, the process looked both ridiculous and shameful.

Mr. John Scopes was put on trial in Tennessee for teaching Darwin's theory of evolution to a high school class. Seemed like a strange reason for a trial, but he was convicted and fined $500.

In England, Winston was made Chancellor of the Exchequer and returned the country to the gold standard. A lot of his countrymen had told him doing so would be disastrous for the economy, Reg included. Later, Winston told us he felt politically cornered. His decision plunged England into a period of huge unemployment, deflation, and labor strikes. Winston believed it was the greatest mistake of his life.

The very first Macy's Christmas parade was held Thanksgiving Day that year. The three-hour march included professional performers, bands, and live animals from the Central Park Zoo. A half million people lined the route and enthusiastically greeted each entry. When the participants reached the Macy's store on Thirty-Fourth Street, an elf came out on the balcony above the main entrance and was crowned; it didn't seem very Christmas-like, but the crowd loved it.

1925

That year, New York displaced London as the largest city in the world.

F. Scott Fitzgerald's *The Great Gatsby* was published in April to mixed reviews. The author thought it was his best work, but it sold so poorly that when he died fifteen years later, he believed he was a failure. It wouldn't be until World War II that the book enjoyed a revival and became so popular it was often be referred to as the great American novel, sad for him that he wasn't appreciated during his life.

Adolf Hitler was found guilty of leading his failed coup and sentenced to five years in jail. He would only serve nine months though and used the time, pacing back and forth in his cell, to dictate his book *Mein Kampf* to his pal Rudolph Hess.

Lost World was the first movie to ever be shown on a flight between London and Paris that year.

That July, Reg had planned a trip to England for Sperry and wanted me to join him. I wasn't very enthusiastic until he suggested that when he finished his work, we could sail to Montreal and visit Ebus and Monty. I was thrilled and, of course, immediately agreed! I hardly ever got to see Ebus anymore and was really looking forward to her company and seeing her life in Montreal. I also thought it would be lovely to share a bedroom with my husband again. By then we'd been married ten years, and separate beds were typical among the upper class when one didn't want any more children. This arrangement wasn't very cozy though and seemed to create an emotional distance between my husband and me.

We sailed on the *American Banker* and enjoyed a wonderful stay in London, then boarded the *Doric* for St. Albans, Vermont and on by train to Montreal from there.

I did some thinking during the languid hours sitting on the deck of the *Doric* watching the ocean roll by. I began to realize how increasingly guarded I'd become in my conversations with Reg. I know I was protecting myself from saying something strange about David or Leonardo. It had also made me quieter and less spontaneous. Big secrets seem surrounded by this fog. Seeing all the ramifications of having to be so guarded really made me sad. Though every memory of that afternoon filled me with regret, history cannot be changed. It's also very destructive to continually dwell on sadness and regret for what you wish hadn't been. I tried to comfort myself with the reality that all of us have such places in our lives. Somehow, we often don't think other people share similar tragedies but they do. We always think of ours as singular.

We had an especially lovely visit with Ebus and Monty, though we stayed in a hotel because their apartment was quite small. I hadn't realized how much I had missed my sister's sense of the absurd, creativity in the face of adverse circumstances and her continual use of French idioms in her conversations. "Mon Dieu!" was my favorite. Happily, after we moved back to Long Island and had a bigger house, she and Monty would often visit. On New Year's Eve, we hosted a small dinner party that year. Leonardo came with his brother, Telesforo, and Telesforo's girlfriend, Grace Hegger Lewis. She was charming and entertained us with tales of her careers as a *Vogue* editor, beauty consultant for Elizabeth Arden and a published author. Her father had owned an art gallery on Fifth Avenue when she was younger, and she had a great many interesting stories about the artists who frequented his shop. Before she met Telesforo, Grace had been married to Sinclair Lewis for a decade. Reg and I extended a standing invitation for both of them to join Leonardo whenever he came up to see us. Though

Grace was a born New Yorker, I noticed she spoke with an English accent. It seemed slightly odd but was an affectation of the time that many people seemed to have adopted. She and Topi, as she often called him, were married five years after we met them and seemed quite happy together.

1926

That year, Reg decided Shippan Point was just too far from Sperry and he thought we should look for something on Long Island. It took us a few trips, but we finally settled on a property in Kings Point. It too was on a peninsula, with Little Neck Bay to the west and Manhasset Bay to the east, with just two miles between them. I suppose after our house in Connecticut, we had become accustomed to enjoying the lovely sea air and the water being so close. The house was a little bigger than our last one and had three floors. Sperry was only fifteen miles southwest and considerably more convenient. Mummah sold her house in Shippan Point as well and came to live with us. If one compared our Kings Point location to Fitzgerald's *Great Gatsby* novel, we had moved to Jay Gatsby's West Egg. Supposedly Fitzgerald developed this story after living in a house just down the road from our new one. The North Shore of Long Island came to be called the Gold Coast at the turn of the century because so many wealthy industrialists built very large homes in the area—and I do mean *very* large. Looking at some of them certainly brought to mind those portrayed as Daisy Buchanan's and Jay Gatsby's. During the period he wrote the novel, many wealthy, fashionable residents living near him and his beautiful wife did indeed throw the sort of Roaring Twenties parties Mr.

Fitzgerald wrote about and probably as a young writer, he and Zelda would have been guests at some of these soirees.

In early May, Richard Byrd and Floyd Bennett made the first flight over the North Pole. They would receive the Medal of Honor for this achievement, though many people expressed skepticism about actually having been able to do such a thing; apparently it was nearly impossible then to determine exactly where the North Pole was on the ground.

In 1926, Mr. Sperry decided he wanted to see more of the world with his wife. He resigned as president of the company he'd founded sixteen years earlier and became chairman of the board.

Rudolph Valentino, the very famous silent film star, died of appendicitis on August 23 in New York. I could not believe the huge crowds that swarmed onto the streets to publicly mourn his passing. The city had to muster a hundred mounted police to control the100,000 hysterical fans who lined the route of his cortege as it proceeded to a church in the Theatre District. In spite of these efforts, a twenty-four-hour riot erupted the next day as his casket was taken to Grand Central Station for shipment to Beverly Hills, California. There he was given another service and final burial. Of course, everyone knew him as an actor, but he was really a more multidimensional man. In his early years, he had earned an agricultural degree but later supported himself as a paid dance partner at Maxim's in Paris. He starred in thirty-one movies during his film career, one of which was the first picture to make a million dollars. As movies with sound made their entrance, he was given a voice test but immediately deemed unsuitable because of his heavy Italian accent. How silly, I loved accents and think it would have added to his sex appeal.

Right after Valentino's funeral, I remember Mummah received a letter from Papa's sister, Aunt Mable. She wrote that her son Rollin had been very depressed for the last several months. She'd taken him to the doctor, but there didn't seem very much he could do for him. Five days later, Rollin had shot himself. As she read that line in Aunt Mable's letter, I was absolutely shocked, especially as he was only in his early twenties. I couldn't imagine how devastating that must have been for Aunt Mable as his mother. I remember thinking, *how could any mother get over such a terrible thing?*

After Mummah reading the letter out loud, she kept holding it but seemed to be thinking of something else. When she noticed I was watching her, she said, "One day I have something to tell you ... but not just now."

Rolls-Royce Phantom

1926

A lovely summer drifted into fall, and one Saturday morning we were having breakfast in the dining room. It was about a week before my thirty- fourth birthday. Quite unexpectedly, Reg announced that on his last trip to England he'd bought me a birthday present and it would be arriving that morning. As if on cue, there was a knock at the front door and before the butler could tell us who it was Reg pushed back his chair and cheerfully announced, "That must be my surprise!" Then he pulled out my chair and as the butler held open the front door he escorted me to the foyer. To my great astonishment, there in the drive was a very shiny, navy blue Rolls-Royce! Immediately my dear husband proclaimed, "Happy birthday, Edwina!" I was absolutely speechless! What an amazing present... and superlative timing; so like Reg. The moment greatly reminded me of when he presented me with my engagement ring. Then he asked Mummah to go find the children so we could all take a ride. When Reggie, Bill, and David appeared, he proudly announced, "This is Mummy's beautiful blue birthday present! Shouldn't we all take a ride and try it out?" Of course, they got very excited and ran around the car as Reg's driver held the back door open for them. They scrambled in, with five-year-old David getting an assist from Mummah. Then Reg held the driver's door for me and politely queried, "Driving lesson, Mrs. Gillmor?"

As Reg gave me instructions, the children investigated how the windows worked, felt the seats, looked at all the dials, and opened and closed everything that could be made to move. I was quite overwhelmed. Reg also seemed terribly thrilled that his "little" gift had arrived exactly as he'd planned. At one point, he had me stop the car and took a photograph. I love that picture, with Mummah and the boys in the back, though you can't see David above the window. I am in the driver's seat and wearing a hat, of course!

On Christmas Day, Japan got a new twenty-five-year-old emperor. As might have been expected of such a young man, he would turn out to be even more warlike than his father. By then, Japan had the ninth largest economy in the world and the third largest navy; they intended to make use of the latter too.

1927

That January, you could call London!

In March, a South African farmer discovered a diamond in one of his fields. Within a year, over one hundred thousand fortune hunters descended on the region to search for more. Prior to then, South Africa's main industrial exports were corn and cement! The Diamond Rush would last ten years.

May 20 in Garden City, Long Island, twenty-five-year-old Charles Lindbergh took off from Roosevelt field at 8:52 in the morning. He was attempting the first solo flight from New York to Paris. It took him thirty- three and a half hours to cover the 3,600 miles, but he arrived the next day at 5:22 in the afternoon. Of course, it was an amazing accomplishment, but after we heard his description of the flight, it seemed a miracle he'd survived. Apparently, he'd done a little too much preflight partying the night before and hadn't gotten very much sleep before boarding "Flight 1 to Paris." When he landed in France, he thought he'd been awake for fifty-five hours! Well, not exactly; he'd slept some during the crossing! As he recounted, he flew the first nine hours at an altitude of only six hundred feet. Small planes now generally descend to that altitude to land, so that's very low. He also admitted that during the first six hours, it was a real struggle to stay awake. Once over the Atlantic, he ascended to ten thousand feet but confessed that, after eighteen hours in the air, he thought he'd fallen asleep and reawakened continually and by the twentieth hour was actually hallucinating! After the twenty-third, and still alive, he was wide awake; probably because of all those naps! After returning to the States, he was given a hero's welcome and a tickertape parade down Fifth Avenue.

Another flying record was set that June when two navy pilots flew 2,400 miles from California to Hawaii in just under twenty-six hours. They carried over 1,100 gallons of fuel, forty of oil, and rations of soup, chicken sandwiches, tinned beef, water, chocolate bars, and most importantly, lots of coffee. They had also decided an inflatable raft would be good to have though if forced to attempt a water landing, their plane would have immediately gone under and taken them and their boat with it.

Laughably, when they finally decided they were hungry, they couldn't find the food. Upon first sighting the airfield in Hawaii, it was 6:30 in the morning but they noticed thousands of people waiting to welcome them. This discovery was immediately followed by the distinct puffs of smoke from an artillery salute. Such an elaborate greeting at that hour spoke volumes about the hospitality of the island's people.

For the first time in US history, the government decided it needed to oversee the safety of the country's food and drugs. The FDIA came into being. Rather comically though, those letters stood for the Food, Drug, and Insecticide Administration!

On my family's many Atlantic crossings, we often encountered Gertrude Vanderbilt Whitney and her husband, Harry Payne Whitney. When we first met, I was quite young, and Mrs. Whitney was in her early twenties. I knew she was the daughter of Cornelius Vanderbilt II and that her childhood summer home had been that extravagant Italian palace in Newport, the Breakers. Her Yale-educated lawyer husband was also quite wealthy and had interests in oil, tobacco, and banking. He also enjoyed a collection of yachts, was a top polo player, and had a stable of racehorses. The year Reg and I were married I remember one of his horses won the Preakness. As Mrs. Whitney had a considerable fortune of her own, she was able to pursue her own interests and often avoided the boats and horses. She regularly visited Paris and developed a keen interest in art, particularly sculpture. She had even studied with Auguste Rodin! In New York, she also kept a studio in Lower Manhattan where she worked.

Existing art galleries of the day were only interested in displaying traditional pieces, so Gertrude often bought the work of unknown, emerging young artists, particularly women, to support and encourage them. Sometimes she'd also hold exhibitions to showcase these acquisitions and invite the public. Eventually, she amassed a collection of several hundred pieces and decided to approach the Metropolitan Museum of Art about donating them for a special wing of American Art. For whatever reason, they refused her gift. Never one to abandon something she believed in, four years later she founded the Whitney Museum of American Art. I loved Gertrude's spunk.

Gertrude also loved to entertain and often staged rather over-the-top parties at both her New York house and country estate in Westbury, ten minutes from our home. These were usually Jazz Age events like those Mr. Fitzgerald wrote about and were all the rage among of some of the wealthy. During the summer of 1927, she invited us to one of her productions in Westbury.

As our car approached the property, there was no mistaking it as a Whitney party. Lights were in the trees, lively music could be heard from some distance, and people in outrageous costumes were everywhere. Yes, this was the place!

Gertrude and Harry met us at the door dressed in jewel-encrusted outfits, she wearing exotic pointy shoes with bells, and Harry sporting a turban. Gertrude's ensemble was decidedly more elaborate and must have reflected the evening's theme. Mummah and I were just modest flappers but Reg had refused all suggestions about costuming himself. Gertrude, then in her fifties, was still quite attractive and looked fabulous! After the usual pleasantries, she showed us into a large room full of tables on which were set blocks of clay, rotating sculpting stands, and tools of the craft. She then explained that she was hoping that after a little champagne, some of her guests might discover their hidden artistic talent and there might be another Rodin among them. Our accomplishment would be ours to remember the evening; party favors were quite the thing then.

Then Mummah, Reg, and I went out to the garden where a full orchestra was playing. Elaborately costumed waiters were also passing drinks while wild animals were parading about in their own jeweled outfits. As we wandered among the other guests, we saw a veritable circus of jugglers, musicians, and exotic animals performing under giant palm trees and splashing fountains. It was all quite amazing and must have taken a great deal of time and expense to arrange; Gertrude had outdone herself! As we each collected a glass of champagne from a passing tray, I remember suddenly noticing a full-grown elephant in an ornate robe and crown, then a monkey in an emerald-green vest with a matching hat, of course, hats are always de rigueur? Though I never saw it, Reg also said there was jaguar. The whole thing looked like a movie set, but I suppose that was the idea. In spite of all this outrageousness though, Gertrude was always a sincere and gracious hostess. After we looked around a bit and chatted with some of the other guests, I announced I was going to find my inner sculptor and left Mummah and Reg in the "zoo."

Gertrude Vanderbilt Whitney

1917

Almost immediately I decided on a subject, and hardly any time seemed to have passed before I had nearly finished the figure of a dancing girl. She had her hair up, and her hands behind her back like Spanish women do. I didn't think it was too bad and was also surprised because I hadn't found it very difficult.

After dinner, Gertrude asked everyone to join her in the studio. She walked among the tables and made pleasant comments about each piece, not knowing which of her guests had done them. When she came to mine, she was very complimentary and remarked how adeptly the artist had handled various things. I was certainly flattered but also slightly amazed because she herself was an accomplished sculptor. I convinced myself she was just being nice, even as Reg was positively enthralled by his wife's newly discovered talent and kept beaming at me.

We returned to the garden, and Gertrude came over to ask if I had done something. I said, "Yes, the dancing girl." Well, she launched into my "amazing natural ability," how I must "develop it" and even talked about finding me the perfect mentor with whom to study. It was lovely of her but it all seemed so considerably out of my usual realm, it was slightly ridiculous. I really didn't take her comments seriously but thanked her. After she left our little group, I never gave it another thought.

I guess I'd forgotten how determined a woman Gertrude Vanderbilt was and just how many people she knew in the art world. Within a week, she called to tell me she had found the perfect teacher and had already spoken to him! Yikes! As she went on about this and that, hardly allowing me a moment to respond, she told me my mentor was a well-regarded sculptor and he was looking forward to meeting me at his New York studio. I was positively stunned! She had sprung it on me so suddenly, I felt I just couldn't say I wasn't interested, so I kept those thoughts to myself. I felt I had to commit after she'd gone to so much trouble. She told me that my teacher Paul Manship would be working on several projects in his studio for which he'd already received commissions and a number of other sculptors would also be there assisting him, so I wouldn't be intruding. She said it was actually an ideal situation, because he could help me begin a piece, go back to his own work, and then return later to check how I was doing. This sort of teaching would encourage me to create my own style rather than copy his.

On the first day I visited him, he gave me a tour, discussed the work that was being completed, showed me drawings of some of his commissions, and explained what happened at every stage of a piece. I remember a large sculpture in the middle of the skylight studio which would eventually be a memorial to the servicemen that had died in World War I and was to be installed at the American Cemetery in France. He also showed me some smaller pieces that included busts and bas-relief plaques, the sort of sculpting used on coins and medals. Some of his work was of women in flowing gowns, which I thought especially beautiful. These made me think Gertrude might have chosen him as my mentor because my dancing girl was slightly similar ... very slightly.

I would study with Paul on and off for nearly twenty years. He was a wonderful teacher, always encouraging, and his suggestions about composition and detailing were very helpful; I still feel very lucky to have had him as a mentor. He never insisted on a specific schedule and always welcomed me whenever I was able to return. I did many female figures, some quite large, and also some animals; one was of our Springer Spaniel, Harry. Paul also encouraged me to try bas-relief, and I treasure a small plaque I did of Reggie as a baby. In the forties, I began a life-size bust of Reg but was unable to finish.

Through my study of sculpture, I acquired an entirely new sense of myself and my value as a person. It was also lovely to feel one had some special ability. Gertrude's Hollywood garden party gave me a certain respect for myself I might never have known otherwise. Her gift would be with me the rest of my life.

As the years passed, I couldn't help but notice Leonardo's enduring interest in David. He was almost always there for his birthday and at Christmas. Whenever he joined us, he always had time to talk to David or encourage him in whatever he wanted to show him; it really felt like he was fathering him. It was also easy to see David had special feelings about Leonardo as well. It was amazing to see how just a small amount of interest from a male adult could have such a strong impact on a young boy. Reg was certainly a master in the business world, but he didn't seem to have any interest in his sons. Perhaps that was how his father was with him? Even if Leonardo was not his father, David had that sort of relationship with him, and it would continue throughout their lives.

In the fall that year, the Columbia Phonographic Broadcasting System began transmitting to forty-seven radio stations across the country. The company would later change its name to CBS.

The Holland Tunnel linked New Jersey to New York City under the Hudson River that fall.

Two days after Christmas, America's first musical, *Showboat*, opened on Broadway. Florenz Zeigfeld was the producer, so it featured an army of his trademark showgirls dressed in lots of sequins and huge feathered headdresses. It was fabulously extravagant!

Edwina -Self-Portrait

1928

Out in Los Angeles that March, a dam holding back thirty-eight thousand acres of water broke, and a forty-foot wall of water plunged toward the Pacific Ocean fifty-four miles away. Six hundred people in its path were killed as they slept snugly in their beds.

By June, two new bridges also linked Staten Island to New Jersey and Long Island.

Another useless treaty, signed by fifty-four countries, outlawed "aggressive" war; what could that possibly be; badminton rackets only? The document was officially called the General Treaty for Renunciation of War as an Instrument of National Policy. Both Germany and the Soviet Union ratified it, but both countries would secretly conspire together to build "experimental centers" where Hitler would build a huge fleet of airplanes, train pilots, and develop chemical weapons— all violations of the Versailles Treaty they both signed ten years earlier. And because it was in the Soviet Union, it would be completely hidden from Allied eyes. The GTRWINP, see above really long name, would not save any nation from being overrun by Germany... not even the Soviet Union.

It seems the world's most powerful countries, those not run by dictators, are the only ones who can prevent war, but only with constant vigilance and cooperation. They must work together to limit aggressive authoritarian leaders from acquiring advanced weaponry and attempting to take control of their neighbors. When this becomes impossible or these peace-loving countries won't shoulder the burden, it will be the end of all of us. Treaties can only be a beginning.

The Scottish scientist Alexander Fleming discovered the antibiotic penicillin and for the first time it was possible to treat diseases like pneumonia, syphilis, meningitis, and diphtheria. Previously, becoming infected with such things meant certain death. Fleming's discovery also meant that many of the wounds incurred in war were no longer fatal. Mr. Fleming was awarded the Nobel Prize in Medicine seventeen years later for his remarkable discovery. I suppose it took that long to truly understand all that penicillin could do.

A devastating hurricane swept through Florida and up North Carolina with winds of 160 miles an hour; an astonishing four thousand people in its path lost their lives. Better weather forecasting would greatly reduce these kinds of weather-related deaths.

Sperry Gyroscope went through some dramatic changes that December. First it was sold to North American Aviation, a holding company composed of a number of aircraft manufacturers and airlines. General Electric then briefly took control of North American, and the Sperry Gyroscope Company became incorporated. I didn't exactly understand how that affected how it functioned, but the following year, Sperry Gyroscope Inc. and Ford Instrument were spun off and became the Sperry Corporation, and Reg was elected president at forty-one. He had joined Mr. Sperry when there were only two people in a very small shop; it was still difficult for me to believe that just sixteen years later it had transformed itself into such a huge company.

William Sims Gillmor

David Spear Gillmor

1929

In San Francisco, a woman was actually arrested for wearing men's clothing; ridiculous! I suppose they'd run out of bank robbers, murderers, bombers, and mobsters to arrest.

I will never forget February 21, 1929. Margot was in Palm Springs, California with Herbert when he called to tell us she had contracted meningitis. The very next day he called again and said she was dead! We kept thinking there must be some mistake. She was perfectly healthy when we saw her just a few days before. Then, very quickly Herbert began calling Mummah insisting she make all sorts of arrangements for Margot's funeral, and he hadn't even boarded the train for New York! He even announced in the *New York Times* that her funeral would be the day the train pulled into Pennsylvania Station. We couldn't imagine why he was in such a hurry. It was very difficult for all of us but particularly Mummah. He kept calling her several times a day and demanding she do this and that. There simply wasn't enough time to make all the arrangements and the service had to be re-announced for the following day. It was very strange. Margot was just forty-one, and her son only fourteen.

Her funeral was held in the same church where she had been married just fifteen years before. It was heartbreaking for all of us. I couldn't tell if it was for Herbert.

As her husband, he had the right to decide where she was to be buried, and he chose a plot in Sag Harbor, way out at the end of Long Island. At the time, it seemed an odd choice, as even his parents hadn't lived anywhere near there in years. It almost felt like he wanted to keep her away from us. There were other unusual things about Margot's death, but at that point, we hadn't discovered the strangest one. Of course, when anyone is interred, the marker isn't there when the graveside service is conducted. So on the anniversary of her death, Mummah and I went to visit her grave. To our horror, the director's records indicated no one with her name was buried in that cemetery! Only after walking among the headstones and reading a great many did we discover why. Her headstone bore the name as "Margaret," not Marguerite! It was then that I began to understand why Herbert might have wanted to rush everything and also keep Mummah busy by demanding things. He didn't want an autopsy! That might have discovered another reason for her death. He also might have buried her so far away so we wouldn't discover the wrong name on her headstone when it was finally installed. Lastly, if we did find her grave, we wouldn't be able to have her exhumed for an autopsy because the records clearly indicated one "Margaret Spear Soames" was buried there, not our Margot. I was a horrible, sickening end to my beautiful sister's life.

I did a little research after that terrible discovery and learned that bacterial meningitis is usually deadly, but it can be the result of a blow to the head. An accurate diagnosis can only be made with an autopsy. It seemed Herbert was not just a weasel but one without a soul. (Author's note: Herbert Jerome Soames married again the following year. All mention of his ever having been married to Margot were removed from the family's history.)

Twenty-six-year-old Laura Ingalls created a most unusual aviation record that year. She did 980 continuous loops in a single-wing, open-cockpit Gypsy Moth over a field in Oklahoma. Three months later, she managed an astonishing 714 barrel rolls in the same aircraft which actually had folding wings! But even more astonishing, eleven years later she was tried as a Nazi spy and sent to prison though she staunchly insisted she was only doing publicity for Hitler.

That was the same year flight attendants first served food to passengers on a Pan American World Airways flight; they were all men. United was the first to hire women for these positions, but they insisted they had to also be trained nurses; that actually brought to mind disasters, not happy flying. After the Depression, these jobs were one of the few open to women and, consequently, were in great demand. In 1935, Transcontinental and Western Airlines advertised for forty-three female flight attendants and two thousand applied. Eventually, they began calling them stewardesses, and the requirements took on a very different tone. You couldn't be taller than five foot four, older than twenty-six and weigh over 118 pounds. Once you were hired, you also had to have a physical every three months but that wasn't to make sure you were healthy. It was to determine if you were still attractive enough! I'm sure they never checked pilots to assure they were good-looking. It was so difficult for women to find work then that they put up with that sort of nonsense.

The very first Academy Awards were given that year. Contrary to the lavish ceremonies that would later characterize the presentations, the first one only took fifteen minutes. *Wings* won for Best Picture.

The Vatican somehow managed to get itself declared a country; I guess that was the ultimate solution to the difficulty of separating of church and state policies; make them one!

Then Germany announced it wasn't going to pay its World War I debts! I guess that money had gone to "research" in the Soviet Union?

Americans increased their cigarette use by inhaling a billion more than the year before. Of course, no one imagined then that it could be harmful or even kill you. Britain's King James I was the first national leader to come out against smoking back in the early 1600s. But German doctors in the early 1900s were the first to link smoking to cancer, and the Nazis were the first to initiate an actual antismoking campaign. Hitler disapproved of smoking but he wasn't worried about its health risks; he thought it was morally irresponsible—certainly an unusual attitude for someone who oversaw the murder of eleven million people.

The Graf Zeppelin returned to Lakehurst, New Jersey from its first round-the-world trip of twenty-one days. Almost exactly ten years later over the same field, the spectacular explosion of the Hindenburg would, for all practical purposes, end the use of dirigibles for transportation.

In September 1929, the first "all blind" flight was made by aviation pioneer Army Lieutenant Jimmy Doolittle at Mitchell Field on Long Island. The term refers to the pilot's use of only his instruments to fly his aircraft. Lt. Doolittle wore a hood to prevent him from seeing anything but the dashboard and never looked outside. This is now called IFR and wouldn't have been possible without the artificial horizon, directional gyroscope, and the many other instruments Sperry invented to facilitate flying. As airplanes became faster, human reaction time was also unable to respond quickly enough and instruments became absolute necessities. Lt. Doolittle was the first to recognize this need and developed the first programs to teach instrument-only flying. It was the combination of Sperry's advanced instrumentation and Lt. Doolittle's IFR programs that made all-weather commercial airline travel possible. Trans World Airways was the first to use IFR flying.

The new country of Yugoslavia was formed in October from Serbia, Montenegro, Slovenia, Croatia, Bosnia, Herzegovina, and Macedonia. Time will prove the union a poor marriage.

October 29, 1929, brought complete devastation to the US economy. The stock market collapsed and signaled the beginning of the Great Depression. In two days, the total value of all the stocks listed on Wall Street dropped $30 billion and would eventually be worth only 89 percent of their pre-crash value. The nation's banking system also began to collapse; over the next three years four thousand banks around the nation failed. The economy wouldn't fully recover for seventeen years.

It was after the crash that I learned what Mummah had wanted to tell me earlier after she'd received word of my cousin's death. We were having tea in the library, the boys were away at school, and Reg was in England. It was a lovely fall afternoon and I was admiring all the beautiful shades of lavender in the hydrangeas outside the French doors. We had stopped talking, and suddenly I became aware that Mummah was looking at me. When I turned toward her, I was surprised to see how sad she looked. Actually, I was immediately reminded of the way the headmistress at school looked the morning she told me Papa had died. At first, Mummah seemed reluctant to speak, and then she finally said there was something she had wanted to tell me for a long time but had waited for the right moment. She now supposed there would never be such a moment.

Reggie - David - Bill

She began by telling me that the evening Papa died at the train station, he hadn't been alone; she was with him. They had been to the theatre together. Because I was young and often away from the family, I probably hadn't noticed that Papa had been quite depressed. She said they'd talked about him seeing a doctor, but he kept telling her it was nothing. Gradually, she began to think it wasn't about something that happened at work or any particular event but a sadness that seemed to pervade everything, sort of nothing in particular and everything in general. But every time she brought it up, he'd brush her concerns aside and say, "Maybe later."

Then she went back to that night at the theatre in Chicago. They had taken the train home as usual and it had stopped at Evanston. Papa got off first and helped her down. Expecting him to follow her, she walked toward the station, but when she got to the door, Papa wasn't behind her. As she turned to look for him, she noticed the train just starting to leave for the next station. Suddenly she heard the brakes screech and it slowed. Then people began screaming and a crowd began rushing toward the the engine. She wasn't really very interested though, she just wanted to find Papa. Then she saw a conductor that knew them walking toward her. He asked her if she would come inside the station. As she stood in front of him, he calmly told her there had been an accident. As she wondered what that could have to do with her, she heard him say Papa had been hurt and a doctor had been called. He asked her to wait there while he found out how he was doing.

She quietly waited in the station for what seemed like a long time before the conductor came back. Talking very softly, he told her the doctor had done his best, but Papa was severely injured. Then he told her how very sorry he was, that there was nothing the doctor could do for him and Papa had died. As her heart dissolved in despair, he lowered his voice and quietly added, "I'm so very sorry, Mrs. Spear. I saw the whole thing, but I wasn't close enough to stop him. I feel you would want to know that your husband intentionally stepped in front of the train. Please know that I will never speak of what I saw to anyone. You have my solemn word; I will insist it was an accident."

I was numb with despair. My poor Papa had somehow been so desperate. I felt so terribly sad and wanted to put my arms around him and tell him how much I loved him. What could possibly have made him feel that was the only thing he could do? Of course, nobody can know what someone is thinking at that moment but after years of turning it over and over in mind, I would come to understand a little better. Such a loss does leave a hollow place in your heart though and it never ever goes away. You can only get used to it being there. Dear Papa had been gone twenty-two years by then, but I felt as if his loss had just happened…

November brought the opening of the new Museum of Modern Art in New York. Abby Aldrich Rockefeller, the wife of John Rockefeller II, was the driving force behind it. As her husband had disapproved of the project, he refused to finance it so she funded it entirely with only her own money; wealthy, determined women seemed to be a hallmark of that time. The museum was first located on the twelfth floor of a building at the corner of Fifth Avenue at Fifty-Seventh Street. Mummah and I thought we'd like to see what "modern art" meant, so we roped Reg and Leonardo into taking us to the opening reception. The post-Impressionist work of Vincent Van Gogh, Paul Cezanne, and George Seurat was among the pieces. They were different but also interesting and certainly provoked some lively conversation during dinner afterward at Delmonico's in Lower Manhattan. What with our differing opinions about what we'd just seen and the restaurant's famous Lobster Newburg, it was a lively and delicious evening. We also couldn't resist capping the evening off with one of the Delmonico's spectacular Baked Alaska they'd also invented. It arrived at our table after flaming its way across the entire dining room. We all shared it and it was enormously yummy!

Commander Byrd was at it again. In November, he claimed to have flown over the South Pole this time. Now, no one believed him.

In late November, my family was hit with yet another tragedy. It was a Saturday afternoon, and eight-year-old David was upstairs taking a nap. When I walked through the front hall, I heard him screaming just as his nanny was coming down the stairs. I asked her what was the matter with David, and she casually answered, "Oh, he just doesn't want to take a nap." I still cannot understand how anyone could hear that sort of screaming and believe it was just a prank. I asked her to please check on him. A moment later, she came running out of his room yelling, "Mrs. Gillmor, there's been a fire! David's hurt."

We rushed him to Doctors Hospital in New York, where we were told he had severe burns over almost the entire left side of his body. He had secretly taken some matches to his room and while playing with them had ignited the mattress. In those days, mattresses were made of straw! I try never to imagine the terrifying scene in his bedroom that afternoon.

David would spend nearly an entire year in the hospital and endure endless painful skin grafts. I was sick with worry the whole time. Reg rented a small apartment on Eighty-Ninth Street next door to the hospital so we could be near him as often as possible. I stayed with him at least part of almost every day. It was a grueling experience.

Meanwhile, Mummah bought a larger house in Forest Hills to be closer to the station, where I could catch the train to the city and Reg would be closer to Sperry. She also took charge of Reggie and Bill, which was a huge relief. Dear Mummah seemed to spend her whole life helping those she loved. It was certainly a time when I couldn't have managed without her. Reg visited the hospital whenever he could, as did Leonardo. David seemed especially cheered whenever he appeared and it was almost the only thing I could count on to make David smile. Though the apartment was close by and I'd go there at night, I never slept very well and was almost as tired the next morning.

On New Year's Eve that year, Guy Lombardo combined an old Scottish folk song with the words from an eighteenth-century poem by Robert Burns. It would be the very first time "Auld Lang Syne" was played. Though it quickly became a staple for welcoming in another year, I cannot ever hear it without thinking of David in the hospital.

1930

In the Soviet Union, Joseph Stalin began nationalizing farms; they were now "owned" by everybody. Essentially, this meant that though the farmers did all the work, the state distributed the products to Stalin's cronies.

Thousands of Russian farmers promptly fled the country for Poland.

That was also the year that the last farm in New York City at 213th Street, was sold to a developer. It's really hard to think of the city as farmland now.

In Massachusetts, Brooklyn-born Clarence Birdseye had just started testing his flash-frozen foods on retail customers. They included meat, fish, fruit, spinach, peas, and oysters. Frozen, defrosted oysters didn't actually sound very appealing. Mr. Birdseye had originally been a taxidermist but when he became a scientist for the US Agricultural Department he learned his freezing process from the local Inuits in Labrador. Mrs. Marjorie Merriweather Post became his staunchest supporter and used his frozen foods extensively on her huge yacht as she traveled around the world. Everyone who dined on them marveled at how she managed to serve such "fresh" food so far from the sources of such things. After years of trying to convince the board of her Postum

Cereal Co. they should invest in Mr. Birdseye's company, she finally succeeded and they bought 51 percent of the company. Goldman Sachs bought the remaining 49 percent. Two years later, however, Goldman decided frozen food wasn't going to be a good investment and sold all their shares back to Postum; good work, guys!

John Rockefeller II had been planning a twenty-two-acre business complex in the heart of Manhattan. After the stock market crash, however, he found it impossible to obtain the necessary financing. In 1930, he decided to rely solely on his own ability to borrow the needed capital. The fourteen-building Rockefeller Center would be the largest construction project ever undertaken in the United States by a single individual.

The planet Pluto was discovered that February and was named after the Greek god of the underworld. Its orbit was at the outer most edge of our solar system.

In New York, a Swedish model who had taken up acting appeared in her first "talkie" film, "Anna Christie." Greta Garbo's most memorable line, delivered in a surprisingly husky voice, was "Gimme a whiskey."

The income of the average American family in 1929 had decreased 2 percent; quite surprising considering the stock market crash of the preceding year. As most Americans did not have enough money to buy stocks, they were spared the catastrophic losses suffered by those who were able to invest in such speculating.

In March, Mr. and Mrs. Sperry were visiting Cuba when she became ill and died quite suddenly. They had been inseparable partners in everything and I immediately thought Mr. Sperry wouldn't do well without her. Just three months later, he also died of surgical complications. We attended both their funerals at Plymouth Church in Brooklyn and their interments beside each other in Greenwood Cemetery. It was the end of an era and a very warm friendship for both Reg and me.

In May, construction began on the first building in Mr. Rockefeller's giant scheme.

The sixty-six-story Chrysler Building officially opened and though it was the tallest skyscraper in New York for just eleven months, I still think it's the most beautiful one.

Winston's party lost the election that year and he was immediately unemployed.

In August, New York Supreme Court Judge Joseph Crater disappeared after having dinner with his mistress and a friend. He was last seen walking down Forty-Fifth Street alone. Surprisingly, no one missed him for nineteen days, not even his wife. Only when he didn't appear to preside over a trial did the police launch an investigation. They found $5,000 ($70,000 in 2013) was missing from his safe, two of his girlfriends had abruptly left town, and a third had been murdered. Though his disappearance was rumored to involve corruption at City Hall, no trace of him was ever found.

David

1930

In late October David was finally well enough to leave the hospital. We took him home the day before his ninth birthday. There to greet him was a beautiful Irish setter, a gift from Leonardo. David had never had a dog and was thrilled, though mostly he just seemed to be happy he was home. A year is a long time in the hospital, particularly for a child. He looked thin and pale and very delicate, though taller and more handsome. We had been especially worried that the accident would impair his ability to walk, so the doctors encouraged him to exercise. He took up tennis and in no time seemed completely recovered; the scarring on his side would always remain though. He seemed to greatly enjoy this new activity and became quite good at it. To celebrate his miraculous recovery, we had his photograph taken with that beautiful dog; it always reminds me of how relieved I was that he was OK.

Reg began talking about how he needed to go to England for Sperry shortly after David came home. Though at first he didn't say anything about my accompanying him, gradually he began pointing out how I needed a change of scenery. Then he was suggesting how wonderful it would be to see our old friends and wouldn't I like to see all the changes they'd made in the city since the war…we could even visit the same places we'd known when we lived there? He painted such an enchanting picture I finally agreed to go with him. I really thought we'd only be gone a month at the most, but the trip ultimately stretched to nine. Reg's mother died while we were away and we were unable to attend the funeral. Jane and his father had been married shortly after he returned from the Civil War, an incredible sixty-eight years.

1931

Even though we were in England all those months, I still read about what was happening in the States. Hungarian actor Bela Lagosi was becoming famous as Dracula, the "Star Spangled Banner" was officially made the country's national anthem, and the Empire State Building had opened and immediately became the world's tallest building at 1,245 feet and one hundred floors. It would also have a million square feet of office space that needed to be rented but most of the building would stay unoccupied for decades.

One-eyed Texas aviator Wiley Post and his Australian navigator Harold Gatty flew around the world in a little more than eight days. It wouldn't have taken them so long if they hadn't needed to replace their propeller twice. The president awarded them the very first Distinguished Air Medal for their achievement. Two years later, Mr. Post made the same trip alone using Sperry's autopilot and gyrocompass in place of Harold and shaved off a half a day!

Al Capone was finally sent to prison, not for the murder, robbery, and racketeering he'd spent his life perfecting but tax evasion. He was given a sentence of eleven years but was granted early release after seven. I guess it was because he was such a nice man?

Conte Di Savoia

Georgic

The Paris De Strasse

Europa

New York

Conte Di Savoia Gyrostabilizers

1932

1932

Britain had been developing a submarine aircraft carrier since 1927. Yes, it does sound like a most improbable invention. By 1932, they finally thought they'd mastered such a thing. It involved a single seaplane with folding wings mounted on a catapult under the deck. It was launched after the U-boat surfaced; the last phrase in that sentence is the critical one. One day the crew was practicing and trying to beat their previous launching time. They got at little over zealous and raised the catapult before the deck had fully cleared the water line. The ship immediately filled with water, sank and the entire crew went down with it. Though Britain abandoned the concept, the Japanese loved it and eventually built forty-two.

In February, the United States awarded the first Military Order of the Purple Heart to servicemen who had died or been wounded in a foreign military action.

That same month, Austrian-born Adolf Hitler was granted the German citizenship he needed to run for president of the country. Could that have meant that some minor official in a government office could have stopped World War II simply by stamping a red "No"? Mr. Hitler immediately ran for president and was defeated but it would mark the beginning of Hitler's march toward controlling everything in Germany. His Nazi Party then began actively promoting German Nationalism, extreme anti-Semitism, and the overthrow of the democratic Weimer Republic in power at the time. Just eleven months later, he was appointed to the position that would place Germany's destiny entirely in the hands of one insane man.

In New Jersey, the baby son of Charles Lindbergh was kidnapped from his nursery one night, and a ransom note was found on the windowsill demanding $50,000. The news was instantly splashed across the front of every newspaper in the nation. Rather than let the police handle the case, Lindbergh himself took charge. Eventually seven ransom notes would be delivered, Lindbergh would be duped out of the money he paid, and two and a half months later, his son's body was found on the Lindbergh property, most probably killed immediately after being taken from his nursery. At that point Lindbergh let the police take over and a short time later a German immigrant was arrested. It was discovered that he'd left a criminal record in his home country and $15,000 of the ransom money was in his house. He was put on trial, found guilty, and executed three years later. The crime resulted in legislation that made kidnapping a federal crime.

In 1932, an American researcher accidentally discovered how to combine molten glass with compressed air and fiberglass was created.

By that year, Sperry gyrostabilizers had been installed on a thousand merchant ships and the company's workforce had expanded to one hundred thousand with operations around the world.

The Dow Jones plummeted to $41.22, the lowest level of the entire Great Depression. For comparison, in the 1940s that number would usually be between $146 and $206.

By August, the results of Stalin's agriculture policies had become dramatically visible, though only to Russians. Widespread famine had led to such mass starvation that dead bodies were littering city streets. The rest of the world wouldn't know this for years because Stalin prohibited photographs of these poor people to leave the country; he said they were "propaganda." The very definition of propaganda is the use of lies to create a false impression.

It was Labor Day in New York City and a steamship was backing out of its berth to take two hundred ironworkers to Riker's Island where they were building a new prison. Suddenly an enormous explosion lifted the ship out of the water and blasted debris and bodies everywhere. What was left of the vessel immediately sank. As crowds gathered on the pier in search of their loved ones, seventy-two bodies were pulled from the water. Ensuing investigations discovered the ship had actually sunk forty-four years earlier and was refloated, renovated, and put back in service. It also revealed that the ship's owner was not the captain, as expected, but his teenage son. The boy, who had been working in the concession stand at the time of the accident and was still in the hospital recovering from injuries. Apparently, after questioning the seaworthiness of his purchase, his father had decided to put the boat in his son's name to limit his liability in the event of some catastrophe. When the boy was finally released from the hospital, he was put on trial for negligence. In the end the judge ruled him not guilty and held his father liable.

In late September, Reg went to Genoa for the sea trials of the new Italian liner *Conte di Savoia.* She had been equipped with three enormous Sperry gyrostabilizers to eliminate the normal pitch and roll experienced by passengers in rough seas. This was the first time this problem had ever been addressed but they did add six hundred thousand pounds to the weight of the ship and cost the Italian government $1 million. There had also been some problems during the trials, so Reg decided to sail to New York on her maiden voyage. It was not a pleasant trip.

Somewhere along the way a valve jammed and a large hole was blown in the hull below the waterline! The loss of 2,200 lives seemed eminent but was averted by the quick action of a clever crew member. The incident seemed to foreshadow the tragic end that ultimately awaited this beautiful ship.

When World War II began, she was taken out of service and stored in Venice. In the later stages of the conflict, the German army retreated through the area and set her on fire. She was then refitted to transport Italian troops. In 1943 the Allies bombed and sank the vessel but two years later she was refloated. After another five rusting in place, the gorgeous *Conte di Savoia,* filled with the very best Italian craftsmanship and design, pride of Italy, ended as nothing more than a huge pile of scrap metal.

Now we come to the second mistake the Allies made that led to World War II, the first being their failure to enforce the Versailles Treaty armament restrictions on Germany. At a world disarmament conference held in 1932, Germany was actually allowed to rearm beyond the limits stipulated in the Versailles Treaty! This was especially strange because Hitler had already been rearming Germany for the previous five years with the help of Stalin. The decision by the disarmament attendees practically sent a letter to Hitler saying, "We are so afraid of confronting you we'll overlook the armament restrictions placed on you by the Versailles Treaty.

Now please be good enough to stop your aggressive posturing. You're scaring your neighbors."

Confronting Germany couldn't possibly have been as bad as the destruction that rained on the world during World War II.

In New York City, Radio City Music Hall opened two days after Christmas. It was the first building to be finished in Mr. Rockefeller's huge complex and it was named for its first tenant the Radio Corporation of America, later to become RCA. The theater could seat over six thousand people and was handsomely decorated with Art Deco designs of aluminum, glass, chrome, and leather and several impressive murals. The stage also became famous for its advanced hydraulic elevator that was able to raise a full orchestra or an ice-skating rink up from the basement. It was really an astonishing thing to see, especially if you weren't expecting it. It was such an engineering feat that the US Navy used the same system on its aircraft carriers during World War II. The building also became home to a large radio studio and later stage sets for television broadcasting. The first performance in the theatre was a variety show, but the format proved unpopular. Within a week, the program was changed and the precision dance team the Rockettes began appearing after a film. The line of high- kicking girls quickly became the theater's hallmark and is still one of New York's major tourist attractions.

Before the end of the year, the two newly minted countries of Hejaz and Nejd joined together to become Saudi Arabia. Instantaneously it became one of the world's poorest nations. Four years later oil was discovered. After a period of development, the hunger for petroleum would transform the country into one of the world's richest.

1933

The people of German began enthusiastically supporting their new leader. Huge crowds cheered Hitler as he vigorously told them only he could return the country to its former greatness. After an election January 30, both Nazi and Communist candidates gained a huge majority of seats in the legislative house, the Reichstag. This forced the president to appoint Hitler chancellor. He promptly introduced legislation to give him near complete control of the government but the Reichstag refused to pass it. Hitler wasn't going to let that stand in his way. He arranged to have the building where they met, set on fire! This seemed to "encourage" their cooperation. The next day they passed the measures that made Germany a one-party state, nullified most of the country's civil liberties, ceded Hitler the power he'd sought and made him dictator of the country. His first move was to greatly expand the secret police and appoint Hermann Goring head of security. This followed a proven formula for taking over a country. Then Goring began liquidating all Nazi opposition and Hitler started to implement his violent and aggressive campaign against the country's Jews. His first concentration camp, Dachau, opened the day before he was elected Führer.

As his plans for Germany moved forward many people in the West became alarmed and boycotts of German products were organized. An anti-Nazi rally was also held in New York that filled Madison Square Garden and attracted an overflow crowd of 50,000 in the streets outside. Simultaneously, similar protests were held in seventy cities around the world. I thought these huge public outcries would have had some effect on the world's leaders, but over the next twelve years neither the United States nor any other large nation intervened to protect these people. Meanwhile, inside Germany Hitler's depravities increased to include atrocities the world would never have believed possible.

Many still wonder how the German population so enthusiastically supported Hitler's leadership. At that time, Germany had not fully recovered from the economic ruination brought on by the combination of the 1929 Wall Street Crash in the United States and the catastrophic effects of World War I on the country—not, I must add, the punishments inflicted by the Versailles Treaty. Hitler recognized that a great many Germans were angry about the circumstances of their daily lives and carefully crafted speeches to capitalize on this discontent. He charismatically referred to the earlier prosperity they had enjoyed under an autocratic ruler, blamed the punitive damages of the Versailles Treaty for their suffering and gave voice to the angry sentiments many Germans felt about the loss of their former glory. Of course, he left out any references to the fact that the primary cause of the country's economic collapse was the war that Germany itself had started. His charisma as a speaker, coupled with his angry rhetoric, spoke to the uneducated masses. They heard the words they wanted to hear and Hitler gave their frustrations a voice. It was the perfect combination of rhetoric in the perfect political climate and gave Hitler the power he wanted. Their new democratic government was also so locked in bickering that it wasn't functioning and Hitler told the crowds that their suffering was also the result of this form of government. A master manipulator, he kept reinforcing that if they followed him and him alone, his leadership would return Germany to its former greatness and prosperity. Hitler clearly understood his audience and delivered simple statements they could easily understand. Before long they were gladly raising their right arms to proclaim him their exalted savior. Of course, he didn't tell them he wasn't interested in Germany's prosperity, just absolute power over their country and the rest of the world.

Prometheus - Skating Rink

Rockefeller Center - New York

With his new political power as chancellor, Hitler began passing laws that eventually abolished all the rights of Germany's Jewish citizens. First he limited the number of Jews who could attend schools and universities, then the number of Jewish doctors and lawyers who could practice and what they could charge. This was followed by forbidding Jewish lawyers to take new cases, prohibiting Jewish doctors from treating non-Jewish patients, and even prohibiting Jewish actors from appearing on the stage or in films. Many more laws restricting the lives of the country's Jews would soon follow.

Thirty Rockefeller Plaza, the seventy-floor centerpiece of Rockefeller Center, was finally finished and the four of us went to the opening ceremony. A thousand-foot mural by Diego Rivera covered the walls of the two-story lobby. Though it was titled *Man at the Crossroads*, I don't think Mr. Rockefeller had that particular crossroad in mind. Mr. Rivera had apparently failed to convey some of the details of his painting before its unveiling, particularly a scene in which Vladimir Lenin was clearly depicted. Mr. Rockefeller was not pleased and privately asked that the Bolshevik be painted over. Mr. Rivera refused. After a great deal of back and forth, the artist was paid and the mural removed. It was eventually replaced with *American Progress* by Catalonian artist Joseph Maria Sert. Having seen both, I greatly preferred Mr. Sert's vision. His mural covered not only the walls of the lobby but the entire ceiling as well; giants were realistically painted standing on parapets supporting the ceiling on their backs. It was absolutely spectacular!

Outside in front of the building on Fifth Avenue, Mr. Rockefeller had commissioned Lee Lawrie to design a sculpture. Though it wasn't in place then and wouldn't be for another four years, it would be a mammoth four- story Atlas carrying a huge sphere of circles representing the heavens. It was grandly heroic and certainly a fitting greeting to the formal entrance of Mr. Rockefeller's huge complex in the heart of Manhattan. It too was not without controversy though. Some people began saying the face of Atlas resembled Italian Dictator Benito Mussolini. The sculpture was so stylized and angular, it seemed ridiculous that anyone could make such a comparison. Someone later wrote that Atlas's face was what Mussolini wished he looked like. Fortunately, Atlas kept his face as Mr. Lawrie had designed it.

In the center of the complex, there was to be an open area with formal gardens and a sunken terrace that would be transformed into an ice-skating rink during winter months. When the first building was dedicated, Paul Manship's golden figure of Prometheus wasn't ready and wouldn't be installed until the following year but, of course, I was there for the dedication! Even though the fountains weren't finished, Paul's sculpture was spectacular and received a great deal of critical acclaim. I remember thinking how ironic the compliments were because Paul didn't think it was one of his best pieces. Over the years though, city residents and visitors alike seemed to have loved its presence and what it represented particularly for Americans. It is still one of New York City's most loved and recognizable landmarks.

When Prohibition finally ended, Reg and Leonardo decided to celebrate with a special "research" project. Once and for all time, they would determine which gin really made the best martini. But this would be no casual pour and shake, or stir and drink study. First they purchased a case of every brand of gin they thought was most likely to be the winner, in short a truckload. I wasn't certain of how it had been determined that such large quantities of test material were necessary, but oh well. Then they enlisted Leonardo's new friend Genevieve Duffy as their lab director. She had been hired because she was willing to adhere to the exacting laboratory protocols demanded by the researchers, and because she looked quite striking in a lab coat. Highly accurate methodology and standard scientific practices of the day were strictly adhered to, ensuring total accuracy, of course; Genevieve used eyedropper. Each test was conducted blind, as they say, so the volunteers never knew what they had drunk, excuse the pun. They just marked their little cards. The participants seemed to greatly enjoy the experiment and often remarked, "I think I need another, just to be sure." After all that measuring and sampling, to this day I'm not entirely certain of their conclusions; maybe Beefeater?

That was our first introduction to Genevieve. Though she was from Brooklyn, she didn't have that unusual accent, seemed very refined, well educated and also quite well traveled, particularly in Europe. She was just eighteen when we met her but very poised. I suppose as the actress she was, one had to master such things or being on stage wouldn't ever attract you. Actually, she appeared in many New York productions and later would even form a theater group called the Sperry Players. Genevieve folded right into our lives as Leonardo's perpetual girlfriend and would remain so for as long as I knew her. She was lovely company, so it didn't matter that she was half Leonardo's age. During the summer, two British men managed to fly over 29,000- foot Mt. Everest in the Himalayas between Tibet and Nepal. They accomplished this amazing feat in a two-seater biplane with an enlarged propeller. It was definitely a triumph, but it also demonstrated the need for pressurized cabins with an independent oxygen supply.

In 1933, President Roosevelt proposed eight New Deal programs to address the huge numbers of starving, unemployed Americans and their families. The Agricultural Adjustment Act (AAA) paid farmers not to plant and to slaughter their excess stock because there wasn't enough consumer demand to continue existing production levels. The Civil Work Administration (CWA) created four million jobs constructing bridges and new buildings the country needed anyway. The Civilian Conservation Corps (CCC) created three million additional jobs constructing new roads, public parks and planting trees. The Farm Credit Administration (FCA) helped farmers refinance their land and cover operating expenses with lower interest rate loans. The Home Owners Loan Corp (HOLC) also refinanced home mortgages at lower interest rates. The Tennessee Valley Authority (TVA) provided flood control, hydroelectric power and economic development in the particularly devastated areas of the Tennessee Valley, Alabama, Mississippi, Kentucky, Georgia, North Carolina and Virginia. The Works Progress Administration (WPA) provided more construction work building roads, hospitals and schools, as well as work for artists, writers, actors and film directors. The National Industrial Recovery Act (NIRA) developed industry codes to protect workers, ensure fair competition and pricing, and encouraged the development of new businesses. Though the NIRA also addressed dangerous working conditions, extremely long workdays, and the starvation wages characteristic of the Robber Barons, the US Supreme Court declared it unconstitutional the following year.

In early October, a United Airlines plane exploded over Indiana en route from New Jersey to Chicago. All seven people aboard were killed. It was the first recorded incident of sabotage on a commercial aircraft. Investigators found a bomb had exploded in the baggage compartment and concluded it was the work of the Chicago mob though no one was ever prosecuted.

1934

In New York, the year began with a new mayor, Fiorella La Guardia. His installation marked the end of seventy-five years of Tammany Hall corruption. Mayor LaGuardia was a remarkable man and had made the most of his modest upbringing before his election. He was born in Greenwich Village to an Italian Catholic father and a Hungarian Jewish mother, who raised him as an Episcopalian. In his early adult years, he worked for the State Department in Hungary, Italy, and Croatia and also as an interpreter on Ellis Island. At the same time, he was earning a law degree at New York University. He also persevered through some major personal tragedies. He married his first wife in 1919 but just two years later, she died of tuberculosis and left him with an infant daughter. Before the year ended, his child was also dead after contracting spinal meningitis. As mayor, he would become so loved and admired that he was not only elected to a record three terms but an airport was named for him while he was still in office.

February brought New York a massive taxi strike; 2000 cabdrivers parked in the streets in Times Square demanding the right to unionize. This virtually shut down the city. Forty-five days later when their demands weren't met 4,500 did it again.

Hitler violated the Treaty of Versailles again by introducing conscription followed by full-scale rearmament. Britain and France protested but in the end chose to avoid a confrontation. Hitler then began dramatically increasing the amount of money he spent on defense though the rest of the world probably wouldn't know that. By 1939, Hitler was spending

$7 billion a year while the United States was allocating $1 billion. Then I guess he was ready so he publicly declared Germany was not going to abide by any of the terms of the Versailles Treaty; he really hadn't anyway though.

The year 1934 saw the beginning of severe dust storms in the Midwest. They eventually stripped all the topsoil from one hundred thousand acres of farmland in Texas, Oklahoma, Kansas, Colorado, and Arkansas. The tilled land in those states was reduced to windswept desert, with visibility often down to three feet. These storms had actually been created by the newly invented gasoline-powered tractor and combine. Their use dramatically increased the number of acres a single farmer could cultivate but this also removed the native grasses that had held the soil together. When a severe drought hit those areas, the natural winds that swept across the prairie stripped the topsoil off otherwise fertile land and it became impossible to grow anything in those over-plowed states. Rural life in those places was devastated. The dust storms eventually became so large and widespread that black clouds of dust even appeared in Washington, DC, and New York City. The Dust Bowl lasted six incredible, sad years into 1940.

On May 23, the three-year crime spree of Clyde Barrow and Bonnie Parker ended when police ambushed the pair on a rural road in Louisiana. The six officers that laid in wait for them fired a total of 130 bullets from eighteen guns; that's twenty-one shots for each man. Was that really necessary? After the smoke cleared fifteen sets of license plates were found in the car; I suppose they wanted to be sure they fit in with the locals, no matter which bank branch they chose.

Hitler had all Germany's anti-Nazi leaders murdered, including some he only imagined were rivals. Single-party systems always demand absolute allegiance.

In July, bank robber John Dellinger was shot as he left a movie theater in Chicago. J. Edgar Hoover's relatively new FBI had been pursuing him for sometime but their overzealousness had killed two innocent people in the process. Mr. Hoover might have needed some good press just then, particularly as his agents had only recently been allowed to carry guns. Dellinger's death certainly fit the bill. Almost immediately after he was killed, however, rumors began leaking from the morgue that threatened to undermine Mr. Hoover's accomplishment. First the dead man's fingerprints didn't match those on Dellinger's fingerprint card. Then the offending card disappeared. It also became apparent that the corpse was taller than Mr. Dellinger and had the wrong color eyes. When Dellinger's father arrived to identify his son, he immediately said, "That's not my boy." All these issues were soon resolved—sort of—when the corpse was buried under five feet of concrete and reinforced steel. More talk after the unusual burial implied that Mr. Dellinger had made a deal with the FBI in return for allowing another man to "die in" for him. He was also given a new identity and was supposedly living in California under the newly formed Witness Protection Program.

During that summer, Reg told me about his education plans for Reggie and Bill, then eighteen and sixteen. He thought Reggie should study engineering and attend the Massachusetts Institute of Technology and Bill should go the Naval Academy. He also talked about the Severn School in Bowie, Maryland, that was founded to prepare young men who intended to enter the Academy. He thought both the boys should go there in the fall to properly prepare them for the schools he had chosen. He thought the discipline at Severn, though not as strict as the Academy, would develop the character and determination needed to be successful in those schools. Having never had a brother, I could only assume it was the father's prerogative to determine the educational and career direction of his male children.

Only after going on at length about the reasoning behind these choices, did he ask for my opinion. I said I thought Reggie seemed a good candidate for MIT and the Severn School might encourage both of them to be more focused but I also told him that I didn't think Bill had the temperament to flourish at the Naval Academy. I decided not to remind him how he himself characterized his years there as unpleasant.

It would have only served to give him a platform to champion "the good education" he'd received there and how it had connected him to Mr. Sperry and a career he loved. He probably would also have added that his father had made the choice for him and he saw no reason why he shouldn't do the same for his sons. I knew I was on the losing team from the outset.

Bill and Reggie both went to Severn that fall with Bill staying two years and Reggie one. Reggie would get accepted at MIT and Bill to the Naval Academy. But none of those plans would turn out as he'd so carefully arranged. Sometimes the road ahead has some sharp turns that cannot be anticipated.

Over the years, it has often amazed me how many men repeat the behaviors of their fathers, even when they clearly remember the distress they brought them growing up. Maybe it's some sort of manly adversity program designed to instill masculinity in sons through hardship and struggle?

August 19, there was an election in Germany and 89.9 percent of the public voted to give Hitler complete control of the country; so much for thinking most Germans weren't onboard for his persecution of Jews. It seems to me now that this support might have arisen from some German character trait that wanted an authority figure to organize everything and tell them what to do? Or perhaps the German educational system didn't encourage actual thinking. Only poorly educated people could fail to see the consequences of a single person being handed such power over them and their country. It seems impossible that intelligent people wouldn't see the enormous possibilities for abuse by allowing this to happen. Hitler must have been very excited about this development because the very next day, he required all military officers to take an oath of allegiance to him that took precedence over their pledge to defend Germany. The handoff was complete and nearly irrevocable. As years of strange laws, serious discrimination, and enforced racism were followed by abductions, confinements, starvations, unspeakable cruelties and millions of deaths would follow. Few dissenters among the population would or could stand up to Hitler after that.

In the states newspapers reported on the opening of a new island prison off the coast of San Francisco. I only remember this because the authorities had decided the inmates at Alcatraz would not be allowed to talk!

Back on the east coast of New Jersey, a terrible shipwreck happened that September. The *Morro Castle* carried over seven hundred passengers as it struggled through a storm pummeling it with sixty mile an hour winds. At some point, the captain became sick and had to go to his cabin to lie down. At short time later, he died. Then a fire erupted in first class and quickly spread out of control. By 3:00 a.m. the ship had lost all power, radio communication, and its ability to steer. Some of the crew panicked and, rather than help the passengers, abandoned ship. Nearby vessels attempted to rescue those on board but were greatly hampered by both the storm and the darkness; 139 people eventually lost their lives trying to escape. Strangely, it was never determined how the captain died or how the fire had started. Years later, a new investigation laid the blame for both on the deranged chief engineer.

1935

The American branch of Alcoholics Anonymous was founded that year. It was based on principles developed by a Lutheran minister in England.

Several laws were also passed that tried to address some of the cutthroat business practices the country's industrialists had been using against their workers. Several other laws including the Public Utilities Act were enacted to curb monopolies and increase taxes on corporations and the wealthy.

The "King of Swing" Benny Goodman made his first public appearance in Los Angeles that summer. His lively music soon swept across the country and made you want to dance!

In September, a category 5 hurricane slammed into the Florida Keys with winds of 185 miles an hour and produced an enormous twenty-foot storm surge that devastated the islands. The WPA had some workers and their families in the area and sent a train to rescue them. When it finally arrived, all but the engine had been swept away. Torrential rain and fierce winds moved up the west coast of the state and killed two hundred people. Another four hundred died as the storm moved through the Carolinas and into Virginia.

George and Ira Gershwin's opera *Porgy and Bess* premiered on Broadway that October. It was based on Du Bois Heyward's novel *Porgy* and was hailed as America's first opera. The music included both the jazz and blues that originated in the United States. The music was so unlike traditional opera, however, that the *New York Herald Tribune* called the production a "half-opera." And critics gave it mixed reviews.

To commemorate the first flight of the Wright brothers thirty-two years earlier, a DC-3 flew from New York to Los Angeles in eleven hours; hard to believe aviation had made such incredible strides in such a relatively short period of time, especially considering the fact that no "flying machines" had existed in the world during all the world's previous centuries.

Hitler's newest anti-Semitic laws revoked the citizenship of all German Jews and prohibited them from marrying, voting, holding public office, going to a hospital, or having their names appear on a war memorial. He also dismissed all German military officers that were Jewish, prohibited Jewish doctoral candidates from taking their final exams, announced that any Jew who held a job must be fired and any business that was owned by a Jew must be immediately sold at below its market value. He also made it mandatory that all Jews register their property, both domestic and foreign. I'm sure that was to make sure he could locate and confiscate all of it. To address anyone who protested Jewish families being taken away, Hitler said they were being taken to special camps for their protection. He also instituted a precise formula for determining exactly who was Jewish; all you needed was one Jewish grandparent, and away you went. It didn't matter if all your other relatives were Christians and you yourself had been a practicing Christian your entire life. It must have been truly horrifying to find yourself and your children trapped in Germany with no way to escape the horrifying danger that was always just outside the door.

I still have a great deal of difficulty understanding how non-Jewish Germans allowed their friends and neighbors to be forced from their homes, put on railroad cars, and never seen again. Perhaps by then some of them were also afraid of Hitler? Too late friends, you already enthusiastically gave him the power he now wielded over you and everyone in Germany. Watching newsreels of German rallies and seeing Hitler's enthusiastic supporters numbering in the tens of thousands, cheering their adoration was really strange and scary. Such images made it difficult to imagine any Germans had reservations about their violent, racist Führer. It certainly made me wonder, even as I remember living among Germans when I was a child; but then I wasn't a Jew.

Reggie

Bill   David

Camp - Rangley Lake - Maine

1936

By the beginning of 1936, another world war looked inevitable. Italy had already signed on to defend France. Based on my previous experience, these sorts of agreements can dramatically change over time though and this one will. As things began to look more and more sinister, the nations lying at Germany's borders seemed as if they were pretending not to notice Hitler's posturing. Some actually acted as though they wanted to be Germans.

Discrimination against women took many forms in the United States then, as it still does. The case of a New Jersey mother seemed especially sad for both her and her children. She was denied custody of them because she was an avowed communist and didn't believe in God. They were awarded to her ex-husband, with the judge asserting "so he could bring them up as Americans."

The Winter Olympics were held in Germany that year, but a number of nations threatened to boycott the games if Hitler continued to say that Jews and blacks wouldn't be allowed to compete. Because Germany so desperately needed the money the event would generate, he eventually backed away from such statements and even ordered the "Jews Unwelcome" signs removed from restaurants and stores. Over six hundred athletes from twenty-eight countries would compete, with

Norwegian figure skater Sonja Henie winning three gold medals. She would also go on to collect ten world titles and later, rather oddly, become the highest-paid actress in Hollywood.

In March, Hitler marched German troops into the demilitarized zone created to protect the Netherlands, Belgium, and France from Germany aggression. Great Britain did confront him but somehow he convinced them he just needed a little more land to grow Germany's economy. It was sort of true; he just left out the part about needing to be in a better position from which to attack those countries. Britain had suffered so terribly in the last war they might have been hoping a larger nation would confront Hitler instead of them.

Margaret Mitchell wrote forty-six books, but when she published *Gone with the Wind* that year it won her more acclaim than any of her other works. It portrayed the struggles of plantation owners in the South during the Civil War; "down south" they call the conflict The War between the States. The book was hugely popular and won her the 1936 National Book Award for Most Distinguished Novel and the Pulitzer Prize for Best Fiction the following year.

June brought record-high temperatures and severe drought to the Midwest. North Dakota actually reached a high of 120 degrees with Ohio just ten degrees lower. Soil in those areas registered two hundred, hot enough to cause sterilization! Tragically, the extreme heat caused the deaths of five thousand people.

Congress passed a law that made the eight-hour day and five-day workweek standard across the nation. It also prohibited children from working for companies with government contracts though they could still hold jobs in other businesses.

In 1936, Reg hired a new secretary. The only reason I remember that is because, rather quickly, she seemed to become a regular member of our household. At first it seemed a little strange as no other woman from the office had ever appeared at home before. Reg introduced her by explaining that she had just moved to New York from Illinois and thought she might enjoy meeting some young people her own age; she and Bill were both eighteen. As both Bill and Reggie always seemed to be away at school, that didn't make any sense. She was actually very nice though. Mummah and I enjoyed her company so we didn't question why she spent so much time at our house. Reg was traveling more and more for Sperry and was always off to some board meeting across the country or on the other side of the world, so I suppose she helped him manage all that as she always traveled with him. She would also make all the arrangements when I met Reg in Washington, arriving with a car and driver, even entertaining me when he was in a meeting. When he'd return from a trip he just brought her home and she'd stay the weekend. She was a gracious guest and in no time at all, seemed like part of the family. In fact, when she decided to get married, Bill's wife even lent Virginia her wedding dress.

That year the average American family lived on $1,337 though 38 percent of them lived below the poverty line of just 25 percent less. It seemed sad that only $340 separated the two groups, many of them must have been in desperate circumstances.

For the first time in history, we could watch the Summer Olympics in Berlin on television. It was very exciting especially as few of us would ever have the opportunity to attend them. During the opening ceremony, it was discovered that the flags of Haiti and Lichtenstein were exactly the same. Lichtenstein promptly added a crown to theirs. Forty-five countries participated with over 3,900 athletes in attendance. I noticed the equestrian events were the only ones in which men and women directly competed against each other. In a cycling competition, a German fouled a Dutchman, something that would normally have disqualified him; Hitler made sure he received his medal though and he was only punishment was a fine. The black sprinter and long jumper Jesse Owens won four gold medals but when it came time for the presentation, surprise, Hitler had left the stadium. He must been annoyed that a black man had beaten his "superior Aryans" and four times. The American runner John Woodruff gave an absolutely stunning performance when he found himself boxed in during the 880-meter race. He opted to get around the group by slowing his pace and actually went on to win! The thirteen-year-old American diver Marjorie Gestring also won a gold. After watching an English and a Czechoslovakian woman compete in the shot put and the javelin, the president of the Olympic Committee requested that a system be instituted whereby female athletes could be examined for "sexual ambiguities." I wasn't sure what those were, but a year later, those same two "women" had sex re-assignment surgery and took female names.

The year 1936 brought me and my family another horribly devastating event in late August.

In Western Maine, the Rangeley and Kennebago Rivers converge near the small town of Rangeley Lake. Local fishermen had discovered that extraordinarily large brown trout frequented the lake, driven there by the convergence of the two rivers. As news of record catches spread, wealthy sportsmen from New York, Boston, and Rhode Island began flocking to the area during the summer months. Gradually, they began bringing their families to enjoy the fresh air and natural beauty of the area. As these visitors appeared to have money to spend on their hobby, the locals decided to rent them boats and provide guides, supplies, and provisions. Gradually they also learned their visitors enjoyed other forms of recreation and before long the town was building tennis courts and bike trails. Eventually they added a hardware store, a library, a bank, a pharmacy, several grocery stores and a movie theater. The town even began holding community dances for their summer visitors, inviting traveling orchestras to entertain them under the stars and established a cadre of chefs-for-hire to accommodate the fancier tastes of these visitors. The lake became so popular that a bus service was started, a rail line was constructed and a seaplane service could even run you to New York City and back for a meeting. Then some families decided to build their own "camps." These didn't include tents and campfires, however. They were huge log mansions outfitted with all manner of rustic accoutrements manufactured by the locals including log- and-branch furniture, snowshoes, oars, canoes, animal heads, and forest curiosities which were used to adorn the walls, hang from the ceilings and nestle in the rafters. Some of these "cabins" were truly magnificent constructions designed for a style of backwoods living no one could have ever imagined before.

Reginald Everett Gillmor II

1936

The early twenties was the heyday of Rangeley Lake and in 1923 we sent the boys to camp up there; Reggie was seven, and Bill was five that year. Many American parents today would think that was too young but it wasn't unusual then. Mummah would take the boys up on the train and then stay for a week or two with friends. Sometimes Reg and I would rent a house on the lake for a month and go with them. I remember the house we especially liked had a little boathouse with a motor launch. We would often tour the shoreline and look for wildlife. If one took a canoe instead, there was no sound but that of the oars. Then the solitude would sometimes transport back in time to before the settlers arrived and I could even imagine an Indian in his canoe silently glide around a bend, bare- chested with a feather in his hair. It was so serene and peaceful up there, very different from our life in New York. Though Reg usually didn't stay very long, Mummah and I enjoyed ourselves immensely.

In 1936, we hadn't rented a house, but twenty-one-year-old Reggie wanted to spend the summer there before he entered MIT that September. Mummah said she'd be happy to go up with him and rent a place. Unexpectedly they received an invitation to stay with the Porters for the latter half of August. Bill had graduated from Severn and was spending his summer at the Naval Academy's required cadet training program, while fourteen-year-old David was at home with us in Kings Point. After Mummah and Reggie arrived we began receiving regular correspondence detailing their activities. Reggie wrote that he was especially enjoying the fishing and having fun entertaining the Porters' two grandsons. He never mentioned anything about their mother. Mummah talked about what lovely people they were and what a wonderful time they were having. Reggie also wrote to Bill at the Academy. He did mention how much he was enjoying "her" company and eventually confided to Bill that they were in love but swore him to secrecy. Later I learned he wrote to his brother, "We're planning a life together." It's hard to believe she actually told Reggie she would leave her husband, but somehow, he believed she would. Mummah was completely in the dark about all this.

By the end of August, most families were packing up to return to their city lives. When the young wife told Reggie she would always remember their time together, he must have realized it had only been a summer fling and was devastated.

August 31, Mummah called. She was so upset I could hardly understand a thing she was saying. Later, the newspaper would report that he was taking the bullet clip out of his twenty-two pistol when his thumb slipped and a single shot struck him in the head. That was kind of them, but it seemed he had intentionally killed himself, just as Papa had stepped in front of the train and Rollin had also pulled the trigger. I dropped the telephone and kept screaming, "No! No! No!" Everything became a blur of despair and desperation.

September 1, Reg and I flew to the lake in a seaplane and returned with Mummah and Reggie. It couldn't have been more horrible; I had to take a sedative to get through it all. I held myself together as best I could, but I was in a daze. I will be forever grateful for having Mummah beside me. She made all the funeral arrangements even as they tragically must have reminded her of Papa's death twenty-nine years before. Reg, as usual, was composed but I could tell he was devastated as well. The service and Reggie's burial were at All Saints Church in Kings Point in the afternoon; he was the first in the family to rest there surrounded by a little hedge down the hill behind the church. In those days, a suicide was both a terrible tragedy and publicly shaming. Sometimes a church wouldn't even let you hold a service if they knew. For that reason, we felt compelled to keep Reggie's death as quiet as possible. The enforced silence caused me even more suffering. It almost felt like we were pretending he'd never been our son.

It was for the same reason that we didn't ask the Naval Academy to allow Bill home for his brother's funeral. But it was a mistake to not allow David to attend; Reg had insisted. David was respectful but I could tell he was very angry with his father. I deeply regret not stepping up to insist that he be there. The funeral was very small and even if some people might have wondered why Reggie's brothers weren't there, I was too distraught to have paid any attention. In the end, I don't think anyone's opinion mattered; it was our grief, not anyone else's. The absence of both my sons made it much more painful; we should have all stood together that day. Bill would suffer terrible nightmares for a long time and David vowed never to attend any funerals again; that would include his own father's twenty-four years later.

Considering how proud we were of him, Reggie's thirteen-word obituary in the *New York Times* seemed tragically small:

Reginald Everett II, beloved son of Reginald and Edwina Gillmor, died suddenly August 31st.

Men seem better at going on with life after such a loss but it was very difficult for me as his mother. An older person who dies has had time to shine and make the best of their talents but so many dreams are lost forever when a child dies. I don't think a mother can ever fully move past the death of her child. Time might help her get used to it but the loss will be with her forever…it will never go away.

Fortune Magazine Advertisement

1937

Book 5
1936–1946

1936

My life had to go on though for my family's sake and Mummah was still there to help me. That first year was such a terrible struggle though.

I tried to fill my mind with other things. As I have always been interested in what was going on in the world, I tried to make "being informed" my new manta.

In October, the *New York World-Telegram*, the *New York Times*, and the *World-Telegram* began a publicity stunt that really captured my attention. Together they sponsored a race around the world with one reporter from each paper tasked with circumnavigated the globe in the shortest amount of time. The only stipulation was that they could only use commercial airliners. As they hopped from city to city, their respective newspapers published their progress and reports of unexpected layovers, detours, cancellations, and weather delays. It certainly made for suspenseful reading and anticipation of what the next day would bring, especially when they passed through places our family had been. The *World-Telegram* reporter was eventually the winner with a time of eighteen days and twelve hours. I guess they hardly saw a thing and probably even lost track of where they were on occasion.

On October 25, the Statue of Liberty had her fiftieth birthday. It was hard to believe such a feat of engineering in metal could have been accomplished in 1886; Mr. Gustave Eiffel of the tower fame helped the French sculptor Bartholdi with the construction of his piece and France gave it to the United States as a symbol of their friendship. It would become a symbol of the freedom our country extends to our citizens and those who wish to settle here.

President Roosevelt ran for president again and received a record 62 percent of the popular vote, as well as, 98 percent of the Electoral College! In Germany, Hitler made it mandatory that all boys between ten and eighteen join Hitler Youth except, of course, Jews. In the Soviet Union, Stalin was becoming even more aggressive about eliminating those he imagined opposed his regime. He went after people in the country's intelligentsia, military, members of the Communist Party, the wealthy, even some poor, powerless peasants. He clearly intended to rule by fear and used assassinations, firing squads, gas, starvation, and exposure in freezing Siberian labor camps to impose his will.

In the United States, General Motors workers went on sit-down strike for the right to unionize. Eventually, the strike mobilized 45,000 workers in six states who refused to work but occupied the company's plants in order to keep them from hiring replacements. Supporters from outside the factories delivered meals to the strikers, sometimes at no charge. The occupation lasted six weeks but the workers finally won. Prior to then, GM hired spies to pose as plant workers and report any attempts to unionize. By the time it was all over, five hundred thousand workers had joined the United Auto Workers.

1937

Heavy rain in Indiana caused the Ohio River to overflow its banks in Cincinnati, Ohio, by eighty feet and forced two hundred thousand people from their homes. One town even moved three miles away from its former location to spare themselves future flooding. Kentucky had eighteen inches of rain in sixteen consecutive days but in their part of the river, the floods were accompanied by swift-moving sheets of ice.

By March it had been seven months since Reggie's death. Though I had tried to busy myself, there was always something that reminded me he wasn't there. Reg suggested I sail with him to England; I think he was beginning to worry about me. I decided a change of scenery might help, so I agreed. I had to laugh when he told me we would be traveling on the *Europa*. Reg had crossed the Atlantic on that ship so often, I told him I expected to see his name on the cabin door. We only stayed a week and returned on the beautiful *Queen Mary*. The trip was a definite thought changer and the ship was enchanting. I lost some of my sorrow in her beauty. I was feeling much better when we sailed into New York Harbor and stood in the crisp morning air on the forward deck as the city slowly appeared out of the mist.

In June, Bill returned from his first year at the Naval Academy. He looked very distraught and unwell. His face told me the experience had not been a good one but I said nothing to him or Reg. He needed time to find his voice. Finally he got the courage to talk to his father and after a sentence or two, he was saying he didn't want to go back. Reg listened then launched into a prerecorded message, about what an honor it was to have been chosen from among all the other fine young men who had applied. Bill also listened but didn't seem to be the least bit interested in changing his mind; I don't think Reg noticed that. As Reg went on with his convincing, now and then, Bill quietly repeated he didn't want to go back. I watched their interaction with sadness as I knew if Bill succeeded, the price he'd have to pay for his victory might be his relationship with his father, the man he most admired and respected. I kept silent though. It seemed better for Bill to assert himself without my support and Reg wouldn't have listened to me anyway. Several days passed before Reg told him he could resign, but this single event changed the very air between them and nothing would ever be the same.

Bill never spoke to me about it, but I knew he felt he'd greatly disappointed his father. Not only would it break the limited father-son connection that had previously existed, it would also deal a lasting blow to Bill's self-esteem. The subject was never spoken of again and Bill never talked to his father about going to another college. The whole event was so tragic. Reg never gave me his thoughts about the situation or voiced his disappointment either. I'm sure that was part of the "Annapolis thing" that had been so successfully drilled into him; do your job and don't complain. It seemed so heartbreakingly final and was very upsetting. I always believed it was a father's obligation to resolve disagreements with his sons. It demonstrated leadership and compromise, skills we all surely needed in life. By not doing so, Reg not only told Bill he was wrong but that there was no way to make things right again. It also seemed so heartless, almost like Reg had given up hope that Bill would ever be a success. Sadly, I came to believe Bill carried his father's message with him for the rest of his life.

Bill got a job as an insurance agent and continued living at home. July 2, Amelia Earhart and her navigator disappeared over the Pacific Ocean while attempting to circumnavigate the globe. The historic flight began in California, traveled east to Florida, then south toward South America, across the Atlantic to West Africa, Pakistan, India, Singapore, Thailand, and Australia. When they landed in New Guinea twenty-seven days later they had flown 22,000 miles and only 6,200 remained. After taking off for tiny Howland Island they seemed to have had trouble finding it. Her last radio transmission was estimated to be four hundred miles southwest of their intended route and was most probably near Nikumaroro Island. If their plane crashed and they somehow made it there it might have proven a deadly experience. The island has very little fresh water and some of the fish in the surrounding waters can be toxic during different seasons. For the next seventeen days many searches were mounted at a total cost of $4 million, but the pair were never found. Over the years there have been rumors that the flight was a clandestine spy mission directed at Japanese military maneuvers in the Pacific. The departure from her publicized route might have been explained by such a mission but it is still a tantalizing mystery after all these years.

In a discrete program began in 1937 Hitler had forcibly been sterilizing black German children, some as young as twelve, without their parents' knowledge. About the same time, he opened his Buchenwald concentration camp where some prisoners were intentionally injected with typhus, supposedly to attempt cures. Others were actually poisoned to determine what quantity was lethal! Inmates who thought hard labor might be preferable faced death by hanging, random shootings and dying from the deadly combination of overwork and starvation. Two priests were even crucified there! In August, Hitler made it illegal to speak any language other than German. I'm sure that was to prevent Jews from having conversations in Yiddish that Nazis couldn't understand.

By the end of 1937, the Wall Street Crash had led to a 19 percent unemployment rate. Unbelievably, that was an improvement over the 25 percent of 1933.

Reg appeared in an advertising campaign for Sperry that I came across quite by accident in *Fortune* magazine.

Frances Ethel Gumm had been singing with her two sisters in their family's vaudeville act since she was seven. By 1935 Frances had changed her name and stopped singing with her sisters when she came to the attention of Metro Goldwyn Maher Studios. They signed her to a contract when she was just thirteen. After some minor singing rolls, she sang at a birthday party for Clark Gable. This performance led to a starring role in the musical film *Broadway Melody*. Don't remember Frances? I'll bet you know her stage name, Judy Garland.

1938

Benny Goodman brought his distinctive music to Carnegie Hall that January. The sold-out concert included Lionel Hampton, Duke Ellington, and Count Basie and would later be recognized as the most important performance in the history of jazz. Though it gave the genre some degree of legitimacy it would still be a decade before it was regularly heard on the radio.

The Arabian American Oil Company, ARAMCO, made the first oil strike in Saudi Arabia that March; the country would never be poor again.

Hitler invaded Italy as a Viennese cardinal directed all Catholic clergy to "unconditionally support the Fuhrer"; truth is really stranger than fiction.

The April issue of Time magazine featured an article on Sperry. Among other things, they referred to Reg as the "lean, blue-eyed, Annapolis man." They also reported that the company's annual earnings were $2,469,576. Two years later, the May issue of *Fortune* ran a huge sixteen-page piece on Sperry that included a great many photographs and a small one of Reg. The boys thought it was very exciting to see their father in such a prestigious magazine.

Reg told me J.P. Morgan had been trying to duplicate Sperry's success by forming a company to produce his own version of a gyrocompass. He said that they had been forced to abandon the project because they were unable to duplicate the precision required.

In early May the Cloisters Museum and Gardens opened on a promontory overlooking the Hudson River north of Manhattan. It had been designed specifically to house John Rockefeller II's collection of medieval art. Mummah and I went to see it and were surprised to discover the buildings looked so authentic it was hard to believe it hadn't been there five hundred years. The original site was four acres but Mr. Rockefeller bought an additional fifty-two that surrounded the museum to ensure the views from the grounds would remain pristine forever. Our visit was so enjoyable and the setting so lovely we vowed to visit every year.

The House Committee on Un-American Activities was formed that year with the intent of investigating subversive activities by American citizens. Rather quickly it turned into a sort of Salem witch hunt focused writers, actors, singers, directors and radio commentators. Under intense questioning the committee forced each witness to explain personal aspects of their private lives and in the end it seemed that even reading a book about communism could be grounds to blacklist a person and almost guarantee they'd never work again. This Thought Police group forced many talented people to move abroad or use pseudonyms in order to secure employment, including Charlie Chaplin, Orson Welles, and that wonderful baritone Paul Robeson. I was amazed to learn that the committee refused to investigate the Ku Klux Klan. I supposed that meant that some committee members were Klansman? It was a scary time in America. After the United States joined World War II, it would be the same committee that oversaw the internment camps for Japanese Americans.

In 1938 Congress passed more laws to prohibit children under eighteen from working in manufacturing or mining and children under sixteen from holding jobs during school hours. Another law reduced the taxes on large corporations and raised them on small businesses. This certainly sounded like it was specially designed to discourage new business, reduce competition and increase the profits for large businesses. Wouldn't that lead to ever-larger corporations and increase their ability to control supplies and pricing? I didn't think America was founded on such ideas. It began to seem like special interests in congress were exerting undue influence on our lawmakers. America's strength lay in competition and new ideas that could produce better products to benefit all of us. Reducing the number of companies that produced products benefited only a few people that owned those companies.

Thirty-two nations met in France to discuss the plight of Jewish refugees. Sadly, the only agreement they could come to was that none of them were willing to allow these poor people to settle within their borders.

The Führer mocked the participants for being hypocritical. I thought just this once, he was right.

On a lighter note pilot Douglas Corrigan requested permission to fly from New York to Ireland in an aircraft he'd spent years renovating. The authorities decided his plane wasn't safe and denied his application. That July, he took off from Long Island and headed for California. In midflight, however, he turned northeast and headed for Ireland. He landed a little over twenty-eight hours later with no problems. When confronted about his course "error," he blamed it on a faulty compass. Irish airport officials confiscated his aircraft and dismantled it though. When Wrong-Way Corrigan returned to New York he was given a triumphal tickertape parade and hailed as a hero... for flying in the face of authority.

All these successful transatlantic flights had always used the northern route through Newfoundland, Britain and then Europe. Until 1938 a flight path across the middle of the Atlantic Ocean had never been attempted. The route had no landmasses on which to stop, was actually longer and the area was plagued by erratic weather patterns that were difficult to anticipate. In 1938 the German airline Lufthansa made a nonstop flight from Berlin to New York. They were planning regular transatlantic service but World War II temporarily shelved the idea.

In September, a swift-moving hurricane dubbed the Long Island Express crossed the island at seventy miles an hour, quickly swept over the sound, and devastated Connecticut, Rhode Island, Massachusetts, Vermont, New Hampshire, and Maine. Winds of 180 miles an hour killed eight hundred people, knocked down two million trees, destroyed or damaged 30,000 homes, 26,000 automobiles and countless bridges; all in just four hours.

Reg told me that two men had invented the world's first copier and approached IBM, RCA, and Kodak about manufacturing it but none of them were interested. I certainly hoped they had copyrighted their invention before presenting it?

November 9 was Kristallnact in Germany. Hitler officially authorized the looting and destruction of all Jewish-owned property. Thirty thousand Jews were also rounded up and sent to concentrations camps. By then the world was being flooded with these poor people fleeing certain death in their homeland. In general, Americans were against allowing them in on the grounds that there weren't enough jobs for new immigrants. I suspect racism was more likely the reason. The newest immigrants to arrive on US shores seemed to always be the most vocal about excluding other nationalities that wanted to settle here after them.

Nineteen thirty-eight was also the year the British company DeBeers began their now-famous marketing campaign to convince women that they couldn't have a "forever" marriage unless they received a diamond engagement ring. At the time, opals, rubies, sapphires, and turquoise were the most popular choices to announce your wedding plans. The De Beers slogan for the sales campaign was so effective it boosted sales of diamonds 55 percent. Most people are not aware that diamonds are not very rare. It is only because a single source, DeBeers, carefully allows only a small, limited number of the stones to enter the jewelry market each year that they are able to artificially create diamond "scarcity" and inflate their value. In reality, rubies have always been much rarer. Because of DeBeers, the minute your diamond leaves the store it's real worth plummets 50 percent.

Before the end of the year, Hitler was now publicly declaring he intended to kill all the Jews in Europe.

1939

France and Great Britain announced they would defend Poland from a German invasion; very chivalrous but dangerous. Sensing trouble, Britain suddenly announced conscription for men eighteen to forty-one.

April 1 Francisco Franco declared himself dictator of Spain and following Stalin's fine example, immediately began executing all Spanish citizens opposed to his rule. This initial purge brought about the murder of 100,000 people. For the next thirty-six years, Franco maintained absolute power over life in Spain and would also execute 400,000 more Spanish citizens in his own concentration camps.

In Flushing, the 1939 World's Fair opened April 30 on land previously referred to in Fitzgerald's *The Great Gatsby* as the ash dump. Over two hundred thousand people attended the opening ceremony presided over by President Roosevelt. The exposition had actually been the brainchild of a group of retired New York City policemen who thought it would lift the spirits of both New York and the country. Though only open a year, an astounding forty million people toured the site.

The first food stamps were issued that April.

On May 13, the liner *St. Louis,* the same ship on which we spent our honeymoon, left Hamburg, Germany, bound for New York. Its departure was an especially joyous one for the 915 German Jewish passengers as it meant they had escaped Hitler's deadly grasp. They were hoping to settle in America or Cuba. Upon reaching New York, however, only the ship's twenty-two non-Jewish passengers were allowed to disembark. When they departed for Cuba everyone hoped to receive a better welcome. Sadly these poor people were again refused asylum though. In desperation, the captain crossed to Florida but was told his passengers weren't welcome.

Incredibly, the *St. Louis* was actually forced to return to Europe with all his so recently joyous Jewish passengers and eventually Britain, Holland, France and Belgium agreed to divide the refugees among them. What a catastrophically sad and scary trip back to war ravaged Europe. It is estimated that 260 of these poor frightened men, women and children would die in Hitler's concentration camps.

Hitler's Ravensbruck camp was opened supposedly to house only women but 130,000 men, women, and children would be murdered there. Imagine the horror of sixty-four people in your town being murdered every day for six years, and their only crime was that their neighbors didn't like their religion.

For the very first time a diving bell was used to rescue thirty-seven men from a sunken submarine off the coast of New Hampshire.

On June 1 Pan American Airlines began the first regularly scheduled passenger service between New York and England using giant seaplanes called Clippers. Because they departed from nearby Port Washington, we all went out to see the first one take off. With a wingspan of 149 feet and four engines delivering 1,600 horsepower, takeoff made for an incredible display of sound and water. Each plane carried 4,200 gallons of fuel and was able to fly 2,200 miles without having to land. The seventy- seven passengers onboard had seats that could convert to beds, private dressing rooms and even a lounge. They also enjoyed five and six-course meals in a dining room, cooked by five-star chefs and served by white- coated stewards. The cabin had only one class though, "super rich" and a one-way ticket cost $675 (comparable to the 2006 Concorde). After the United States entered World War II the US government leased all twelve of the planes for transporting equipment and personnel to Europe and the Pacific. Because they didn't need a runway they were perfect for the early years of the war but after concrete airstrips were built, they fell out of use. Thirty-five-year-old baseball player Lou Gehrig died May 2 less than a year after he was diagnosed with the incurable disease of the muscles ALS.

That summer, Reg and I decided to send seventeen-year-old David to the Fountain Valley School in Colorado Springs. It had been founded by wealthy New Yorker Mrs. Elizabeth Sage Hare in 1927. She hoped living in the dry air of that locale would improve her husband's asthma. Originally she bought 1,100 acres near the Rocky Mountains and commissioned the Florida architect Adison Misner to design the campus. Among the many physical activities available to the school's students were a stable of horses. They weren't for learning to manage cattle though, but rather to mastering the game of polo. David was very excited about going. So was Leonardo who thought it would be good for him to meet some young men from similar backgrounds and in a completely new environment. During the year he attended, he learned falconry and fencing and was also able to improve upon the bridge Leonardo had taught him during his year in the hospital. He came home with enthusiastic tales of all he'd done and the many new friends he'd made.

In August, seventeen-year-old Judy Garland appeared in the film *The Wizard of Oz*; the public and critics alike loved it!

Germany launched the world's first jet plane that August; an amazing accomplishment even though the flight only lasted seven minutes.

The growing clouds of war had settled over Poland and without warning, Germany invaded the country September first and signaled the start of World War II. Hitler's secret preparations in the Soviet Union during the previous six years allowed Germany to mount a tremendous and unexpected display of power. Britain and France stood by their promise to Poland and immediately declared war on Germany. Australia, India, and New Zealand joined them.

England had been expecting this and September 3 Winston was immediately appointed Lord of the Admiralty, twenty-five years after he had last held the same position. He was then sixty-five but it would be the finest years of serving to his country. For their protection all British children living in London were evacuated to homes outside the city for the duration of the war.

That very same day off the coast of Ireland, Germany attacked and sank the British liner *Athenia*. Three warships, a private yacht and two tankers sped to rescue those onboard but only 117 of the total 1,418 were able to be saved. Because twenty-eight of those who died were Americans Germany feared the event would draw the United States into the war. This led them to deny firing on the liner until after the war. Shortly after the sinking of *Athenia* another German sub sank an English aircraft carrier and 500 more people were killed.

Hungarian physicist Leo Szilard had fled to the United States after Hitler came to power. He knew the Germans had discovered that uranium could be used produce nuclear fission and he was also aware that Hitler was in control of Czechoslovakia's uranium mines. He was convinced Germany was developing an atomic weapon. Consequently, he wanted to alert the United States of the immediate need to begin such a program of its own. He tried to enlist his friend Enrico Ferme to contact the appropriate officials but was unsuccessful. He then turned to friend and fellow physicist Albert Einstein. At that point, Einstein was vacationing near Peconic Bay on Long Island so he went there to discuss his concerns. Eventually these two friends, with the assistance of a presidential advisor, crafted a letter to President Roosevelt expressing their fears. Their advice was ignored. In fact, their behavior led the US government to believe Szilard was a spy working for Hitler and a two-year covert spy mission to track Mr. Szilard's every move.

In October New York Municipal Airport opened in Flushing and was immediately touted as the largest and most advanced commercial airport in the world. Five months later, the facility's name was changed to LaGuardia Airport in honor of the city's much loved mayor.

Though I have never been interested in football, a very unusual game was played that October between the University of Michigan and the University of Chicago. The final score was 85–0! Chicago's coach was so upset he eliminated the university's football program!

The first automobile with air-conditioning went on display that November; it was a Packard.

On November 1, Hitler survived his eighth assassination attempt. I later learned there were actually twenty-seven! Three of his own generals had tried, as well as, two majors, a judge, a cavalry officer, a publisher, two noblemen, a Jew, and a carpenter; five of them had even made two attempts.

Five hundred thousand Soviet soldiers invaded Finland that November. Though the Finns fought bravely their sixty-two planes and thirty tanks were no match for the 3,543 and 515 of the Soviet Union. During the three-month battle, 26,000 Finnish soldiers were killed but the Russians lost 126,000. Finland finally surrendered to avoid the deaths of even more countrymen.

That Christmas Montgomery Ward distributed free coloring books to children that came to the store with their parents. It marked the first appearance of a reindeer with a glowing red nose named Rudolph.

In 1939 Solomon Guggenheim opened his Museum of Non-Objective Art in a former New York automobile showroom. All the abstract artwork on display was from his private collection and considered very avant- garde. During the opening reception Bach and Chopin were played over a speaker system. Mr. Guggenheim would eventually commission Frank Lloyd Wright to design his now-famous round museum where works by such artists as Kandinsky, Chagall, Klee, and Miro were exhibited.

As the Nazis advanced across Europe top government officials in the Netherlands began to fear for the safety of the country's gold reserves. Finally, they decided to send $223 million worth of gold through France to their West African colony Dakar. They waited a little too long though. After overrunning France, German officers discovered records of the shipment and were able to redirect it to Switzerland, the world's hiding place for valuables of all sorts.

Gone with the Wind was made into a movie and premiered that December and was a huge success. I thought Scarlet O'Hara was irritatingly stupid but apparently a great many other people disagreed; the film won nine Oscars at the Academy Awards the following year. I heard 1,400 women had been interviewed to play silly Scarlet before they finally settled on Vivian Leigh.

1940

Hitler made it illegal for Jews to travel on trains; I guess he made an exception for those heading to concentration camps. It had been just over three years since Reggie's death and he was never far from my thoughts. At first his framed photograph on the piano flooded my mind with grief every time I saw it. After a time though I found seeing his face made me feel better, almost like he was still with us. Then I collected all my favorite pictures of him and displayed them in the rooms I frequented most often. Gradually on seeing them, I would smile at the memories it brought back. Since then, I have learned that great sadness can never be erased. Time makes it less painful but only because one becomes accustomed to it, it will always be with you.

In February, the Soviet Union agreed to supply Germany with grain and raw materials and in exchange Hitler was to send Stalin industrial equipment. A year and a half later, Hitler would attack his "friend" in an attempt to take control of the Soviet Union. Hitler should have read some of Napoleon's writings regarding his own attempts to conquer Russia. The Russian winter was the real enemy.

The same month, off the west coast of Scotland a British minesweeper encountered a German submarine on the surface at three in the morning. The U-boat immediately dove but depth charges forced it to the surface again. While most of her crew was surrendering, others were seen throwing things overboard. Then they scuttled the vessel. Further investigation discovered the men were tossing pieces of Germany's highly secret code machine Enigma overboard. Apparently, capture of this device was the very reason Hitler had forbidden the machine to ever be taken to sea.

From those few salvaged parts British intelligence was able to theorize how it worked.

Hitler finished Auschwitz that February, but it would be greatly enlarged during the war to include camps II, III, IV and forty-five satellite camps! Over a million people would be executed there and suffer horrible deaths from gas, starvation, hard labor, and diseases brought on by the inhumane living conditions. Horrific decidedly un-medical "medical" experiments were also carried out on its inmates. While 90 percent of the deaths at Auschwitz were Jews, many Poles, gypsies, and prisoners of war were also murdered there.

A British cargo ship was steaming through the English Channel carrying a great many German citizens returning home specifically to fight for their homeland.

A passing German bomber set the vessel on fire and when everyone on board attempted to flee in lifeboats, the bomber machine-gunned them. A Dutch ship came to the rescue but the same bomber attacked it as well and killed nearly 300 more people. Two days later, another overzealous German pilot sank two of his own country's destroyers. Nice work, men!

Two engineers at California's Stanford University invented a radar machine that used microwaves.

The Manhattan Project received its first $6,000 that February.

Stalin invaded Norway and Denmark that March to supposedly protect their neutrality. Two months later, Hitler invaded France, Belgium, the Netherlands, and Luxembourg. While in Poland his soldiers were busy forcing 31,000 Jews into ghettos. I don't think people really understood what that meant during World War II. Certainly a ghetto was a poor area but the Nazis intentionally confined way more people into these slums than available resources inside, could possibly have sustained. Previously 6,000 families might have lived in those blocks but under Nazi control 25,000 were forced in at gunpoint and prevented from leaving with barbed wire barricades and military guards. The severe overcrowding led to a great many deaths from starvation, lack of water, medical supplies, and exposure. Those that survived these deprivations were then loaded into open railroad cars meant for cattle and shipped to concentration camps. In an attempt to escape such a fate, some people took to hiding. German police dogs were then used to find and force them into the open where they were immediately shot. In the end, some Jews still managed to evade capture so Nazis soldiers set the entire ghetto on fire and watched as it burned to the ground; too horrible a death to even imagine.

On May 10, Neville Chamberlain resigned as prime minister and Winston immediately replaced him. Both Reg and I thought he'd be just the kind of leader the country needed at this critical time. As with the First World War, Winston again believed Great Britain would not be able to fend off Germany without the help of the United States. President Roosevelt wanted to help England but at that time 80 percent of the public was against entering another war. The best the president was able to offer were shipments of munitions and equipment that Britain would have to buy.

One of Winston's very first decisions as prime minister was the implementation of a secret campaign to persuade Americans it was in their interest to join the war. With the knowledge of President Roosevelt, the State Department, and a very reluctant FBI Director Hoover, Great Britain leased three floors at 30 Rockefeller Plaza for British Passport Control. BPC was in reality the BSC; British Security Coordination and its work had nothing to do with passports. The staff was taxed with writing pro-British and anti-German propaganda for American consumption, disguised as "real news." They distributed this "reporting" to US newspapers and radio stations across the country as well as BSC's own radio station, WRUL. In return for allowing this operation, BSC was prohibited from hiring Americans. That rule was quickly ignored and Reg soon told me both the State Department and Mr. Hoover were irate about this violation. The agency also had a fleet of agents on the docks monitoring passenger liners for contraband materials that might be headed to Germany. A major Nazi supply route existed between South America and Italy, and those ships often stopped in New York. BSC also maintained a residential suite at Hampshire House on Central Park South and a secret Camp X on the Canadian side of Lake Superior. Its director William Stevenson was a close friend of both Winston and Roosevelt. At one time or another, BSC had as many as three thousand employees working from Rockefeller Plaza. Cooperative newspapers included the *New York Herald Tribune*, the *New York Post*, the *Baltimore Sun*, and radio commentator Walter Winschel. BSC was the largest covert spy operation ever undertaken by Great Britain.

Actually, at the time BSC began its operations at 30 Rockefeller Plaza, Reg also decided to take an office in the building. This seemed slightly odd as he already had a very nice one just across the bridge in Brooklyn. As president of Sperry, I didn't think he would have had time to work for BSC, but perhaps that was the reason he was never home, and why Virginia needed to travel with him.

Leonardo really seemed like a much more likely agent, especially because of his connections in South America, Italy, and Malta. Having family in Argentina would certainly have given him good cover too. At that time, the Mediterranean island of Malta was also a strategic position from which to monitor ship traffic of all flags traveling through the region. Then again, both Reg and Leonardo were in official positions that could have been valuable to BSC.

Olla Podrida

DAVID SPEAR GILLMOR

"Gilly"

"Good nature shines from his face."

Red Springs Colony, Glen Cove, New York.
Born at Stamford, Connecticut, November 1, 1921.
Fencing Team.
Came to Lawrenceville September, 1940. Preparing
for a B.A. course at Cornell.

1941

THIS year Dave has had the doubtful distinction of being a Fifth Former in a Circle
house. He sleeps in the Raymond House, but doesn't neglect the esplanade or
Kinnan House during his waking hours. This year Dave turned from building gas
model airplanes to the noble art of fencing. The foil received most of his attention
and, since he has no dueling wounds to be proud of,
we assume that he was rather proficient at it. Dave
has from time to time engaged in the Kinnan House
unofficial bridge tournament. Cornell is the college
of his choice and we have no doubt that, in due time,
he will be bridge champ there. . . . Also the Cornell
boys should have no cause to complain if he brings
dates to their proms of the same type which he brought
to Tommy Reynolds' opening night here. . . . Dave
has an ambition to be an engineer. After he graduates
from Cornell, he will without doubt be a top-notch
slide-rule juggler.

One Hundred Fourteen

David Spear Gillmor - Senior Yearbook

The Lawrenceville School

By the middle of May Hitler was in control of the Netherlands, most of France and Belgium, and Britain no longer controlled any airfields in Europe. Things were looking rather grim. Simultaneously the remaining Allied troops in Europe were being pushed by the Germans toward the Belgian coast and would ultimately be penned in on three sides; their slaughter at the hands of German soldiers on the beaches of Dunkirk seemed eminent. Winston described the situation as a "colossal military disaster" and appealed to those living on the English coast to cross the channel in whatever available craft they had, and ferry as many men as possible back to England. The British people rose to the challenge and in the ten days between May 26 and June 3 800 small boats and a few warships under the relentless bombardment of the German air force succeeded in evacuating 340,000 Allied soldiers. Heroically, another 68,000 stayed behind to defend those beaches and 40,000 of them would be captured. Thirty private vessels and a warship were a sunk in the violent and confusing barrage of gunfire. One ship captain recounted that when he finally made it to England all 340 of his evacuees had died during the trip.

In an attempt to keep German blood pure and Aryan, Hitler had 30,000 mentally and physically disabled Germans executed during the last eight months of 1940. In actuality the real "Aryans" are a race of Persians that Hitler and his propaganda machine and decided to co-opt as their ancient blond, blue-eyed ancestors. Very strange; Persians don't have those physical characteristics either.

June 3 Germany dropped 1,100 pounds of bombs on Paris and the city surrendered the following day. Several weeks later, Hitler began methodically looting the art collections of 70,000 French homes.

That year Goodrich invented the first synthetic rubber; this cheaper substitute for natural rubber greatly added to the affordability and mass consumption of the automobile in America.

For the first time in US history that June noncitizen residents were required to register as "aliens"; funny to think of Leonardo as being from another planet.

As Hitler's armies took control of more and more of France, Winston demanded that the French navy join the British fleet to prevent their ships from falling into German hands. Hitler had promised he wouldn't do that, but who trusted Hitler? Unsatisfied with France's response British troops forcibly took control of eighteen French warships lying in English ports. Then Winston ordered two bombing raids on the French naval base in Algeria during which 1,300 French sailors were killed. This was followed by "suggestions" that the French warships stationed in the port of Alexandria, Egypt join the British navy or be "neutralized." They decided to disarm their vessels until the war was over.

The Battle of Britain began that June In the skies over Britain. A huge contingent of 2,500 German and Italian airplanes manned by 4,300 Axis pilots, continuously bombed English airfields, shipping centers, factories and convoys primarily on the coast. This was the first battle in history to ever take place entirely in the air. It was supposed to signal Hitler's takeover of the British Isles. London endured fifty-seven consecutive days of bombing that damaged Century Guidhall, Westminster Abbey, Buckingham Palace, the House of Commons and eight Christopher Wren churches. During the four-and-a-half month siege two million homes were also destroyed or damaged and 40,000 people were killed. Though the Allies defending the city had only 966 pilots hailing from thirteen countries flying just 1,963 planes, they successfully beat back the German offense. Their defeat was believed to be a turning point in the war and one from which Germany would never recover. It also succinctly put to rest Hitler's dreams of conquering Great Britain.

This German bombing campaign so angered Winston he launched a series of devastating raids on 150 German cities; in Hamburg alone more than forty-two thousand people were killed on the ground. War is a terrible thing for all involved but especially for civilians. Americans often find it hard to think of the enemy as having lives and families, just like their own. But the Allies were fighting so fiercely because the war was in their own countries and they didn't want to live under Hitler's rule. By then, I suspect, many Germans didn't want to either, but they were the ones who'd empowered him in the first place.

After the war ended, it was discovered that two diplomats from the Netherlands and Japan had secretly issued visas to Polish Jews enabling two thousand of them to escape to Japan, China, and South America. There were also some other secret humanitarian operations that successfully saved a small number of Jewish families in spite of the odds.

In July, a German measles epidemic hit Australia that proved particularly devastating to pregnant women. After being exposed to the illness, they later gave birth to children with cataracts, heart deformities, mental disabilities, and hearing impairments. Research after these tragedies led to the creation of a vaccine that when given to young girls protected them from contracting the disease when they were of childbearing age.

By September 1940 the United States had broken the Japanese diplomatic code. The month also marked the first time the United States had ever instituted a draft without the country being at war; men twenty- one to thirty-five were required to register. That upper age limit was eventually extended to forty-five. Even though he wasn't an American citizen then and wouldn't be until November 0f 1944, Leonardo had to register. Pearl Harbor was still a year and four months in the future.

Penterra

1941

During a single month of the German occupation of Paris, Hitler had 700,000 books burned in public bonfires. He also banned the Free Masons, the Rotary and the Red Cross and made it illegal for Jews to own anything. I guess that was so he could legally take their gold fillings.

David returned from his only year at the Fountain Valley School that spring. At the end of the summer, Leonardo, Mummah and I took him to the Lawrenceville School in Princeton, New Jersey. After we toured the charming town and had lunch, it was time to leave. It was especially touching to watch Leonardo and David say their good-byes. It again reminded me of how important a role a father has in a son's life. I could definitely see that Leonardo was as proud of David as if he were his father and the feeling seemed to be reciprocated. Unfortunately, it also made me more aware of Reg's absence in David's life. Sadly, I was equally certain that David believed his father wasn't interested in him either, and easily accepted Leonardo in his father's place. Of course, men must focus on providing for their families and as a result parenting often takes a backseat. Positive interaction between a father and his son is critical to the development of character and values in a young man, though Reg might have thought otherwise.

David, never really one to be sentimental, plunged right in at Lawrenceville. During the single year he would attend he took up with the fencing club, became a star in the school's bridge group and even managed to build several gasoline-powered automobiles. In looking at his yearbook, I also noticed he had acquired a reputation for bringing attractive young women to school functions—the Casanova influence, I suppose.

Just after David left for Lawrenceville, Reg announced he thought we should move from Kings Point and make a new home away from our tragedy. His little talk greatly reminded me of Mummah's after Papa died thirty years before. As our move to the Plaza in 1907 had given us all such a new perspective on life I thought Reg might be right, though I really wouldn't have thought of it on my own then. To my surprise he immediately began telling me that quite by chance, he had stumbled upon a lovely house in Glen Cove on another of Long island's many peninsulas just east of where we were then living.

He went on to relate the unusual circumstances surrounding its being for sale and the very low asking price. He said the house was in an area called Red Spring Colony first developed in 1891 by a group of industrialists. Some had even built very large homes there by 1920. The house he was talking about was built in 1918 by William Beard, supposedly the richest man in Brooklyn. Though he and his wife had a home on Seventy-Fifth Street in the city at the time they used the Red Spring property for sixteen years as a summer place. Then they sold it to David Woodside and his wife, Maude Dorsey of Greenville, South Carolina. They cleverly called it the Villa D'Orsey, a house featured in a 1907 novel called *The Second Generation*; in the book the name was spelled with an "a" instead of her "e."

These little stories was followed by Reg cheerily announced, "Now, to the really interesting part!" The Woodsides had owned the Beard property for six years when they decided to sell it. George Dupont Pratt, president of the Long Island Railroad, lived on a forty-acre estate next door to the Villa D'Orsey, and his daughter Dorothy had just married Samuel Register and he needed a wedding present. When he heard the Villa D'Orsey was for sale he bought it and put the deed in his daughter's name; a rather grand gift I thought. Mrs. Register took a quick tour of her present, however, and announced she hated it and refused to live there. Her father declined to take it back.

So Mrs. Register owned a house she didn't want, for which she had paid nothing and she just wanted to be rid of it. When you see the size of her father's house you might understand why she might have thought the Villa D'Orsey wasn't nearly imposing enough compared to her childhood home. After a short time on the market with no offers, Reg became aware of the house and asked to see it. He found an elegant brick structure that sat atop a hill overlooking Long Island Sound with a caretaker's cottage over a garage and a lovely tennis court. Furthermore, he thought it was really beautiful and Mrs. Register was practically giving it away. Then he looked a little sheepish and confessed he'd actually bought the property that very day because it was such a bargain. He quickly insisted, however, that if I didn't like it he could sell it and make a handsome profit. It would be entirely up to me. As I have always remembered the lovely house Reg found for us in England, so I readily agreed to go see it. Actually, I thought the whole idea was kind of exciting.

Well, it was absolutely gorgeous! The view of the water on top of that hill was really incredible. I loved the whitewashed brick exterior and elegant symmetry of the center front door. Inside the ceilings were high, the public rooms large and the moldings just beautiful. The back of the house faced the water and the entire first floor had pairs of French doors in every room framing that divine view. On the second floor two enclosed porches also faced the water and large beautiful trees were all about the property. The tennis court could be seen from all those windows in the back and it made me think, David would love the house. A little beach was just below the caretaker's cottage and a small dock extended into the water from which one could launch a boat. A tiny bathhouse for changing clothes was also there at the end. I loved everything about the place and expressed my enthusiasm to Reg for having snapped it up. I thought our new home could be just the thing to reinvent our lives and return our family to the happiness we had previously enjoyed.

On the way home I thought about how our Kings Point house had seemed to be located on Fitzgerald's fictional West Egg and now we would be moving to Daisy Buchanan's East Egg.

The sale went through two weeks later and my name was added to the deed. After it was ours, we took Mummah to see it. She fell in love with the property just as I had. Reg and I decided we'd like to make a few changes to both the house and the property before we moved in so Reg cleverly arranged for a lovely Norwegian couple to live there, accomplish the renovations and keep the place safe until everything was finished. Albert and Kate Johnson along with their thirty-five-year-old son would stay in the cottage while Mrs. Johnson cooked and the two men did the work. Albert had just recently retired from a position on the docs working for the White Star Line. Though older he seemed quite fit and skilled at repairing and painting all manner of things. Once again, my genius husband had worked everything out perfectly! The Johnsons were even thrilled to be out of their apartment in the city and near the water they loved.

In the front of the house we had Albert move the driveway away from the front a little and make it circular to accommodate more parking for guests. That also gave more room for plantings under the windows. In the back, Albert extended the second terrace so I could have an English cutting garden to grow seasonal flowers for use in the house. Finally, I would be able to grow all the varieties I loved as the area received plenty of sun. I could hardly wait to see the first blooms.

Inside we redid the floors, painted all the rooms and added a beautiful scenic mural to the dining room in lovely shades of green. While Albert worked away, Mummah and I had a grand time planning where to put all the wonderful things we'd collected over the years and shopped for additional pieces and fabrics to coordinate everything. Reg was a dear and said I could choose whatever we liked. Gradually, as my days were filled with beautiful visions of our new home I began to see that joy could still be part of my life.

Charlie Chaplin's first talkie, *The Great Dictator*, premiered in New York October 15. He was not only the star of the movie but also the director, producer and had written the script and music. It was a satirical comedy condemning Hitler, Mussolini, Fascism, anti-Semitism and the Nazis. It proved to be his most financially successful film even though all his movies were very popular. I suppose people just had to see if a musical comedy about such evil things could actually be pulled off.

In Poland a brave woman began rescuing Jewish children from the Warsaw ghetto. After she enlisted the help of some of her friends she was able to save 2,500 over a two-and-a-half-year period.

President Roosevelt won an unprecedented third term that November after receiving 55 percent of the popular vote. He also carried thirty-eight states.

The Midtown Tunnel connecting Queens and Manhattan officially opened the same month.

Joseph Kennedy was our ambassador to the United Kingdom then but during an interview in England he had commented that because of how the war was going, "Democracy is finished in England." I thought that was an outrageous thing to say to the British public about what he perceived as the fate of the British Empire. Apparently President Roosevelt felt the same way and immediately asked for his resignation.

He had made his fortune as a bootlegger during Prohibition so perhaps he wasn't really a good fit for the position anyway.

The four-month-old Tacoma Narrows Bridge in Washington State became a national celebrity in her own short film that appeared in movie theaters around the country. It seemed a consultant had decided to use smaller metalwork than originally specified by the architect and a forty- mile-an-hour wind proved the choice to be a disastrous one. Galloping Girdy rocked herself apart and collapsed into the river below. It was quite startling to see especially as a driver walked away from his vehicle in the middle of the roadway just before the unimaginable happened.

Forty-four-year-old F. Scott Fitzgerald died of his third heart attack just before Christmas that year. He was at the Hollywood home of his mistress and gossip columnist Sheila Graham. He'd actually had a rather sad life and drank heavily for most of it. Though he was still married to Zelda at the time, and apparently still sent her money, the poor thing had by then been in a mental institution for four years.

Great Britain increased the age of conscription to fifty. I was really shocked; things must be really desperate.

In Egypt three Italian "human torpedoes" managed to sink two huge British warships. I remember these suicide vehicles had been rejected by the British during the First World War as "unsafe"; no kidding.

By November 1940 Mummah was seventy. She suddenly decided she wanted to visit Ebus and Monty in Montreal before Christmas but she promised she'd be back before the holiday. December 1 Reg and I took her to the train in New York even though she was still quite lively and probably could have managed without us. On the platform she seemed particularly animated and cheerful. As I watched the train pulled away though I felt a strange, almost overwhelming sad. I was quite relieved when Ebus called to say she had arrived safely. I spoke to her for a moment but she said she was a little tired and wanted to lie down. That would be the last time I spoke with her. Ebus called again on the thirteenth to tell us Mummah hadn't seemed herself that morning, and by afternoon was worse. She said they called for an ambulance, but by the time it arrived dear Mummah was gone.

All my life, Mummah had been my dearest friend and her death was devastating. Ebus and Monty brought her home on the train. As I stood on the platform waiting for their arrival I couldn't help but remember that Margot and Reggie had returned home the same way. And though I was far away at the time, Papa's death also involved a train. Sometimes our lives have strange connections. Her funeral was in the same church where Reggie's had been just four years earlier; she would be the second one of us to be buried within the little hedge. To stand by Reggie's grave again was also devastating but by then I was determined to persevere, just as Mummah had after being left without Papa and three young daughters. Two weeks after the funeral, Margot's son John married Eleanor Gardner in her mother's apartment on Eighty-Ninth Street and Bill was his best man. The four of us went as we were his only family. It was terribly sad without both Margot and Mummah though. Eleanor was very considerate and made everything small. Her family was quite socially connected, so under normal circumstances, there would have been both a large ceremony and reception. It was obvious John was marrying into a wealthy family as the apartment was large and elaborately furnished with beautiful things. I was happy for him but hoped he was marrying Eleanor for more than just her money, as his father seemed to have done. Of course Herbert was there with his new wife, but it was not pleasant seeing him again.

THE DRAWING ROOM

Drawing Room

Dining Room

Nineteen forty was yet another remarkable year for Sperry; profits had doubled over the previous year. The company's continuing growth still amazed me.

Hitler dropped 124,000 tons of bombs on London December 29 and 30. The raids caused so many fires they took to calling it the Second Great Fire of London. The first had been in the seventeenth century.

1941

In Washington Charles Lindbergh gave a speech before Congress in which he urged the United States to sign a neutrality treaty with Germany. Hitler must have been afraid the United States would join the Allies. Lindbergh's plea seemed rather shameful. It certainly identified him as Hitler's friend, more than ours. I suppose Hitler flattered him to be his emissary by telling him he was the epitome of a blond, blue-eyed Aryan; funny how Hitler didn't look a thing like that.

After World War II began I learned some information about Pearl Harbor that would never become public knowledge. That year a cable was sent by the United States Ambassador to Japan to the US State Department on January 27. It warned of a Japanese plan to attack the base. It didn't seem that noteworthy until later when I would learn other things that when all were taken together created a very disturbing picture.

In early February an amusing incident that was unrelated to Pearl Harbor began when a large merchant ship left Liverpool, England for Jamaica. Two days later, gale force winds forced the vessel aground on a sparsely populated island off the coast of Scotland. Fortunately, all the crew survived and were taken in by locals. During idle conversation it was revealed that the ship was carrying 28,000 cases of scotch—64,000 bottles! Well a proper Scot couldn't be expected to abandon that much whiskey especially as the island's wartime ration was severely depleted. A plan was soon hatched and under cover of darkness, local fishermen began absconding with a few cases at a time. Rather quickly, it became apparent that the ship was leaking oil so being the resourceful seamen they were, they adopted some creative measures to protect their clothing using materials they had on hand, as they say. To avoid contaminating their clothes with incriminating evidence they decided to wear dresses! What a splendid picture; burly Scotsmen in flowered dresses hauling heavy cases of scotch in the dead of night with huge waves crashing all about. If caught, I suppose they planned on saying they were just fishing in their regular work gear. No one on the island viewed this as stealing though they were just salvaging abandoned goods. Before customs could arrive, the islanders managed to "save" 24,000 bottles. Agents did catch a few of the ladies "fishing," and they spent a few weeks in jail. But even then there were still a great many cases in the ship's hold. Officials being "official" decided they just couldn't leave them there so as the islanders watched, the wreck was blown up. Local men watched they were heard to mutter, "I can't believe there are men crazy enough to dynamite whiskey." Scotch on the rocks, anyone?

British troops in North Africa blocked retreating Italian soldiers in Benghazi, Libya, and ended up with 135,000 prisoners of war. In the port of Athens, Greece a fleet of German bombers sank seven British merchant ships, sixty barges, and twenty-five local fishing vessels.

March 27 a Japanese tourist arrived in Honolulu but he wasn't there to sightsee. He had been sent to study the US fleet at Pearl Harbor.

Before March ended, President Roosevelt had seized all German, Italian, and Danish ships lying in sixteen US ports.

March 31 we finally moved into our new home. As it seemed a tradition in the area, we decided to name the property Penterra for the five terraces in the back. Albert and his son had done a wonderful job and everything looked beautiful. I busied myself directing where to put each piece of furniture, in which rooms the rugs were to go and hanging artwork. It was more excitement than I'd had in a long time and my melancholy was swept away by our new beautiful home. Every room seemed filled with light and the lovely fresh air from the sound. That divine, ever-present view supplanted all my anxieties and longings. I felt very lucky that my dear husband had found such an exquisite paradise for all of us.

In the drawing room I used a beautiful chintz and put a baby grand piano by the French doors. On the closed top I put a lovely silk shawl Leonardo had brought me from Spain and kept a vase of fresh flowers there beside Reggie's photograph. I had also arranged a large black lacquer Coromandel screen on the wall opposite the fireplace. The covered veranda accessed through the French doors in that room was outfitted with natural rattan furniture done in lovely green cushions trimmed in yellow. The wide front hall had an elegant staircase with its own pair of French doors to the large grass terrace at the back of the house. Another wide hall from the foyer led to the morning room on the front of the house and my studio on the water side with its own pairs of French doors to the grass. Two more sets of French doors were in the dining room with one pair leading to another covered veranda where we often dined in warm weather.

We brought our housekeeper and butler from Kings Point and Kate Johnson stayed on as cook. Albert also continued on as caretaker. We hired a new maid and a Scottish girl as laundress. When the president decided to confine some Americans in internment camps we also took on a lovely Japanese couple to spare them from having to live in a detention center. They would serve dinner in traditional robes and added a special elegance to our dinners as they glided about the room like living artwork. We kept our English custom of dressing for dinner each night with drinks in the drawing room beforehand. I also continued to wear a long dress in the evening as did the other women in attendance.

Upstairs there was a large master bedroom with a private bath and mirrored dressing room for me. Reg had his own bath. I chose gray towels with yellow monograms for his and pale yellow with gray monograms for mine. Back then just about every piece of linen in the house was monogrammed, some with especially beautiful, intricate designs. Directly off our bedroom was a sunny porch. Sitting there in the morning made me feel as if I was perched in the treetops enjoying the breathtaking view of the Long Island Sound, the garden and the tennis court. I often felt Mummah's presence beside me admiring it as well.

I bustled about the house trying to manage things as best I could. Even though I was nearly fifty then, the loss of Mummah had forced a great many tasks upon me with which I was most unfamiliar. It was humbling but gradually, with the aid of lots of lists, I became more confident. And as with most things in life, the more you do them, the easier they become. My beautiful new home became a sort of management training center.

During that time, I came to understand that allowing your mind to fixate on things that make you sad but that you have no power to change is really a choice—a terrible one but one we choose. Doing so spoils the other parts of your life, robs you of happiness in the present and steals your ability to be happy about anything. It will also keep you locked in the past. It is better to put your sorrow away in a special box and take it out only now and then.

I suppose by then I'd accepted that Leonardo was probably David's father. I'd also been lulled into a certain gratefulness that the passing of time had allowed a terrible storm to pass and disappear into the night. Oh, if only that would have been true …

That April Winston warned Stalin that his friend Hitler was planning to attack the "Russian Bear." Stalin still believed Germany was his ally though and paid no attention. Meanwhile Hitler kept his troops busy invading Greece; Stalin had but two months left though. Hitler was also occupied himself dividing up three-year-old Yugoslavia with Mussolini, even as neither had invaded the country yet. After taking possession of his allotted section, Hitler immediately began rounding up every Jew   in sight and shipped them off to his concentration camps. One of the camps closest to Yugoslavia was eight-square-mile Jasenovac, the largest in Europe. In the three years it operated 100,000 people were murdered there. April 20 Hitler enjoyed a fifty-second birthday party in his honor. For the occasion, Goebbels offered a glowing speech in which he declared, "We are experiencing the greatest miracle that history offers; a genius is building a new world." Hitler must have loved the adulation but he'd be dead in four years.

In late April, Bill enlisted in the army and became a warrant officer, the highest enlisted rank; eventually he was an artillery instructor. I knew Bill would have made a fine officer but I suspected dropping out of the Academy and the ensuing sense of failure in the eyes of his father played havoc with his self-respect. Or in deference to his father, he might have decided it would be more respectful if he wasn't an officer. I would never know. Perhaps he'd been offered a commission and declined.

Bill still adored his father but I sadly watched the distance between them grew wider and wider. It was such a tragedy and didn't need to have been that way. As I watched these brief interactions I even decided Bill needed to get away from his father's influence and the army might just be that opportunity.

May 10 Deputy Fuhrer Rudolf Hess, the third most powerful man in Germany, parachuted into Scotland supposedly to persuade Winston to sign a peace agreement with Germany. Later, it seemed the mission might have been planned by Hitler himself though initially it appeared to be solely Hess' idea. Either way it followed other attempts by the Führer to put a nation off guard. Part of Hess's message read, "The war had to end, though Germany would undoubtedly win." Hess was taken prisoner, tried, and sentenced to life in prison for "conspiracy against the world."

All German and Italian assets in the States were frozen May 14, even though the country was still six and a half months away from joining the Allies.

The battleship *Bismarck* was the pride of the German navy. At over eight hundred feet long with a crew of 2,065 and a compliment of sixty-four guns, her distinctive size and visible armaments could easily be identified from both sea and air. While cruising off the coast of Norway with nine escort vessels, a passing squadron of Swedish planes spotted the behemoth and radioed her position to British Command. They promptly sent several ships to engage the fleet. During the ensuing battle a British cruiser was mortally wounded but before she sank she managed to score a direct hit on the huge battleship. At first the enormous hole went unnoticed by the crew, but as the ship steamed away water was forced into the hull and fuel was carried out. Because it would be quite a prize to claim sinking the German giant, no less than forty-two British warships took off in pursuit. Normally *Bismarck* was capable of making thirty knots so no ship would have ever have attempted to catch her, but the gaping hole in her side considerably reduced her speed capabilities and invited a chase. One of the pursuing ships got off a torpedo that knocked out *Bismarck*'s entire electrical system, as well as, two of her boilers. Even those catastrophes didn't prevent the wounded battleship from eluding the pursuing pack.

Killenworth II

Bismarck's captain then decided that the British had given up and gone home so he confidently radioed headquarters regarding his triumphal escape. That communication gave *Bismarck's* position away and four British warships rushed to finish her off. After one of them fired a shot that disabled the ship's rudder, it was essentially all over for the giant battleship as she could only move in a large circle and went helplessly round and round with every available gun taking their turn; Germany's pride was a proverbial duck in shooting gallery. Four hundred rounds eventually set her afire and she sank four hundred miles off the northwestern tip of France nine days after the first torpedo had pierced her hull; 1,900 of her crew went down with her. *Bismarck's* illustrious dominance of the sea had lasted a mere eight months.

In Great Britain, an English engineer successfully launched the first turbo-jet aircraft and it had reached an astounding speed of 370 miles an hour.

Three weeks into June Hitler invaded the Soviet Union; he claimed Stalin was planning to attack Germany and he was only being proactive. After just a week of fighting, the German army was in control of five hundred square miles of the country. I'm sure, Hitler must have been thinking, *that was pretty easy!* Russia is a huge, very cold place, however, and winter was still some months off.

It was then five months before the attack on Pearl Harbor but President Roosevelt froze all Japanese assets in the United States and began drafting men over twenty-one. For anyone who was paying attention it certainly looked like the country was preparing to go to war.

NBC's *Truth or Consequences* became the first regularly broadcast television program in the US.

In Romania German troops with the assistance of the local militia went house to house and shot 12,000 Jews on the spot! Such hatred!!

By then both Britain and the United States had promised to send war materials to help Stalin repel Hitler. I for one thought it was getting difficult to tell who was on the "other" side. In Germany Hitler decried all Jews must wear yellow stars while in public places. He also announced that they couldn't marry or live with non-Jews. In Poland, he opened the Majdanek concentration camp where 78,000 people he didn't like would be murdered.

That August unknown to the public, an FBI investigation discovered that the president of GM Overseas had been secretly supplying torpedo parts to Hitler since 1934, in violation of US law. Hoover concluded, however, that none of this was "disloyal" to America. Somebody must have paid dearly for that outcome.

Pembroke

Winfield Hall

Actually the overseas president of GM had been such an admirer of Hitler that he once said, "Hitler is well-fitted to lead the German people ... not by force, but by intelligent planning and execution of fundamentally sound principals of government." Very strange!

GM's German sales were 40 percent of its European market and the company was also Germany's largest employer; 17,000 in 1934 and 27,000 five years later. Many of those workers must have greatly contributed to the company's bottom line as they were German prisoners and weren't paid anything. After the United States entered World War II, GM went to extraordinary lengths to conceal the profits of its German subsidiary by declaring them "reserves." This strategy also involved making Germany appear to own the subsidiary by falsifying documents. At one point, to keep Hitler's business GM fired all its Jewish employees and terminated all its Jewish-owned dealerships. In gratitude Hitler awarded GM's president the Eagle with Cross medal, Germany's most prestigious foreign collaborator honor for Service to the Reich. In cooperation with Standard Oil, GM also gave Hitler the technology needed to produce the high- octane fuel that would maximize engine performance, something Hitler was certainly interested in ensuring for his vehicles transporting millions to his huge network of concentration camps. Germany readily admitted, "Without this technology, the present method of warfare would have been unthinkable." An American company and its American president secretly helped the Nazis wage World War II for eleven years, four of which they fought and killed US boys?

Furthermore, GM's president also flatly stated, "In the interests of making money, GM shouldn't risk alienating its German hosts by intruding in Nazi affairs" and later also remarked, "GM is too big to be impeded by petty international squabbles"; World War II a petty squabble? After the war, GM took a $7 million tax write-off for the loss of its German division and received another $33 million in war reparations ... because the Allies had bombed their German factories. Despicable behavior in my opinion!

After settled in at Penterra, I began to notice some of our neighbors' houses. Actually, they weren't really houses.

The man who gave our house to his daughter as a wedding present had grown up on his property but in a different house. In 1870, his father, Charles Pratt had bought 4,000 acres in Red Spring Colony to ensure that each of his children would have land on which to build homes near him. Three years later he built himself a large Queen Anne style house there and called Killenworth. When he died in 1912 his son George DuPont Pratt inherited it but as he disliked that particular style of architecture, he tore it down and built the much larger stone castle Killenworth II. While some call it Tudor, I thought it much more Dracula.

Down the hill toward the beach from our house was the charming 1906 Italian Renaissance Cedarcroft on a modest seven acres. Bouvier Beale of East Hampton eventually bought it when he married Katherine Jones and they moved in the year after we arrived at Penterra. Bouvie and Chickie became close friends of our family, especially David who was just a year older. They often came to dinner, played tennis at our house, and sometimes even brought over their houseguests. After David married and returned to Penterra their respective children played together on the little beach as well. I have many wonderful memories of our time together. Bouvie's sister, whom everyone called Little Edie, and his mother Big Edie still lived in the family's East Hampton house Grey Gardens. Bouvie remarked once that his mother was getting rather odd and reclusive and he thought she was a bad influence on his sister. I only met the two of them once but they did seem a little different with strange, sort of theatrical behavior. They both also wore unusual, costume-like clothes rather like they were dressed for some stage performance.

Northeast of us was the 160-acre estate of Herbert Pratt, George Pratt's brother. He was the president of Standard Oil when he built his brick Georgian Revival house The Braes in 1902. It looked very like it should have been a university especially with all those enormous marble statues on pedestals all about the property.

To our southwest, there was the truly immense estate of Joseph de Lamar. He had done quite well in the mining of precious metals and phosphate, whatever that is. He'd named his classical French house Pembroke which seemed decidedly English. In 1924, he sold it to Marcus Loew, president of Loews International and owner of the Metro-Goldwyn Mayer film studio. Mr. Loew's son Arthur inherited the estate in 1927 and as a result we sometimes ran into Hollywood types taking in the sun and reading on the little beach.

Also southwest of us was the 1916 Italian-French Renaissance Winfield Hall built by Frank Woolworth. Mr. Woolworth had become quite successful with a chain of stores bearing his name. His stately, white marble home reminded me greatly of the White House in Washington and had a divine spiral staircase in the front hall. In 1929, Mr. Woolworth sold it to Richard Reynolds, who had specialized in aluminum most publicly remembered for foil. Mr. Reynolds promptly changed the property's name to Germelwyn. The name was such a ridiculous word to try to pronounce, I finally decided he had chosen it to make fun of everyone naming their properties.

West of Penterra was Edmund Wetmore's 1900 home, which he never named. Perhaps he was too busy being the president of both the American and New York Bar Associations. The property's next owner, John Nobel Stearns, decided The Cedars sounded nice.

There were also other Pratts living in Red Spring Colony, they just weren't our immediate neighbors. George Pratt's two married sisters Mrs. Walter Gibb owned Old Orchard east of us, and Mrs. Arthur Gibb had Iron Acton northwest of Penterra. Another four Pratt brothers had homes near us as well; Frederick Pratt built Poplar Hill in 1917, Charles Pratt II had Seamore, Harold Pratt had Welwyn of 1906 and John Pratt, the Manor House of 1909.

Chandler Cudlipp Sr., the founder of Goodwill Industries also lived in Red Spring Colony; he started his company to train and employ people with disabilities. F.S. Smithers owned seventy acres and built My Home in 1919; he and his brother founded the investment firm of the same name. In 1894 Edward Ladew built a Colonial Revival house and gave it the Italian name Villa Louedo. His property was quite large and included a number of guesthouses, a huge stable, several formal gardens, and an abundance of elaborate fountains and terraces. William Hester became the property's next owner and changed the style of the house to Georgian Revival and rename it Willada Point.

What with eight families named Pratt living all about us, it really seemed like we'd moved to the Pratt Colony rather than the Red Spring one.

David graduated from Lawrenceville that spring and came home to Penterra for the first time. He walked around the rooms and liked everything but was especially enthusiastic about the view of Long Island Sound and the tennis court.

Reg was busier than ever with both Sperry business and traveling all over the country for board meetings of various organizations including some agencies in the federal government. He also continued bringing Virginia home.

Demand for Sperry products had increased tremendously by 1941. The company now had five times as many employees with many more offices around the world and its products were sold in twenty-five countries.

That August, we had a lovely surprise! Louis "Dickie" Mountbatten called and said his aircraft carrier *Illustrious* was in Norfolk, Virginia getting some needed repairs and he suddenly found himself with free time on his hands. Could we put him up? He promised to be an exemplary guest and entertain us. Of course, I was delighted and told him he could stay as long as he liked. By then he was forty-one, a commodore in the Royal Navy and actually the captain of *Illustrious*. He arrived in his uniform and looked quite dashing. There's something about a uniform that always makes a man more attractive. He stayed a week or two and did amuse us with interesting tales of this and that, most of which we had to swear never to repeat. With my memory, the minute he said that I promptly filed them away in the attic of my mind and couldn't have found them again with a gun to my head.

One story that wasn't so secret involved his former ship the *Kelly*. Apparently, it had as he put it been shot out from under him twice! His friend Noel Coward was so taken with the story of the *Kelly* that he wrote a script featuring the ship and it was being made into a movie called *In Which We Serve*. It would be released as a patriotic film the following year and was designed to rally British troops and their families. Audiences and critics alike loved it but the Admiralty decidedly did not. Among themselves, they referred to it as *In Which We Sink*. Mr. Coward directed, produced, and wrote the music for the film and also starred as Louis.

When Louis asked to visit I thought perhaps his wife Edwina might join him but he told us she was quite busy supervising the St. John Ambulance Service in England. Apparently, Edwina had transformed herself and become a devoted charity worker.

As repairs to *Illustrious* took longer than anticipated Dickie left us and made a little excursion to Pearl Harbor. That's what he called it though Hawaii was nearly five thousand miles away. He would soon be in charge of the Pacific Theatre there but fortunately had left before the Japanese arrived.

In Germany widespread protesting complete with press coverage had somehow convinced Hitler to stop executing mentally handicapped Germans. Sadly, by then 70,000 had been shot. I was surprised that anything could have caused him to change his mind. I've come to think negative attitudes about him did seem to bother Hitler, something now known to be typical of highly self-centered, egotistical people, particularly the mentally ill. Back in World War I Hitler had served as a messenger in the army but was eventually evacuated to a hospital though not because he'd been wounded. It was a psychiatric ward! Nice, now he was the leader of a huge army trying to take over the world!

The movie *Citizen Kane* starring Orson Welles was released that April. It told the story of an idealistic man bent on social service. As the film progresses, however, he turns his attention to the ruthless pursuit of money and power. It was rumored to be based on the life of newspaper magnate William Randolph Hearst. Mr. Hearst must have recognized himself because he forbade any mention of the movie in his papers and refused to publish any advertisements for it.

In early September, Hitler personally supervised the first test of his newest way to kill large numbers of people. Eight hundred Russian POW soldiers were herded into an underground room at Auschwitz and Cyclon B gas was pumped in; they all died. He must have been thrilled and began routinely using the gas on enemy troops at the front. When the wind direction changed, however, he sometimes liquidated his own soldiers too. He won't have any problems using it in his concentrations though.

As Hitler's armies marched further and further into Russia they eventually slaughtered 40,000 Polish and Ukrainian Jewish noncombatants along the way. By early September his success in the Soviet Union must have had Hitler feeling very optimistic about soon controlling the entire country. His armies occupied 2,000 miles of front lines by then and had blockaded Leningrad. This kept supplies from reaching the city and lasted so long, a million Russians died of starvation and disease. The Siege of Leningrad left such a horrible memory in the minds of the survivors that after the war they returned the city's name to St. Petersburg.

In November off the coast of Gibraltar a German U-boat sank the eight-hundred-foot British aircraft carrier *Ark Royal*. Of the 1,500 men aboard miraculously only one died. In Luxembourg, now under Hitler's control 60,000 Jews were forced into cattle cars and sent to concentration camps. Hitler must have been afraid he wouldn't be able to kill every Jew in Germany because he banned them from leaving the country. I don't believe the world was aware at that time of the magnitude of Hitler's exterminations and certainly not the kinds of depravities being carried out in his concentrations camps. I would like to believe that if these unspeakable atrocities had been publicized we would have been done more to save these poor people and their children. Remembering the sad plight of the *St. Louis*, I wasn't sure though.

Britain raised the age of conscription to fifty! Yikes!

The US government set up a 20,000 acre munitions depot in the Oregon desert. The war was being fought almost entirely in Europe and we weren't even part of it?

Before the end of the year Thanksgiving was officially declared a national holiday.

In October three northern California counties along with one in southern Oregon decided to form the new state of Jefferson. They even elected a governor!

October 2 the German army began a two-hundred-day battle to take Moscow. After six months of fighting, the Nazi commander in charge conceded defeat. The loss was the first failure Hitler would ever publicly acknowledge. Eventually the entire Russian campaign would be abandoned but not before the lives of five million German soldiers and 8,700,000 Russians were wantonly wasted.

By the end of November, developments surrounding the coming attack on Pearl Harbor had become quite disturbing. Secretary of State Cordell Hull called his friend, newspaper correspondent Joseph Leib. He was frantic and said he had to see Mr. Leib right away. When the two met Mr. Hull pulled a transcript from his pocket and showed it to Mr. Leib. It described in detail a pending Japanese attack on the naval base. Then he told his friend he had just had a terrible argument with the president about Roosevelt's refusal to do anything to stop the attack or even warn the base because he thought the United States must join the Allies in order to stop Hitler. As secretary of state Mr. Hull felt he was powerless to countermand his country's commander-in-chief so he pleaded with Mr. Leib to take the transcript to the press. He also made his friend swear he'd never reveal the source of his information. Mr. Leib immediately went to the United Press office with the evidence but someone there contacted FBI Director Hoover who insisted the story was not to be published. By then, however, some newspapers had already printed it on their front page so Mr. Hoover sent agents to confiscate all the copies they could find. They missed one, ironically it was the *Honolulu Advertiser* of November 31. For some reason, the editor decided not to name the location of the attack though.

That very same day the head of Chinese Intelligence, our ally at the time, sent messages to both the United States and British State Departments detailing the planned assault. He sent it again on December 1. This was the same day Japan officially declared war on the United States, Britain and the Netherlands. I'm not sure which of these countries they actually informed but the United States wasn't one of them. Somehow we seemed to know anyway; December 2 US Intelligence stopped monitoring conversations inside the Japanese consulate.

December 4 the aircraft carrier *Enterprise* left Pearl Harbor for Wake Island. Simultaneously a huge fleet of Japanese warships left Hiroshima— six aircraft carriers carrying 414 planes, twenty-three submarines and twenty-two support ships. They headed for a position 250 miles north of Hawaii. The enormous armada was even spotted by a passenger liner that radioed their sighting to authorities on the mainland.

December 6 the aircraft carrier *Lexington* and five cruisers also left Pearl Harbor. When the last translated Japanese message referencing the attack on Pearl Harbor reached President Roosevelt at 9:00 p.m. that night, the president remarked, "This means war."

On December 7 at 7:48 in the morning Pearl Harbor was attacked by 353 Japanese planes and five submarines. The raid lasting two hours and sixteen minutes and sank four US battleships, destroyed 188 airplanes, and killed 2,471 Americans. Ten other ships and 159 additional airplanes were also damaged.

In the ensuing years I have become aware of even more information about the attack. Prior to the surprise assault on the base the United States had intercepted no less than fourteen Japanese messages that they decoded. Each clearly stated the day of the attack, the location of the staging area and the intended target, the time it was to begin, even the ships that were to be attacked first. President Roosevelt had shown each of these messages to Secretary of War Henry Stimson, Secretary of State Hull, Secretary of the Navy Frank Knox, Army Chief of Staff General Marshall, and Chief of Naval Operations Admiral Harold Stark. The commander of the Southwest Fleet General Douglas Mac Arthur was even informed eight hours before the attack. Commander in chief of the Pacific Fleet at Pearl Harbor Admiral H. E. Kimmel was, however, told nothing. At a cabinet meeting before the assault, Secretary Stimson questioned, "How can we maneuver them to fire the first shot without too much danger to ourselves?" CNO Stark could have easily ordered the US fleet out to sea to prevent their destruction but he decided against it; he didn't want to alarm the Hawaiian people! I'm sure they were a little more than alarmed when hundreds of Japanese planes swooped down out of the morning sky bombing and strafing everything in sight!

That morning as the first Japanese planes attacked his base at Pearl Harbor CPF Admiral Kimmel stood at his office window and watched his fleet being destroyed. He reportedly tore off his four-star shoulder boards because he knew his career as a naval officer was over. Ten days later he would be relieved of his command and in February 1942, a presidential commission found him guilty of dereliction of duty and reduced his rank to a two-star general. Reg told me he had known Admiral Kimmel at the Academy and he was a fine man.

A Court of Inquiry also found Admiral Stark guilty of neglecting to brief Admiral Kimmel and he was relieved of his command as Chief of Naval Operations. Undersecretary of the Navy James Forrestal later commented regarding Admiral Stark, "He shall not hold any position in the US Navy which requires the exercise of superior judgment."

After the United States entered World War II it seemed as though the entire world joined the Allies; Great Britain, China, the Netherlands, France, Luxembourg, Australia, New Zealand, Thailand, Greece, Norway, India, and the Soviet Union were united against the Axis Powers of Germany, Japan, Italy, Finland, Slovenia, Albania, Lithuania, Romania, Bulgaria, and Hungary.

These developments must have made Hitler a little nervous. In December he publicly declared Germany really wanted peace with Britain but Roosevelt was preventing it because he wanted to be dictator of the world. Hitler had such complete control of Germany by then he could say anything and probably count on no one daring to confront him with the truth.

After a few cases of typhus were found at the Bogdanovia concentration camp, the commandant ordered all 40,000 of his prisoners killed. Many were shot but others were locked in buildings that were then set on fire while others were simply left outside without clothing or food to freeze to death; unspeakable crimes so casually committed and intentionally designed to inflict maximum suffering in the process. Something had gone terribly wrong in the German mind.

Looking back on the two horrific wars I witnessed it does seem difficult to avoid such conflicts. I think this is partly because there will always be men with an intense desire to control others. But it does appear that there are things that can be done to prevent such conflicts from escalating into war. A few powerful nations, under intelligent leadership, must maintain a constant awareness of the political landscape in volatile areas of the world and derail fanatical leaders before they amass enough power to threaten other countries. They must also confront aggressive leaders before they disrupt areas in their own countries and then launch their armies into countries that border them. If these behaviors are not stopped in their initial stages, war becomes the only alternative. Considering the seemingly inevitable evolution of more and powerful weaponry early intervention is the only defense against annihilation.

In 1941, the Native American Sioux, Iroquois, Ojibwe, Navajo, and Choctaw nations declared war on Germany as well. By then the indigenous Indians native to North America had been reduced from an estimated one million when European settlers arrived to little more than 350,000 but 20 percent of them volunteered to serve even before the draft was instituted. Because large numbers of them did not speak English, however, they were rejected. Undeterred, many learned to write their names and say a few words in English, hoping that would be enough. When this failed to qualify them they organized remedial English classes; which resulted in some being accepted for service. One basic training officer was quoted as saying, "The Indian is the best damn soldier in the army; they proved to have an acute sense of perception, better endurance, and superior physical coordination." Another 45,000 Indians contributed to the war effort by taking jobs in the defense industry, agriculture, civil defense, the Red Cross, and women's aid groups. Native Americans would also buy $50 million worth of war bonds to demonstrate their support.

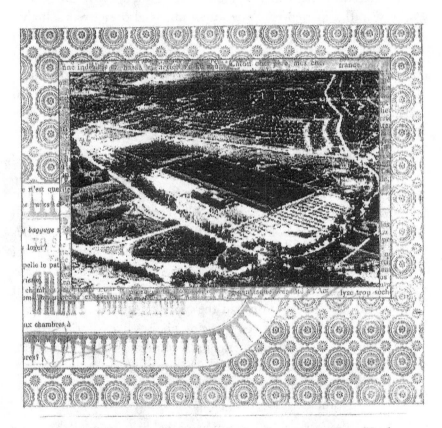

Sperry Gyroscope Plant - Lake Success - New York

1941

The Navajo language was also used extensively in the field to transmit coded messages. This led Hitler to send spies to their reservations to learn these languages. Goebbels even resorted to declaring that the Sioux were actually Aryans to elicit their cooperation. Indians also invented some very colorful names for the German "chiefs"; Hitler became He Who Smells His Moustache, Mussolini was Gourd Chin.

World War II also increased Indian integration into white America and lessened the racial barriers against them. As a direct result of their World War II experiences, American Indians also enjoyed a higher standard of living, better education levels and health care. Increased job opportunities for Indians also resulted in greater respect for them among the non-Indian population. Many left their reservations and decreased their dependence on tribal dictates. In some ways this is sad but no one should be denied the opportunity to improve their lives just to preserve a way of life.

When David returned from Cornell that Christmas, he kept talking about joining the navy and becoming a pilot. At that time, many young men were very enthusiastic about fighting for their country. They often feel quite differently after having actually experienced the battlefield and are not as eager to volunteer for the next one. The war memories of those who've actually fought are often so traumatic they don't want to talk about them. This spares younger generations from the details of real combat, details that might make them more hesitant about believing in war as a solution and the glory of fighting. Newspapers often encourage young men too by using phrases like "patriotic duty" and the "camaraderie" of the experience. A country's leaders should also be careful to avoid waging war that the public perceives as unnecessary or unjust; backlash from drafting men to fight and die in such conflicts can last a long time.

David's desire to be a navy man probably touched Reg's heart especially as Bill had already joined the army. I was against him leaving Cornell and felt strongly that he should finish his degree but I suspected he might have thought if he waited three years, the war might be over and he'd have missed all the "excitement." Sadly, he simply was not going to listen to me about this subject. Finally Reg gave in but insisted he finish his first year; it would be his only year of college.

In 1941, Bill met Mary Louise van Zandt, a lovely young woman originally from Plainfield, New Jersey. Her parents had moved to nearby Sands Point the year before we arrived at Penterra. Bill was twenty-three and "Mary Lou" twenty when they decided to get married. The ceremony was on December 27 in the lovely Zion Episcopal Church in nearby Douglaston. Mary Lou's great-great-great-grandfather had built the church and given it to the small village of what was then called Little Neck. I was thrilled to have her join our family and thought she and Bill were a wonderful match.

That year, Sperry moved out of its Brooklyn building to a much larger ninety-three-acre complex in Lake Success fifteen minutes from Penterra. Actually the US government felt Sperry was so critical to the country's war effort that they purchased the land and paid for construction of the new plant according to Reg's specifications. Sperry would lease the facility until after the war when they bought the entire property.

A new weapon was invented that year at a secret Harvard lab. Some "clever" technician had thought to combine highly flammable petroleum with a gel that when ignited could be propelled from a flamethrower. Unbelievably, it was specifically designed specifically to stick to human beings! The mind is capable of inventing some really horrific things.

As soon as the United States entered World War II Hitler immediately stepped up his U-boat campaign to block us the transport of men and supplies across the Atlantic to Allied armies. It seemed we were slightly unprepared for these attacks on our merchant vessels and warships. That first year we lost hundreds of ships to these underwater wolves. Finally Great Britain and the United States banded together to form convoys that were escorted by military ships and accompanied by aircraft surveillance units that could locate U-boats and bomb them. The American public was kept in the dark about most of the huge losses prior to the use of these protective measures and the fact that German submarines were actually been prowling within twenty miles of our East coast. We tried to enforce blackouts at night in coastal areas because our navigational beacons and the electric light glow from populated areas silhouetted ships and aided Germans U-boats in spotting vessels and guiding their torpedoes. Many Americans resisted these suggestions though.

Winston spent Christmas in the United States that year. He and Reg had the opportunity to meet privately in New York and afterward when he stayed at the White House.

1942

January 1 the United Nations was formed with twenty-six member countries. Their stated goal was "complete victory over the savage and brutal forces of Hitlerism seeking to take over the world." I thought that was an amazing statement unanimously arrived at by a large and diverse group of nations that was directed at a single national leader and form of government. It's hard to get even a few countries to agree on a single issue. All of them also agreed that nothing less than complete, unconditional surrender on the part of Germany would be acceptable.

The movie *Yankee Doodle Dandy* opened in New York with James Cagney singing and dancing into American hearts. The premier performances the first week of January were promoted as a fundraiser for the war and managed to raise $4,750,000 not only by selling tickets but special sheet music, records, ties and even evening dresses. There were also contests to see who could sing like Mr. Cagney.

By 1942, Hitler was promising to rid the entire world of Jews. France's liner the *Normandie* had been sailing the Atlantic since 1935.

She had twelve decks and could carry 3,300 passengers and crew. Her modern art-deco interiors featured huge public rooms with wide staircases and high ceilings. The dining room alone was quite grand at over 300 long, could seat seven hundred people at one time and was also resplendent with twelve twenty-eight-foot lighted Lalique crystal columns and twenty foot doors. Our newest immigration laws of the early twenties had begun to severely limit the number of people crossing the Atlantic in second and third class so the French had designed the *Normandie* specifically for upper-class Americans.

As the war approached, her home country thought the liner should take refuge in New York Harbor. Five days after the attack on Pearl Harbor the United States seized the 980-foot ship and began refitting her as a troop carrier. During the reconstruction process the ship's state-of- the-art fire control system was disconnected and on February 9 a welder accidentally set some life vests on fire. In no time at all the entire ship was ablaze. While attempting to put out the fire a huge amount of water was poured on *Normandie* and after twelve hours, the unthinkable happened. The beautiful liner gently rolled over on her side. It was a pathetic sight; a masterpiece of human accomplishment reduced to nothing more than a huge coffin sleeping next to her pier. At first there was talk of righting and restoring her but from past experience, I doubted that would happen. Eight months later, she was sold for scrap metal.

In the middle of February "exclusionary zones" were established on both the East and West Coasts of the United States. Apparently some Americans, specifically military men, Native Americans, white farmers, and the California American Legion felt threatened by Americans of Japanese, German, and Italian descent. Suddenly these nationalities were prohibited from living in those zones. Both President Roosevelt and FBI Director Hoover did not consider them a threat but that didn't stop these poor people being carted off. These isolated, guarded camps were in parts of the country most Americans would have refused to live but as many as 100,000 Japanese Americans were forced to abandon the homes and businesses they'd worked hard to establish. If you were just one-sixteenth Japanese or Korean you could be subject to internment; sounded eerily like Hitler's formula. Of course, infants and children had to go with their parents but the elderly and the mentally ill were also deemed dangerous. Though Japanese immigrants were the largest group affected the law was not applied equally in all areas of the country. In Hawaii where one-third of the population of 150,000 was Japanese there were such strenuous objections that only 1,800 were relocated. Many Japanese living in Oregon, Washington state and Arizona were also allowed to remain in their homes, while 17,000 Germans, Italians, Latin Americans and 3,800 Buddhist and Christian priests were forced to live in these austere camps. I'm also reasonably certain that most Americans were never aware that 62 percent of the detainees were American citizens.

As all these imprisonments were going on an estimated 20,000 Japanese American young men had volunteered to serve their country and were dying alongside other American boys.

That February Hitler had a list compiled of all the European Jews still alive. Then he came up with a brilliant new "natural" way to kill more of them. His Hunger Plan combined hard labor with food deprivation! I guess he believed dying from deliberate starvation was natural? And this man was actually chosen by his people as their leader?

March 1, 1942, the Rent Control Program began in New York City to help lower-income families find and keep housing. It froze rents and specified that a landlord could only raise them 7.5% every two years, but only if a new tenant rented the space. It would have dramatic unintended consequences for the city that would last for decades. The law stated that for the duration that a tenant rented the space the landlord could not raise the rent. But it permitted the tenant to sublet his apartment to anyone he wished and as the subletting tenant was not renting from the landlord, he was not considered "new." This financially trapped the owner of the apartment between his ever-increasing taxes and maintenance expenses and the stagnant income his unit generated. Over time it seemed to me that less rental property might be built and a landlord renting a space for the first time might need to ask more to compensate for not being allowed to raise rents to as his expenses rose.

By 1942 Britain was drafting women as old as forty-five!

As part of an aid package the United States gave Great Britain some obsolete destroyers, one of which was the *Buchanan*. England immediately rechristened her the *Campeltown* and began a special remodeling mission. Two of her funnels were removed and the remaining two were racked. A forward gun was added, as well as, eight cannons on her upper deck. The facelift turned the former destroyer's exterior into that of a German torpedo boat. Inside, a special compartment was also added to conceal four and a half tons of explosives. When all this redecorating was finally complete the *Campeltown* set out across the Atlantic flying German flags and using German communication codes.

By the end of March the *Campeltown* was approaching the German occupied dry dock at St. Nazaire, France. Just as she closed in, the crew hosted the British Union Jack and rammed the locked gates and 622 British commandos stormed ashore. They immediately set to work destroying everything in sight. When the *Campeltown*'s explosives were finally set off the docks were rendered useless and 360 German soldiers were killed in the blast. Sadly, 384 brave Englishmen also lost their lives but the success of the raid meant Germany could no longer use the convenient facility to repair of its warships.

The American public would not learn of the Battan Death March until January 1944 but it began April 10, 1942. The actual number of US and Allied Filipino soldiers who had surrendered to the Japanese in the Philippines, and were forced on that horrible trek would never be known. It could have been as many as 80,000. These POWs were forcibly marched sixty to seventy miles for six days with their hands tied behind them. Their abusive Japanese guards randomly shot, bayoneted and ran over them with trucks while others were even be headed by Samurai swordsmen on horses. If one of their fellow prisoners fell, their comrades were not allowed to help him; they were simply abandoned on the trail to die. The men also endured many hours sitting in the blazing sun with little water or food. After the war, however, the Japanese commander in charge of the POWs was executed by firing squad for allowing his men to treat his prisoners so inhumanely. The apparent reason for the cruel treatment could have been the Japanese belief that any soldier who surrendered forfeited his right to be treated as a human being. Apparently, the world had altogether different customs regarding POWs.

In Europe, a highly decorated Austrian officer working for Hitler's army when his men committing atrocities against their Jewish prisoners and ordered them to stop. Even though he had previously been awarded Germany's Iron Cross for bravery, Hitler had him shot. What a message this sent to German officers and the men under them.

Back in the United States antisubmarine aircraft squadrons began regularly patrolling the East Coast from Maine to the Chesapeake Bay.

Forty-five-year-old Lt. Jimmy Doolittle organized the country's first air raid on the Japanese mainland. The limited capabilities of the aircraft of the day coupled with the great distances involved made for some intense planning and unexpected last-minute changes. The mission involved two aircraft carriers, fourteen support ships and sixteen bombers. The bombers were to take off from the carriers but would be unable to re-land because the decks were too short. They planned to bomb Tokyo then head for China, refuel and then return to US territory. Things went wrong even before the convoy reached the launch coordinates when a Japanese reconnaissance plane discovered them. Doolittle felt the raid must immediately launch even as they were still 200 miles away from their intended location. April 18 the bombers successfully hit Tokyo but their compromised fuel supply forced fifteen of the planes to crash in enemy territory; this resulted in the deaths three crewmen. The eight survivors were then captured and three more were shot. The remaining seven crewmen were imprisoned and endured three years of severe deprivation that resulted in the death of yet another man. Eventually they were rescued. Though only one bomber managed to land safely in China and though everyone survived and they were well treated, they were not allowed to leave. Finally, they managed to escape. For all that effort, numerous deaths and suffering, in actuality the raid had caused very little damage to the Japanese capital. Doolittle himself believed he would face a court-martial when he returned home. In the states, however, news of the raid was greeted by the public with enormous enthusiasm and served as a great morale booster to the country. When the survivors finally made it home President Roosevelt awarded them the Distinguished Flying Cross and Doolittle also received the Medal of Honor and was promoted to brigadier general.

In early April the Battle of the Coral Sea began in the South Pacific. It would be the first air war fought entirely from aircraft carriers during which neither side ever saw the other's ships. The Japanese started with more ships and men but lost more of both. Though the United States lost 656 men, sixty-nine planes and one aircraft carrier we were eventually the victor in the four-day battle. More importantly the defeat halted Japan's plans to expand their presence in the Pacific.

Hitler decided he didn't like seeing pregnant Jewish women so he ordered all of them executed!

Winston sent two huge raids of two thousand planes each to bomb Cologne, Germany. The bombings destroyed sixteen thousand buildings and were thought to have killed 486,000 people on the ground. Hitler must have been stamping his feet like a spoiled child; in retaliation he ordered the execution of all concentration camp prisoners. Stupid man; he probably didn't have enough soldiers left to do that. He was always making himself look like an idiot, to say nothing about him being a mentally ill, egocentric, paranoid, psychotic, racist and a power-mongering butcher. The German people didn't seem to think any of these characteristics were dangerous in a leader so I guess they liked them.

By June 1942 reports finally began reaching the West about Hitler's use of gas chambers to kill people. I'm sure most people thought they were so awful such things couldn't possibly be true.

Later that June the United States opened the Office of War Information; it should really have been called the War Propaganda Office. At that time most Americans didn't understand why we were at war and were hesitant about becoming involved. Still others were completely apathetic or distrusted the Allied nations. The OWI was formed specifically to "encourage" public support for World War II. It even sounds strange to say. Among OWI's projects were newsreels that were shown in movie theaters before the featured film. They also dropped 180,000,000 leaflets behind enemy lines supposedly to taunt Axis soldiers. They were printed with such slogans as "You're surrounded" and "Will Italians die for Mussolini and Hitler, or live for Italy and civilization?" OWI also printed magazines, matchbooks, and seed packets promoting the virtues of American life that were distributed abroad.

"Radio Free Europe" was also part of OWI. It often featured people commenting about the war and what was "really" happening. Of course, sometimes that involved suggesting what OWI "wanted" to be happening. One of the agency's most successful broadcasts operated out of a house in Luxembourg where actors portrayed a group of loyal Germans trapped behind enemy lines.

The supposedly casual conversations of these "ordinary" people were designed to discourage German soldiers. The actors, probably real spies, discussed such things as how badly the war was going for Germany, the deaths of soldiers they knew and their country's poor leadership.

OWI also ran a sophisticated radio campaign bent on demoralizing Japanese troops while simultaneously aiding resistance groups in the country.

These efforts by OWI caused some controversy at home and people began characterizing them as manipulative. They were, but the reality was that much of the rest of world was fighting for its very existence while at home we could watch from a safe distance. OWI also started the Office of Strategic Services which later became the Central Intelligence Agency. A strange and almost *Laurel and Hardy* sabotage operation was launched by Germany that June. Eight US citizens were recruited and sent to Berlin for a month's worth of intensive training. Actually, I don't think a month could be characterized as intense enough for these particular agents.

The first batch of four arrived in the middle of the night on a beach in Amagansett at the eastern end of Long Island. Their "intense" training was immediately evident; they wore German uniforms. They did change their clothes after landing but burying them attracted the attention of the local Coast Guard who immediately began searching for them. They managed to elude capture though and boarded a Long Island Railroad train for New York where they rented two rooms and went to sleep. The next morning, "Laurel" went to the window, opened it, and motioned for "Hardy" to come look at the view. Then Laurel told Hardy they were now going to come to an agreement but if that wasn't possible, one of them was going to leave by the door and the other by the window. Laurel said he thought there was little chance of the mission succeeding and, as he hated Nazis anyway, he was going to the FBI to tell them everything. Hardy smiled broadly and said he hated Nazis too and he'd go with him! Boss Laurel said fine but Hardy must stay there to make sure the others didn't get into trouble before he returned. Then he went downstairs, called the FBI's New

York office and asked for J. Edgar Hoover. He was passed from person to person, however, each thinking he was some sort of crackpot, and he never reached the director. Four days later, Laurel took a train to Washington, went to the FBI office there and asked to see Mr. Hoover. Again, he was shuttled from office to office, until finally the assistant director agreed to see him for five minutes. By that time "Laurel" was so angry he immediately opened the suitcase he'd been carrying and dumped the mission's entire budget of $84,000 on the man's desk. Then he told him that the four of them had been assigned to blow up two factories, two bridges, a hydroelectric plant and a train yard.

Meanwhile, another team of four "crack agents" were deposited on a beach in Ponte Verde, Florida. They wisely decided that it would be better to land in civilian clothes but kept their German hats on. They got into town, perhaps without their hats, and boarded a train to Chicago. Laurel's confession ended the entire operation though and all eight were arrested. Eventually, they were put on trial, found guilty, and six were executed.

The US Army developed a shoulder-fired rocket launcher that weighed only twelve pounds and could destroy a tank. That might be a very dangerous weapon in the wrong hands.

Off the coast of Maine an American merchant ship carrying 1,600 tons of automobile parts and 4,000 tons of war materials was making its way to New York Harbor. The ship was being escorted by four other merchant vessels and six military escorts. That's quite a lot of protection? The American ship being guarded by the convoy was also carrying Two Soviet envoys. A passing German U-boat spotted the eleven ships and scored a direct hit on the one in the middle. Though it stayed afloat for seven hours it did finally sink. In its hold was actually seventy-one tons of platinum and gold supposedly worth over $53 million then. It was Stalin's payment to the United States for war materials we'd sent him to fight his German friends. To this day it is believed that the cargo was never salvaged. I guess no one wanted to go to all that trouble for some rusty auto parts.

Winston secretly came to Washington again that June most probably to discuss the Manhattan Project. Its facility at Oak Ridge, Tennessee would eventually employ 130,000 people and cost the United States $26 million ($2 billion in 2013 dollars). Incredibly 90 percent of the budget was used to produce the uranium needed to arm just two atomic bombs. The project also had a research center in Los Alamos, New Mexico and a team of spies that fanned out across Europe to find and seize nuclear materials, "encourage" the defection of German nuclear scientists and escort them back to the US.

June 25 Winston launched a 1,000 plane raid on Bremen, Germany and dropped 2,100 tons of bombs that flattened an aircraft factory, destroyed 572 houses and killed eighty-five people.

David returned to Penterra after his first year at Cornell and promptly enlisted in the navy. He was immediately sent to Officers Candidate School in Chapel Hill, South Carolina where he entered an accelerated training program designed to speed up the graduation of much-needed officers. He trained in open cockpit biplanes and was eventually stationed in Pensacola, Florida where he became a flight instructor and taught acrobatics, the sort of skill required in a dogfight. The first time he came home he was a new man. Besides looking very handsome is his uniform, he absolutely sparkled with enthusiasm for flying.

That summer we invited Jeanne Fisher to spend a few weeks with us. David had met her at an intercollegiate social while at Cornell. He told us he'd enjoyed her company so much that first evening that he sent her two- dozen roses the next day; definitely a Casanova move. She was charming and pretty, and both Reg and I liked her very much. David seemed quite taken with her, too. He took her home on the train and stayed with her family for a week. It seemed like a promising relationship.

Hitler apparently wasn't satisfied with just killing Jews; he ordered that all the women in Ravensbrook be sterilized; only a crazy man could think of such things while battling to take over the world. In France, as Catholic leaders loudly protested, French police loaded 13,000 Jews on cattle-cars trains bound for Auschwitz and Treblinka.

July 21 the US Navy established the Women Accepted for Volunteer Emergency Service. Although they were officially the United States Naval Women's Reserve they were most frequently referred to as WAVES.

In a small Polish town German troops arrested two hundred Jewish children living in an orphanage, many just two years old. The director was told to prepare them for deportation the next day. In order to keep them from being frightened about the journey the director told the children they were going on a holiday in the country and to wear in their best clothes. As they boarded the train together he held their hands and talked to them about their new adventure. All of the children and the man that loved and cared for them were killed in the gas chambers at Treblinka. Nothing seems too horrible for the Nazi mind.

As I learned of more and more atrocities committed by Germans during that horrible war I began to think that there must be something in German culture that stamps out the ability to be empathetic. Perhaps Hitler had understood this and used it to control them. I do know they have strong feelings about maintaining order, making rules and following them. But my greatest dismay will always be the barbarity of the German people who so enthusiastically supported and carried out the orders of their sadistic lunatic leader. They owe a great deal to the world for all the suffering they caused.

David & Jeanne

Bill & Mary Lou

The British liner *Queen Mary* had been requisitioned during the war to carry troops. On October 2 she was steaming for Scotland with 10,000 American soldiers on board. To deter a submarine attack she was maintaining a prearranged zigzag course and her three British escorts were altering their direction accordingly. Unfortunately, one of them was twenty-four years old and her captain was finding it impossible to keep up with the liner's twenty-eight knot speed. He decided a straight course was the only option he had to keep his ship within antiaircraft range of the liner. It wasn't long, however, before disaster struck when the older ship crossed the bow of *Queen Mary.* The resulting collision cut the smaller vessel completely in half and it sank in just six minutes. All 338 sailors on board went into the water but as the *Queen Mary* couldn't risk the lives of all those much-needed US soldiers she continued on course and wasn't able to stop. Neither of her remaining two escorts could leave the liner unprotected so no rescue of the men thrown into the ocean was possible. It was several hours before a ship could return to the scene but sadly by then 245 had drowned.

Reg told me an amusing story about Admiral Nimitz when he was the commander in chief of the US Pacific Fleet at Pearl Harbor. At some point in a staff discussion the name Guadalcanal came up. As he didn't know that it was; he checked a *National Geographic* map!

In Minsk, Poland Hitler's troops shot a group of 12,000 Jews. Imagine twelve thousand people standing in a field where you live. Then picture them all being machine-gunned and dropping dead on the ground in front of you!

A new singing sensation appeared with Benny Goodman in New York City that September. The concert brought out 5,000 screaming girls because twenty-seven-year-old Frank Sinatra was performing with the band. A return engagement on October 1944 would produce a crowd of 35,000 and nearly caused a riot outside the theater.

On November 29 coffee was added to the list of rationed goods—a very upsetting thought for me personally; I wasn't sure I could leave my dressing room without it! You were allowed one pound every five weeks; that was about half the amount most people normally used.

December 1 gasoline was also rationed. Most people were only allowed three gallons a week but if you had a job that required traveling you could get eight. This led to the cancellation of the Indianapolis 500 race for the next two years.

As part of the Manhattan Project the Italian physicist Enrico Ferme produced the first controlled nuclear fission explosion December 2 in a squash court under the University of Chicago's football stadium. It involved very small amounts of the key ingredients and only produced enough energy to light one light bulb but even a small miscalculation would have had disastrous consequences.

David asked Jeanne to marry him and they were engaged just before Christmas.

1943

Reg and I were familiar with the work of Croatian-born electrical genius Nicola Tesla and we were saddened to hear of his death January 7 at the New York hotel where he lived. Mr. Tesla had invented over three hundred electrical devices that would revolutionize American life including AC current, fluorescent light, laser beams, remote controls, x-rays and the wireless radio. He was also very civic minded and believed his discoveries should be used to improve the lives of people all around the world, especially the poor. It was for that reason he published diagrams of the wireless radio he'd invented. He imagined doing so would enable everyone to make their own radio and freely communicate when they needed help. He never considered that someone might construct one and claim they had invented it but that's exactly what Guglierlmo Marconi did. Even after the US Supreme Court declared Marconi's patent invalid in 1934 and recorded Mr. Tesla as the rightful inventor many people were even taught in school that Marconi was the inventor. Mr. Tesla felt his most important discovery, however, was that the Earth itself could conduct electricity. Strange as that sounds he proved it in a demonstration by lighting two hundred lamps from a location twenty-five miles away without using any connecting wires. Then he devised a way to provide free electric power to the entire world using a series of towers. J.P. Morgan agreed to finance his project and a single 187-foot tower went up in Shoreham thirty miles east of our house. When Mr. Morgan realized there would be no way to charge for electricity delivered this way he withdrew his support and Tesla's dream collapsed.

Strangely after Mr. Tesla's death US government agents entered his apartment and took all his papers before his relatives could claim them. Someone must have thought Mr. Tesla's work was very important.

The king of Italy suddenly "woke up" that January and refused to surrender Italian Jews to German troops.

January 27 Hitler got his first taste of the combined air power of the United States and Great Britain. Only then did Germany experience the kind of destruction Hitler had been inflicting on other nations. During the next two years urban Germany would virtually be reduced to rubble. The day after that first raid Hitler began drafting men between sixteen and sixty-five and women seventeen to fifty—certainly an able-bodied group.

Leonardo - Best Man

1943

In early February the trial of the popular actor Errol Flynn ended. He had been accused of raping two teenage girls. As expected he used the familiar defense of attacking the moral character of his accusers and was acquitted. I hoped it would at least scare him but he seemed to continue this predatory behavior. At some point he even openly commented that he liked his women young. His devoted fans, however, refused to believe he was capable of such a thing or else they didn't care. Later he actually got another young girl pregnant. Things didn't end well for her either.

Shoe rationing finally ended that February. During the two years it was enforced you were only allowed three pairs a year. At the time, I remember thinking there were probably a great many Americans who wouldn't have enough money to buy three pairs even every other year.

In Germany the small, nonviolent intellectual White Rose Society at the University of Munich erected a sign that proclaimed "Out With Hitler! Long Live Freedom." Hitler immediately had the three young leaders including a twenty-two-year-old woman arrested publicly beheaded!

Sergei Rachmaninoff, the famous Russian composer and pianist, died in Beverly Hills at the end of March. He had composed some of the most beautiful pieces including my favorite his Third Piano Concerto.

The British began a concerted bombing campaign against the city of Berlin that dropped fifty tons of bombs every day on the city for eighteen days. It involved as many as 760 planes and left 175,000 people homeless. Can you imagine the noise and devastation! Personally, I thought the Germans deserved it for putting this man in control of their lives and the cruelties they had inflicted on so many people not only in their own country but numerous others around the world. The bombing must have had an effect on the army defending the city. Nazi soldiers were suddenly forcibly conscripting fifteen-year-olds in the streets.

The team of Richard Rogers and Oscar Hammerstein brought New York a breath of spring with their first musical *Oklahoma*. Together they would produce many more of them that delighted Americans for decades.

In March German troops began rounding up Jews in Greece. During the next five months 44,000 were sent to Auschwitz and Birkenau.

The Warsaw ghetto in Poland was created by the Nazis in 1940 and by 1943 the number of Jews confined within those barbed wire walls had reached 350,000. During those three desperate years huge numbers of these poor people were shot, sent to concentration camps, died of disease and starved to death. In mid-April 1943, several thousand Nazi soldiers entered the ghetto and attempted to force the remaining 50,000 into open cattle cars destined for Treblinka but it was believed that 13,000 more chose to hide instead. Nazis henchmen with dogs hunted them down and forced those they could into the open with smoke bombs, where they were immediately shot. Supposedly another 6,000 had still managed to evade detection so the soldiers set the ghetto on fire and stood guard as it burned to the ground; what horrible deaths. Hearing of the slaughter a group of other locals expressed their defiance by attacking a train carrying Jews headed to Auschwitz and set 236 free.

April 24, 1943, David and Jeanne were married in her hometown of Centreville, Maryland, at St. Paul's Episcopal Church. The reception was in the parish hall and even though many wedding essentials were rationed our family was determined to make it beautiful. To complicate matters Centreville is 250 miles from New York City and had a population of only 1,600 so there weren't many resources available locally. We had a lovely wedding cake made in New York and delivered to the church, as well as all the flowers. Jeanne's talented mother not only made her beautiful wedding dress and veil but made all the flower arrangements. Leonardo headed up the transportation and somehow managed to get the photographer and many of our friends to the church, and on time. I was afraid to ask where the gasoline had come from. Jeanne's brother was in the wedding as were Bill and two of David's friends. One of them was Lt. John Towers, the son of one of those first navy pilots at the Curtiss factory. Leonardo wanted a more prominent role in the wedding than just guest and convinced David that he should be the best man. Half the men in the wedding party wore tails and white tie while David, Bill, and David's two friends wore their uniforms; they all looked so handsome. It was a beautiful evening wedding with the church lit only by candlelight.

We all lined up for the customary formal photographs after the ceremony and in one Leonardo is standing off to the side, a little apart from the group. The warmth and affection with which he was looking at David indeed touched my heart. I remember feeling very relieved that everything had turned out all right after all. Alas, just three years later, things won't look so wonderful.

Reg told me about a special British intelligence project named Operation Mincemeat that began April 30 and ended with the body of a dead British Major Martin lying on a beach in Spain. As he appeared to have been the victim of a plane crash and an officer, Spanish fishermen known to be sympathetic to the Nazis, took his body to German authorities. The operation was devised specifically to mislead Hitler into believing the Allies were planning to attack Greece and Sardinia, rather than their real target.

The plan chosen for Operation Mincemeat was apparently one of fifty-one ideas submitted by British agent Ian Fleming—yes, the James Bond Fleming. The elaborate cover-up began with the deceased body of an itinerant Welsh laborer named Glyndwr Michael. After he "volunteered", British Intelligence set to work disguising him as a diplomat carrying secret documents. To establish his new identity, Major Martin carried a picture of his fiancée, "Pam," two love letters from her, a receipt for an expensive diamond ring from an exclusive Bond Street jewelry shop, a pompous letter from his "father," an overdraft notice from Lloyds Bank, a letter from a family attorney, a book of stamps, a St. Christopher medallion, a set of keys, a pencil stub, a used bus ticket, two-week-old theatre ticket stubs, a receipt for four nights at the Navy and Military Club in London, a receipt for a new shirt, a personal letter from the Vice Chief of Imperial Staff and a letter of introduction from his commanding officer, none other than our Dickie, Vice Admiral Louis Mountbatten. All these things were even on authentic stationery, a time-consuming task by itself. Lastly, it was deemed vital that Major Martin must be found wearing good-quality underwear. Actually, I believe that item would only have been important to the creation of a British diplomat.

Ultimately, the mission succeeded, and Germany never suspected Sicily was the real location of the Allied assault.

Winston came to Washington again on May 12 and Reg and he were able to visit with one another again.

By May 19 Hitler triumphantly proclaimed there were no more Jews in Berlin. There was also hardly anything else there either.

Hate is a contagious thing and can be easily taught to the naïve and poorly educated but kindness and compassion can be learned just as easily. That June the British launched a bombing raid directed at Germany's Zeppelin Works and a large radar installation beside it. Completely by accident, the raid also destroyed Germany's V-2 rocket facility in the same complex. Reconnaissance after the bombing noted some unusual results though; lightly damaged buildings had been painted with fake burn marks on the roof and pretend bomb craters had been dug where none had actually been after the raid. It was presumed that the Germans wanted the complex to appear as if the damage to their facility had been so extensive no future bombing was necessary.

In the middle of June the largest tank battle in history began in Kursk, Russia; 2,900 German machines fought 5,100 Russian ones. By the end of the thirteen-day siege 54,000 German and 177,800 Russian soldiers had been killed but the Soviets had the satisfaction of saying they won, in spite of their huge losses.

Mary Lou had our first grandchild on July 15. They named her Pamela van Zandt Gillmor. Mary Lou had come back to Penterra before the birth and Reg's driver took her to Doctor's hospital in New York on the appointed day. We wanted to be sure they both received the very best care.

July 24 marked the beginning of a bombing campaign that destroyed the city of Hamburg. Together the United States and Great Britain bombed the city for eight days, twenty-four hours a day with the English flying at night and the United States during the day. Until then, Hamburg had been an industrial center with a large port, shipyards, submarine pens and oil refineries. So many bombs were dropped that a 1,500-foot tornado of fire was created among the ruins. The death toll was staggering; 40,000 people were killed.

Hitler's terrible thirst for power, coupled with the zealous support of the German people, made such horrific tactics necessary. I'm convinced that nothing less could have stopped him and he would never have surrendered. Egomaniacs seem particularly afraid of failing at anything. War is devastating to all sides anyway but with a completely insane leader who values only his power, the loss of lives is especially devastating. As I had witnessed both the First World War and the Second it was really frightening to see such a huge increase in the physical destruction and the number of deaths between the two conflicts as a direct result of the development of ever more deadly weapons. A World War III will surely kill us all.

Coffee rationing ended that July! Yea!

After only a year and half in existence, 27,000 women had volunteered to be WAVES. I was amazed and decided right then I too should sign up. I talked to Reg about the idea and he was very encouraging. He even volunteered to find out where I should go and within a few days I had an interview. I told the officer I was fluent in French and German and that I had lived in Europe for a decade, some of it in Germany. But he really took notice when I told him what my husband did. Almost immediately after that he asked me if I'd be willing to work in an intelligence office. He said it wouldn't be as glamorous as spying was made out to be though, they just needed someone to sort information and file things. Would I be interested? Was he kidding! It sounded unbelievably exciting! I controlled my enthusiasm though and calmly answered, "That would be fine." He said I could start as soon as he could get me a uniform. I was part of the VIO Program which didn't require me to attend boot camp or participate in any physical training. That seemed a wise choice as I was then fifty and couldn't possibly have done even a single jumping jack. The program would prevent me from becoming an officer but that certainly had never been a dream of mine. He sent me to another office that day where I tried on some uniforms and left with a complete ensemble, including some sensible shoes.

I began working in an office in New York several days a week. I was officially with the Office of Navy Intelligence but I mostly filed documents. Though I did handle intelligence papers and occasionally translated things, I was definitely not a spy. It was there that I made my first pot of coffee! Yippee, a basic survival skill I had definitely been lacking. Though I'd never had a job before, I was very careful about doing everything right and being punctual. I really loved it, especially the interaction with the other people there. The whole thing gave me a sense of accomplishment I'd never experienced before. Rather quickly, however, I determined that no one else arrived in a chauffeured car. I tried to keep that under wraps.

In the beginning of August Hitler's army invaded Italy, until recently also one of his supposed friends. He claimed he was just trying to rescue Mussolini who'd been jailed that June by the country's newly "awake" king. Actually, Hitler seemed to take his time springing his friend. Mussolini's sojourn in the lockup apparently afforded him some time to reflect as he came out believing he'd chosen the wrong side to support and when he was finally released he tried to flee north with his mistress. Some angry Italian partisans captured them both and, as they say, it wasn't pretty.

In August the Danish government declared they would no longer cooperate with the German soldiers occupying their country. They also defiantly sank twenty-two of their largest warships to prevent the Nazis from commandeering them.

By then Hitler controlled Rome and the Vatican and was announcing he intended to kill all the Jews in the city unless he was paid fifty kilograms of gold. Jewish leaders pleaded with the pope for help. Eventually, he offered to give them only some of the ransom and demanded interest and strict repayment terms. Italian Jews ended up paying the ransom themselves but Hitler still sent 1,000 of them to Auschwitz.

In China Chiang Kai-shek arrested the brother of a prominent communist leader and had him tortured to get him to falsely confess his part in a plan to overthrow the government. He steadfastly refused and was executed. His death would have enormous consequences for the country. It provided critical support for the dead man's brother, Mao Zedong, to eventually become the president of China and turn the country into another brutal Communist state.

October 13 Italy declared war on Germany. During the same month Danish citizens clandestinely evacuated 7,200 Jews to Sweden in a series of dangerous boat crossings.

On October 19 the talented sculptor Camille Claudel died in a French mental institution where she'd been involuntarily committed twenty-nine years earlier by her family. They contended she was mad. At eighteen, she had met the forty-two-year-old Auguste Rodin and he invited her to join his studio. She was a really gifted sculptor and he must have recognized her talent. She was also beautiful and soon became his model. Then, as might have been expected she became his mistress and they worked together for a decade. After becoming familiar with the work of both of them I felt he'd often used her ideas and passed them off as his own, even occasionally claiming her pieces as his. She was overjoyed when she became pregnant with their child but he was not and convinced her to have an abortion. It was shortly after that that she seemed to come unhinged and destroyed many of her pieces in a state of great anger. I believe her rage was directed at him. Sadly, this brilliant woman is mostly forgotten by the art world today. That October we heard that the 258-mile Thailand to Burma Railroad, under the direction of the Japanese, had been finished. Outside official circles, it was often referred to as the Death Railway. An estimated 13,000 POWs and 100,000 slaves had done all the work involuntarily and without financial compensation; probably very little food, as well. For every mile of finished track it was believed that 3,700 men had lost their lives. It appeared that the Japanese had some values that differed greatly from those in America.

During the last two days of October German soldiers shot 48,000 Jews at two concentration camps. That was such an astounding number of deaths it is still difficult to imagine how some people are capable of doing such a horrible thing to so a huge group of unharmed other human being? Hitler had been using Vatican Radio to broadcast propaganda so a few apparently reluctant Italian pilots were enlisted to stop him by bombing the Vatican. They couldn't have tried very hard though; not a single building was hit and no one was killed. They did shatter a lot of windows. German Vatican Broadcasting continued its regularly scheduled programming.

Sometime in the middle of November British and Norwegian commandos sabotaged the country's heavy water plant that had been taken over by the Germans. Simultaneously, 160 US bombers attacked the location from the air. Heavy water is a critical component in the production of atomic weapons.

Just before Christmas a group of Allied planes were returning to England after a bombing raid on Bremen, Germany. One of them was limping along with two of its four engines out and its pilot was wounded. Gradually the crippled bomber fell behind the others until it was essentially flying alone. Then twelve enemy fighter planes spotted the crippled plane and swooped in for an easy kill. Though it managed to remain aloft, the German attack had succeeded in knocking out another engine. By some miracle the pilot was still able to keep his plane in the air. At that point the plane had lost its oxygen supply and almost all its hydraulic and electrical power. Half its horizontal tail stabilizer was also gone, the left wing had lost most of its skin and the aileron on one side wasn't working. Of the planes eleven guns only three were operable, but that hardly mattered as there wasn't anyone to operate them; one of the crew was dead, and most of the rest were wounded. The wounded pilot was doing his best to bring his crew home but, at some point, he actually lost consciousness and the plane went into a five-thousand-foot dive. Perhaps the sound of the plane descending stirred him awake and he was able to pull up at a thousand feet. It was at that low altitude that a German pilot on the ground first saw the lone bomber and took off after it. He quickly came alongside and immediately saw how badly the plane was damaged and the wounded pilot. Through the open airframe he could also see all the injured crewmen. The two planes were close enough that the pilots actually made eye contact. The German tried to direct the Allied pilot toward safety in Sweden just thirty minutes away but the American didn't understand him and stayed on course for England. The German knew the bomber would shortly be over the heavily defended North Sea so he decided to fly next to provide some measure of protection for the American from the deadly guns below. Once over open water and out of artillery range, the German saluted and turned for home himself. The American knew a German pilot could be executed for sparing an enemy plane so he always wondered what had happened to him.

Navy Three - Army One

1943

The decorated German pilot made it safely home after the war and years later during an interview he talked about the incident. He said an early commander had warned him if he ever heard that he had fired on someone in a parachute, he'd shoot him himself. Then the German added that the men in the bomber that day were just as incapable of defending themselves. As it would turn out he eventually moved to Canada and the two pilots finally met again. Throughout all the ensuing years since their chance meeting in the sky, each had each always considering the other a friend. Sometimes very challenging situations bring out the best in people. All of us are presented with moments in our lives that call upon us to make the right decision; often we choose the wrong one instead.

I heard another poignant anecdote about an American soldier ferrying German prisoners to England. As he looked at his captives he thought, *My God, they look just like us. What are we doing fighting each other?*

Toward the end of 1943 it seemed Japan might be thinking the war wasn't going very well for them and decided to go for broke. They instituted a program that was based on convincing a few soldiers that they could make a real difference by volunteering for a special mission. As further enticement their families financial compensation if they failed to return from their assignment; that's because no one could return! All of us have probably heard about Kamikaze pilots that flew their planes directly into their targets, but there were also Shinyo motorboats and Kaiten submarines that did the same thing. During training some of the volunteers encountered a few problems and fifteen died. I guess they weren't paying attention in class? That wasn't any reason to stop the program though? Each submarine were essentially a forty-eight-foot torpedo powered by a two-cylinder engine. Once the pilot got himself comfortably inside and the door was closed, there was no changing your mind. The door couldn't be opened from the inside! The designers had thoughtfully provided a self- destruct button though. The Japanese economy was performing so poorly and jobs were in such short supply that sadly many of these men felt they had few other options to support their families. Yikes!

Both Bill and David were able to come home for Christmas that year. I remember being so excited that we would all be together and with a new baby too! When the boys arrived in New York, they went directly to Reg's office in Rockefeller Plaza. I was to meet Reg there too but didn't know they would also be there. What a wonderful surprise to open the door and find my two handsome sons standing there. I think they were kind of surprised to see me in a uniform too.

Someone had a camera and we had fun striking different poses. I didn't notice it at the time, but after the pictures were developed David seemed to intentionally avoid looking at his father in every single photograph. I thought perhaps he was still angry at his father about Reggie's funeral but I was never sure.

Mary-Lou arrived the next day with five-month-old Pamela and Jeanne the day after. We invited Jeanne's family to stay with us over the holiday but only her mother could join us. Her father felt he couldn't leave his patients without a doctor in the event of an emergency. We had a wonderful Christmas and were even able to celebrate Pamela's christening with a church service and a small luncheon afterwards.

New Year's Eve we all sat in the drawing room and raised our glasses to 1944. As I looked at Reg and Leonardo I thought how unusual it was that these two men, best friends for the last twenty-eight years, had both become such a huge part of my life. It would be a long time before I truly understood the enormous impact Leonardo would really have on my family.

1944

The Servicemen's Readjustment Act was passed early that January. Now it is most often referred to as the GI Bill. It provided the sixteen million men returning from World War II with college tuition and low- interest home mortgages. Their participation in this program led to a 50 percent increase in the number of college-educated men in America and the construction of two million new homes for them and their families. The communities created by this building boom were located outside urban areas of the country were called "suburban." The term was eventually shortened to "suburb." It's a shame we no longer offer such assistance to less wealthy young people so they can get an education and buy a home; it's good for them and our economy. I also think it might encourage them to marry, start families and further contribute to the country's prosperity as consumers.

In the Soviet Union, Stalin decided he wanted the land occupied by the autonomous Chechen-Ingush State and forcibly removed all 400,000 of these people, half of which were children. Anyone who protested was shot. Like Hitler he decided to transport them in open railroad cars designed to carry livestock and during the long and arduous journey through remote freezing areas of Russia, 25 percent of them died. I can only imagine how frightened the children must have been as day after day they helplessly watched death claim the lives of families all around them. But that wasn't enough for Stalin; the six indigenous nationalities represented in the purge were completely erased from Soviet textbooks, encyclopedias and maps as if they'd never existed.

Casablanca won the Academy Award for Best Picture though Humphrey Bogart was not chosen as Best Actor.

England took the highly unusual step of barring its citizens from traveling to Ireland. The crown believed the Irish government was collaborating with the Nazis.

Aviation history was made again that March but quite by accident and it didn't actually involve an aircraft. An RAF plane flying over Germany at eighteen thousand feet was attacked by enemy aircraft and caught fire. The pilot immediately ordered his crew to jump but one of the men discovered his parachute was in flames! Rather than face certain death if he stayed he leaped over the side! When he finally woke up he was under a large tree in a huge snowdrift with only a sprained ankle!

I had no idea such a thing existed but the Supreme Court decided "white primaries" were unconstitutional. They were held mostly in Texas and though the ruling discouraged white Texans from trying to block black people from voting. They quickly invented other methods.

In late April off the coast of England, eight British landing craft were practicing for the D-Day. They were spotted by a passing fleet of nine German U-boats that immediately began firing torpedoes at the group. Two of the boats sank and several others were badly damaged. Because the men on board had not been properly trained yet they went into the water wearing all their heavy gear and over seven hundred drowned.

In Europe local Hungarians helped Nazi soldiers load 475,000 of their Jewish countrymen onto trains for Auschwitz. They must have known many of them.

The first eye bank was founded in New York that year. I thought it was astounding that anything so "unneeded" could give a person the gift of sight. What an incredible legacy to leave after your death!

On May 15 three generals mounted another attempt to assassinate Hitler. They were unsuccessful and would be executed for trying to rid the world of this crazed man. Germany's much-loved General Erwin Rommel was implicated in the plot and two months later he died. The public was told he died from wounds received in a battle. He was given the elaborate state funeral of a hero. In reality he had been "encouraged" to poison himself during a visit from Hitler's henchmen for his part in the plot.

Outside Rome the oldest monastery in Europe dating to 579 AD was finally taken from the Germans. The brutal four-month battle had nearly destroyed the ancient structure in the process and 20,000 Allied soldiers had died taking it.

In the Crimea Stalin decided he didn't like the indigenous Tartars who lived there had forcibly evicted all 240,000 of them from their land. He claimed they'd been collaborating with the Germans; seemed rather like Stalin himself was guilty of that but I guess nobody wanted to point that out.

June 6 was D-Day and 156,000 Allied soldiers from thirteen countries stormed ashore onto five beaches in Normandy, France. As they jumped from their landing craft they were immediately confronted by intense German gunfire from gun positions high above the cliffs facing them.   A great many were slaughtered before even before they set foot on the beach. There was absolutely nowhere to hide until you reached the base of the cliffs; it must have been terrifying. The Allied offensive continued for three weeks and though four thousand men lost their lives, six thousand trucks, tanks, fuel and supplies were successfully landed. Eventually the 50,000 Nazis in the heavily fortified bunkers above the beaches fled and left 10,000 of their dead comrades behind. Allied troops would continue pursuing the retreating Germans eventually reaching Germany itself.

In an attempt to save Hungarian Jews the United States recruited a Swedish national to pose as a Hungarian ambassador from Sweden. We supplied him with money and fake diplomatic papers that eventually allowed him to buy thirty-two buildings in Budapest where he hid Jews. The Swedish flag was prominently displayed on all of them and they also bore signs such as "Swedish Research Institute" and "Swedish Library." His efforts saved a thousand people.

In Poland, Soviet troops liberated the Majdanek concentration camp. The guards had anticipated their arrival and evacuated 15,000 of them. Though just 1,500 of the weakest were left, there had been no attempt to conceal the atrocities that were carried out there and the liberators were shocked by what they saw. One US officer described "cruelties so enormous as to be incomprehensible to the normal human mind."

When the people confined in these camps were originally rounded up Hitler described them to the German press as "Enemies of the Third Reich." Most of those dragged from their homes were Jews but others were gypsies, homosexuals, the physically and mentally handicapped, Jehovah's Witnesses, Catholic priests and nuns, political opponents, and common criminals. It is difficult to understand now how ordinary Germans were able to accept that young children, frail old men and middle-aged housewives could really be so dangerous. But they went along with everything Hitler said and newsreels shown in US theaters certainly attest to their enthusiastic support. I have to believe it was racism and bigotry that prevailed.

On July 31 a forty-year-old French aviator took off in his own plane from the island of Corsica just south of France to monitor German troop movements. Though his aircraft was unarmed and considered non- airworthy, he was thrilled to be working for the Allies. He never returned.

Just prior to being stationed in the Mediterranean he had been living in the United States. He had so desperately wanted to fly for the Allies that he'd repeatedly petitioned the US government to allow him to volunteer even though he was over the established age limit. On his fifth attempt, General Eisenhower personally approved his request. Age notwithstanding this French aristocrat had enjoyed an illustrious career flying for the French Air Force and the European, African, and South American Postal Airlines. He and Leonardo had met in Argentina and were good friends. We met him the very first night he arrived in the United States in 1940 and Leonardo brought him to our New Year's Eve celebration. We all thought he was charming and impressively accomplished even before we learned he was a French national hero and an award-winning author. We also felt privileged to be in the audience when he was awarded a National Book Award in 1941. His real name was Antoine Marie Jean Baptiste Roger, Comte de Saint-Exupery but the small book he wrote and illustrated, *The Little Prince*, became far more famous than he would ever be.

Parts of his plane and identification tags were found years later in the Mediterranean. A German pilot then confessed to having shot Antoine down. He must have seen he carried no weapons?

I had been with the ONI about a year when they offered me a special project. They said I would stay in the same office but would be keeping records for only a single mission. They also told me I couldn't be briefed about the work until I accepted but that only made it all the more interesting. The project would later be identified as Benson House and operated out of an ordinary house in the tiny village of Wading River about forty miles east of Penterra kind of next door to Nicolai Tesla's old Wardenclyffe Tower. A couple lived there with their German shepherd, Clifford. The husband was supposedly suffering from highly contagious tuberculosis and his "dutiful wife" was nursing him back to health.

Of course, they might not have been married and he certainly wasn't sick. The dog's name was Clifford though. Two or three other agents also worked on the second and third floors. All their comings and goings were done in the dead of night with Clifford serving as security detail. Though I never saw the place, I would learn the dense trees surrounding the house were laced with radio antennas connected to a shortwave radio. To keep the local electric company from noticing any unusual power usage the radio transmitters were powered by a Buick engine bolted to the floor in the basement with the car's muffler redesigned as a silencer. The house sat on a 150-foot bluff overlooking Long Island Sound which facilitated optimal radio reception. The agents in the house intercepted coded German messages sent from Hamburg and responded to them with combinations of true and false information designed to be confusing. Their German handlers believed they were communicating with their own agents in New York.

The work of this little group produced some remarkable results. They managed to keep the German army from advancing on the Eastern and Italian fronts, masked the size and location of Allied forces and helped to obscure the true date and location of the D-Day landings. It was this relatively small unit that also discovered Hitler's interest in atomic explosions that finally convinced President Roosevelt to initiate a US atomic weapon program.

War often brings together different races and highlights the cultural commonalities among them. One amazing story I learned certainly illustrated this.

The small, strategic Pacific island of Saipan was occupied by the Japanese and US troops were attempting to take control of it. The task had been challenging; in one fifteen-hour battle, 30,000 Americans had been killed. An eighteen-year-old Mexican American marine was among the men stationed there. Because he had been adopted by a Japanese American family and grown up in a poor Los Angeles neighborhood he was both street-smart and fluent in Japanese.

One day while out on patrol by himself, he noticed that a large number of Japanese soldiers seemed to be hiding in some caves on a cliff. Somehow he came up with a crazy plan to get them out in the open. When he would see two guards outside a cave, he'd shoot them both then yell in Japanese, "You're surrounded! You have no choice but to surrender! Come out and you will not be killed! I assure you, you will not be killed!" Anyone who ran out with a weapon, he would also shot. But if any soldier came out slowly he would try to talk them into returning to the cave and convince others to surrender. The first time he tried his outrageous idea, he returned to the base with two Japanese prisoners. His commander was not impressed and told him if he left his post again he'd be court-marshaled. The young Marine, however, decided to ignore the order and went out alone again the next morning. This time he returned with fifty prisoners. His commander thought he was crazy but decided to let him carry on as a free agent. On his next patrol he actually convinced eight hundred men to surrender! This was followed by an even more astonishing success. As group of marines came up over a ridgeline they saw 1,500 Japanese soldiers all still carrying their weapons, standing around the lone private. I can just imagine what they said to each other.

Later, he explained how he talked them into giving up. When a few soldiers would come out of a cave peacefully, even if they still had their weapons, he'd ask them to "Please sit down." Then he'd offer them cigarettes and tell them, "I am here to bring you a message from General Smith, the shogun in charge of this operation. General Smith

admires your valor and has ordered his troops to give safe haven to all
the survivors of your intrepid attack. Such glorious and courageous
military action will go down in history. The general assures you that you
will be taken to Hawaii, where you will be kept together in comfortable
quarters until the end of the war. The general's word is honorable. It
is his desire that there be no more useless bloodshed." Then he would
point to the hundreds of US ships offshore and say, "The American
Navy can kill all of you." The men would then usually mumble to
each other as their leader accepted a cigarette and asked about medical
facilities on the base. The marine would reply, "Yes, we have fine, well-
equipped doctors. How many wounded do you have?" After some
quiet talking among themselves their leader would reply, "So be it, I
become your prisoner." Then he would return to the cave with some of
his men while the single marine would carry on a conversation with a
few of the Japanese he'd left behind. He'd ask them about their families
and where they lived. He would also tell them where he lived, talk
about his foster family, how much he loved them and tell them he
believed the common soldier just obeyed orders and had nothing to
do with starting a war. They'd agree and say how much they loved
American cigarettes. Within an hour or so, more "prisoners" would
usually come out of the cave and join the men sitting in front of the
American private. Later he told his commander that the men didn't
look defeated but rather serious and proud of their decision.

Private Gabaldon was awarded the Silver Star, the Navy Cross,
and the Medal of Honor. He obviously understood Japanese culture
and spoke to those soldiers in a genuine, sympathetic way that took
that into consideration. But this story also provides an example of the
many things people of all cultures share—the desire to live in peace,
have a rewarding and productive life and be surrounded by family and
friends. Then there are those that just want power over others, usually
at the expense of ordinary people.

By August, after a two-year lapse in production, appliances like
vacuum cleaners and ranges were again being manufactured in the
United States. All I could think was, what a great excuse not to have
to clean the house! In 1940 the Nazis had taken over Paris but by
August 26, 1944, they were hastily preparing to evacuate ahead of the
Allied troops marching toward the city. During the years of German

occupation Hitler's men had enjoyed a cosmopolitan Parisian life so unlike their lives in Germany. I couldn't help but think at least some of them must have been sad to leave? Of course while enjoying the "City of Light" they busied themselves sending 13,000 Jewish citizens and their families to Auschwitz. Before the Nazis abandoned Paris, Hitler ordered his military governor to blow up all the city's iconic landmarks and leave everything in rubble. SS engineers had just begun to set up the explosive charges when the Nazi governor in charge surrendered all 17,000 of his men to the Allies and 15,000 American and Free French soldiers liberated the city as huge crowds lined the streets and enthusiastically welcomed them. Some Parisians were not quite so happy though; 10,000 French Nazi sympathizers would be arrested for collaborating with the enemy.

During his confinement as a POW England that same military governor was recorded saying, "We all share the guilt. We went along with everything. We took the Nazis seriously, instead of saying, to hell with you and your stupid nonsense. I misled my soldiers into believing this rubbish. I feel utterly ashamed of myself. We bear more guilt than those uneducated animals."

September 3 the Welsh Guards liberated Brussels and celebrated with a mock funeral for Hitler. Even more residents in that city had supported the Nazi ideology and 60,000 of them fled to Germany as another 56,000 were arrested and prosecuted for enemy collaboration.

That September, a category 4 hurricane hit the east coast of Florida with 145-mile winds and waves of seventy feet; a US destroyer and her crew of 240 were lost. As it moved up the coast a fifty-foot storm surge also devastated the Carolinas and Cape Hatteras. Then it swung out over the eastern end of Long Island and up through Rhode Island, Massachusetts, and Maine where it sank two Coast Guard cutters, a minesweeper, and a lightship. The death toll was over four hundred with most of the losses occurring at sea.

President Roosevelt was elected to an unprecedented fourth term with 54 percent of the electoral college; 68 percent of the press, however, had endorsed his opponent, Mr. Dewey.

In Hungary the Nazis executed a Jewish resistance fighter after torturing him for months. An eighteen-year -old man was also caught in the street without his yellow star badge and was beaten to death. I wondered how a person could be so filled with so much hate that they would be unable to stop themselves from doing such a cruel thing.

At the end of November one night in Maine, heavy snow was falling and it was twenty degrees at 11:30 PM. On a desolate back road covered with deep snowdrifts two men in light overcoats were trudging along lugging heavy suitcases. A passing taxi stopped to ask them if they needed a ride and the two got in. The driver took them to the nearest train station where they boarded a 2:00 a.m. train for Portland. After arriving they shopped for clothes, rented a room, and went to sleep in their new outfits to "un-new" them.

Before their chilly walk in the snow they had been deposited on a local beach by two men in uniform who saluted "Heil Hitler" before pushing off for a waiting submarine. The sleeping men were supposedly spies, but again, Germany seemed way too casual about training. Perhaps incompetence was a desirable trait? If so, these two were stellar choices.

One of them was a former German diplomat of the dinner jacket sort. The other was a Connecticut-born graduate of MIT who had taken a job as a ship's cook in order to cross the Atlantic so he could volunteer to help Hitler; "smart" doesn't mean smart in everything. The two men's mission was to find out about the Manhattan Project, as if wandering around a bus station or standing on a street corner could yield such information. To ensure the success of the project they had also undergone intense though slightly unusual training in how to act American. This consisted primarily of learning the latest dance moves, popular songs, baseball facts and Hollywood gossip...just the sort of things physicists and mathematicians at Manhattan Project would be interested in?

Before departing Germany the MIT agent saw a chance to make a "little" extra money. He convinced his handlers that no American could possibly live on less than $15,000 a year; in reality, the average family managed on $2,200. Just to be sure they had enough to "get by" their German handlers had also loaded them down with $60,000 ($650,000 today) and ninety-nine small diamonds!

Back in Portland after diligently wrinkling themselves the two men boarded a train for New York. Upon arriving they immediately hit the streets to look for an apartment. This took an entire week because they needed a building that wasn't made of steel because that would have interfered with their radio transmissions home.

Meanwhile off the coast of New England the U-boat that had dropped them off headed south. When it encountered a freighter the captain couldn't resist and fired a torpedo that sank the vessel. This alerted the FBI that German agents might be in the area and after a little investigating the taxi driver and the two "snow men" turned up.

In New York, MIT man suddenly decided spying wasn't really the career for him and he fled to Grand Central Station taking both suitcases with him. After stashing them there at baggage claim he went for a drink with some friends. A few beers later he was boasting about being a Nazi spy. Though his friends thought he was kidding one decided to report him to the FBI, who promptly arrested him. His partner eventually turned himself in.

November 29 a surgeon and his female assistant performed the very first open-heart surgery at Johns Hopkins in Baltimore. The procedure had actually been invented by the assistant. How is it that such achievements by women are seldom recognized publicly?

David and Jeanne were expecting their first child August 9 the following year. Babies were still being delivered under total anesthetic then, so the doctor just gave you your child's birthday right after he determined you were pregnant. Much later we learned this sort of anesthesia was good for the doctor's schedule, not the baby.

December 15 the hugely popular trombonist Army Major Glenn Miller was flying to Paris to arrange a Christmas concert for US troops. Tragically his plane disappeared over the English Channel in that famous fog and was never found.

Ten days before Christmas a forty-two-car freight train left Hungary for Switzerland with a very special Nazi cargo. Everything on the train had belonged to Hungarian Jews who were forced by their pro-German government to "voluntarily contribute" their valuables to help finance Hitler's world takeover and the extermination of the Jewish people. The train carried ten thousand pounds of gold, seven hundred pounds of diamonds and pearls, 850 cases of silverware, five thousand rugs, furs, furniture and over 1,200 old master paintings. Everything had been carefully documented and the "donors" had even been issued receipts. In total everything was valued at $350 million ($64 billion today). The secret cargo had to travel barely a hundred miles the trip but was delayed by numerous unscheduled stops, and took three months. SS soldiers alone attempted to wrest control of the train from its Hungarian guards ten times. Finally the caravan stopped just short of the Swiss border where the guards learned the Allies would prevent the train from crossing into Switzerland. As Hungary was on the Axis side of the war, they opted to abandon it just outside Salzburg, Austria rather than risk imprisonment by US soldiers. After the train and the huge number of heavy crates were discovered by Allied troops, everything was moved to a warehouse though a few more things again "disappeared" along the way. Upon hearing that their treasures had been confiscated, the Hungarian government demanded the return of its property. The Allied commander had other ideas and declared everything "unidentifiable" even refusing to allow anything to be inspected. Some of the items were used to furnish the villas of Allied officers, while others ended up for sale in army stores or were distributed to the needy. It was believed Austria had taken possession of the art and gold before the train was abandoned. What was left was eventually auctioned off in New York and brought a mere $52,000 which was distributed to Jewish refugees.

That December, the US Supreme court upheld the validity of wartime interments but also ruled they could not continue. By then those poor people had lost their homes and businesses and were penniless.

In the Philippines, a typhoon with winds of 140 miles an hour, high seas and heavy rain sank three US destroyers, killed 790 sailors, and destroyed one hundred planes on the deck of an aircraft carrier.

In Europe, the Battle of the Bulge began in mid-December. It was named for the shape of the front line on the borders of Luxembourg, France, and Belgium. The forty-day conflict would turn out to be the most difficult battle of World War II but it would also be Hitler's last major offensive. Seven hundred thousand Allied troops with 2,400 tanks fought 449,000 Nazis with 557 tanks. During the brutal fighting

19,000 Americans lost their lives but Hitler may have lost as many as 125,000. More importantly, however, he would be unable to replace these men.

The Women's Air Force Service Pilots were deactivated five days before Christmas. That was a sure sign that things were coming to an end at least in Europe. During World War II, 1,800 skilled WASP pilots had logged sixty million hours ferrying planes, towing targets for live artillery practice and transporting cargo in 12,650 airplanes of seventy- eight different types. Some women had even flown experimental rocket and jet-propelled aircraft. In the process, thirty-eight of these brave and accomplished women had lost their lives. Shamefully the US Army refused to award them any military honors for their service or even allow their caskets to be draped with an American flag! It made me so angry.

1945

By the beginning of 1945, many of US government officials believed the Nazis had lost but that didn't change the need to continue fighting on the ground and in the air war.

In a single hour January 2, the Allied bombing of Nuremburg destroyed 90 percent of the city; tragic certainly, but Hitler and Germany's fanatical support of him made it necessary.

Auschwitz was liberated by Soviet troops January 27. Guards again had anticipated their arrival and forcibly marched 60,000 inmates out of the camp. Some of them were so severely malnourished that 15,000 died on the way to wherever the Nazis thought you could hide that many people. If anyone fell and couldn't get up, they were immediately shot. When the Soviets arrived at the camp they were confronted by 7,000 living human skeletons. During the four years the camp had operated one million Polish Christians, Gypsies, POWs, Slavs, mentally ill, handicapped, religious and political leaders, Free Masons, Jehovah's Witnesses, criminals, homosexuals and Jews had met horrible deaths at the hands of deranged Nazis. Though most people now know about the gas chambers, they probably didn't know about the other vile things Hitler's men did to their prisoners to ensure their deaths were violent, painful and excruciating; deliberate starvation and overwork, firing squads, hangings, even crucifixions were not uncommon. Horrendous living conditions also brought on deadly outbreaks of disease that caused others to die. Then there was the commandant's wife's private bear pit! Some prisoners were also intentionally injected with diseases and poisoned to see how much was needed to kill a person. Eventually the commandant himself was imprisoned in his own camp and executed not for cruelty but corruption and "exploiting" the prisoners—whatever that could possibly have been.

Hitler had somehow gotten his soldiers to commit the most unspeakable things ever known to man.

The day Auschwitz was liberated Nazi soldiers on the Baltic coast killed 11,000 Jews in a small town. Almost simultaneously, a Russian U-boat sank a German liner carrying eight thousand Prussian refugees; all of them drowned.

During thirty-six successive nights beginning in early February the United States filled the skies over Berlin with over a thousand bombers that killed 25,000 people on the ground below. As many as 120,000 survivors were also left without homes. By the end of March there had been 314 Allied bombing raids on the city and at least one-third of Berlin's buildings had been reduced to rubble. Photographs of the devastation made it hard to believe there had ever been a large city there. This is what happens when people choose a maniacal, irresponsible leader... the world fights back.

Dresden, our lovely home for two years, was also bombed on that Valentine's Day. It must have been terrifying to hear the sound of 1,300 planes overhead and see bombs raining down everywhere; 25,000 people were also killed in that raid. Some of them must have been people we knew. Out in the Pacific a thirty-six-day battle to take the tiny island of Iwo Jima from the Japanese was raging in February. During the fighting 25,000 Japanese died but we would lose 7,000 of our own boys. A single Kamikaze pilot caused so many explosions on an aircraft carrier that the ship sank and took 218 sailors down with it.

During two days in early March Allied planes dropped over 1,600 tons of bombs on Tokyo many of which carried that horrible napalm. Sixteen square miles of the city were pulverized, 286,000 buildings were destroyed and 100,000 people were killed.

By March 7 US troops had crossed into Germany for the first time.

Ten days later 1,800 American bombers attacked Berlin.

The United States had discovered a uranium production facility in Strasbourg, Germany but it was in imminent danger of being captured by advancing Soviet troops. To avoid a volatile confrontation with an ally, the United States destroyed it in a bombing raid. Stalin was not happy when he learned about what had been snatched from his grasp; he was definitely someone the United States thought wasn't stable enough to ever possess of such weapons.

By the end of March a report reached President Roosevelt's desk that listed the 349 Americans and foreign residents living in the United States who'd been spying for the Soviet Union. It turned out that some of them even worked for the federal government and the Manhattan Project!

On strategically positioned Okinawa the Allies had amassed a huge arsenal to try to take control of the island; 490 ships, 450 aircraft and 183,000 men 1000 of whom were underwater demolition experts. At one point during the fighting the Japanese had suffered so many casualties that the United States suggested they surrender. Instead Japanese soldiers handed out grenades to the civilian population and demanded they kill themselves to avoid being taken prisoner; five hundred actually did! The battle raged on for nearly two months with horrendous losses on both sides; 12,000 Allied soldiers died and 110,000 Japanese; 92 percent of their army! Their leaders became so desperate for personnel that they forcibly conscripted 40,000 locals. All of them would die, as well as, 150,000 other civilians.

I do not think the American public truly realizes the enormous loss of life that results when a country goes to war. These numbers have only increased with advances in weapon technology. After a generation or two, when all the men who fought in and survived these conflicts are gone, there is nobody to remind succeeding generations of the devastation.

In early April, US troops liberated the Ohrdruf camp in Germany. This was our first look at what Nazis did in their concentration camps. Prior to our arrival, as always, the guards evacuated more than 11,000 prisoners and shot those too sick to walk. They did leave some horrible evidence behind though: living skeletonized human beings and huge piles of corpses that had obviously starved to death. Generals Eisenhower and Patton were notified of the situation and came to see the carnage. I suppose the descriptions they were given must have been so appalling they couldn't believe they were true. After walking among the survivors and seeing the devastation for himself, Eisenhower said, "The visual evidence, the starvation and cruelty left me sick." Patton refused to enter a room filled with forty corpses; he said he'd be sick. General Eisenhower was so appalled he arranged for a group of American congressmen and journalists to come to the camp to view what the Nazis had done. During interviews with the survivors, inmates told of the 3,000 prisoners who'd been shot during the previous three months.

On April 12 in Warm Springs, Georgia President Roosevelt died unexpectedly at his vacation home. At the time, he'd been sitting for a portrait by Long Island's famous Russian-born watercolorist Madame Elizabeth Schoumatoff; her paintings are truly masterpieces.

I thought President Roosevelt had done a remarkable job during an exceedingly difficult time in America. A big part of that success was the result of his empathy for the many American families that had no wage earner, lived in extremely substandard housing, and could barely afford food, much less clothing or shelter. Those living on the edge of poverty suffer terribly when the economy collapses. The president instituted programs that helped these people survive until the Depression began   to abate. The well-off are often so removed from the struggles of the country's poorer citizens that they cannot understand their desperation and often respond callously. Roosevelt's policies were especially remarkable because he had grown up in a very wealthy family and such thinking was contrary to his class. Sometimes people become more empathetic after they themselves experience tragedies over which they have no control. The president, with great difficulty, managed to adjust to permanent paralysis and run for president. This required a great deal of perseverance on his part, a triumph of sheer force of will and determination in the face of almost overwhelming adversity. No one had ever run for president from a wheelchair. Because of he knew what misfortune looked like, the president had the desire to help those less fortunate, who hadn't grown up with the wealth his family had enjoyed. But because of his compassion, generations of Republicans would remember him as a traitor to his class. I always think of him as a compassionate and intelligent leader who set a fine example for all Americans.

The day the president was buried Hitler proclaimed, "Fate has removed from the Earth the greatest war criminal of all time." Mercifully, just sixteen days later the greatest war criminal of all time would be dead.

On April 15 Bergen-Belsen was liberated by British troops. They found 40,000 unburied emaciated corpses and 60,000 barely alive inmates. British soldiers were so appalled that they went to the nearest village and forced residents to walk through the camp to personally see the inhumanities what their country had done in the woods around them. I will never believe they didn't know. Back in Britain upon hearing about the condition of the survivors the government sent food, clothing and doctors and nurses to try to help these poor people. In spite of their efforts another 40,000 died within a month of the camp's liberation. It is difficult to imagine the huge numbers of people murdered at the hands of the Nazis in these camps. If Bergen-Belsen was the town where you lived, 1,000 people would die of starvation, disease or be executed every day … for six years! As Russians troops battled the Germans on their way to Berlin, 3,000 men on both sides died for every mile of fighting! Stalin's soldiers were eventually victorious but the victory cost the country of 110,000 Russians men.

Shortly after President Roosevelt's burial the Allies began a two-week bombing campaign of Berlin; 45,000 tons of explosives would be dropped, killing 20,000 people and destroy nearly the entire city. By the end of the month an estimated 1,700,000 civilians had fled the city in terror. By then the United States had amassed 4,500,000 men on the western side of Germany but the Allies had agreed to stand down and allow Stalin's army of 2,500,000 soldiers, 6,300 tanks, and 8,500 planes to advance on Berlin from the east. As he heard that Stalin was marching toward the city, Hitler declared Berlin was impregnable and must be defended. Easy to say when you're hiding in a concrete bunker underground. The city was so short on soldiers to defend it that SS troops began forcibly conscripting boys in the street as young as twelve and old men who'd fought in World War I, even women.

When they discovered people hiding from their recruitment efforts they immediately hanged them. Bodies were reportedly hanging from trees and lampposts everywhere in the city and frightened young boys were seen at defense positions wearing grossly oversized uniforms and clutching heavy artillery. The remaining civilians still in the city were apparently terrified. It was not so long ago that these same people had probably been among the crowds enthusiastically one-arming their Füehrer. When their own soldiers began telling them the war was going badly for the country because the German people hadn't sacrificed enough. It must surely have been evident that their beloved Nazi leadership had abandoned them.

Amid all these horrible reports, a bright spot appeared in New York when the team of Rogers and Hammerstein gave us the musical *Carousel*. Though the 1909 play on which it was based was set in Budapest, Hungary the setting for the Broadway production was Maine. The music was lilting and lovely, just what we needed. Beautiful things still existed in this cruel world of death and carnage.

April 21 in the French-occupied German town of Haigerloch US officials with the Manhattan Project found the Nazi's prototype nuclear reactor and arrested all the scientists working there. According to the British Germany wasn't able to build a nuclear reactor because they didn't know the mathematical calculations needed and did not possess the needed materials. The Manhattan Project raiders also discovered that Hitler was in control of the largest uranium field in Europe, just as Leo Szilard had warned, and even found evidence that Germany had tested three nuclear bombs. One was exploded on an island in the Baltic Sea October 12, 1944. Two others seemed to have been detonated near a military base in Ohrdruf March 2 and 4, 1945. There were also notes indicating seven hundred prisoners from Ohrdruf and Buchenwald had intentionally been part of these tests and all of them had died.

As a direct result of Hitler's persecution of Jews eight brilliant German nuclear scientists left the country and became part of the Manhattan Project. It seems Hitler might very well have been ahead in the nuclear bomb race, a very scary thought.

By April 24 the Russians had practically surrounded Berlin and many of the remaining German soldiers in the city began moving west to surrender to US forces rather than be captured by Russian troops. When Hitler heard that Stalin's troops were advancing on the city through a subway tunnel, he ordered the entire system flooded. This not only killed those enemy soldiers but also tens of thousands of wounded German troops and frightened civilians who had taken refuge from the fighting in them. I'm sure he didn't give them a moment's thought.

As US troops swarmed toward Munich from the west they liberated Hitler's first concentration camp Dachau. There they found thirty-one freight cars filled with dead bodies. During the twelve years Dachau was in operation including the five before World War II even started, over 35,000 human beings from nineteen countries were murdered there and in its 123 sub-camps. Though the guards certainly used gas chambers and firing squads, they also invented other sadistic ways to kill; injections of malaria and tuberculosis, decompression chambers, forced standing and running, beating, hanging by one's wrists, even intentionally bleeding some inmates to death. The Americans also found a strange "museum" of plaster casts of the physical deformities from which some of the inmates had suffered. By early 1944, the SS seemed aware that Germany was not going to win the war and went to great lengths to remove evidence of their crimes against humanity. A last directive by Hitler authorized prisoners held in northwestern Germany be taken to the North Sea and forcibly drowned! Meanwhile as everything above ground in Berlin was being pulverized, Hitler had been living underground in his custom-built Fuhrerbunker for at least a month. When Russian troops eventually began advancing toward his hideout and he was informed they couldn't be stopped, he married his thirty-three-year-old mistress Eva Braun. They had a lovely twenty-four- hour honeymoon in that desolate tunnel and then he gave her his wedding present, a cyanide pill; such a gentleman. Twenty-three years her senior Hitler then shot himself April 30. Upon learning of his death Goebbels lamented, "The heart of Germany ceases to beat." He then became the Germany's top Nazi but only for a day. May 1 he poisoned his eight little girls then went outside with his wife and ordered his men to shoot them both; fine examples of courageous leadership!

That day marked the death of the Third Reich twelve years, three months and six days after it was created. It was staggering to think that all those cruel deaths and terrible destruction were the result of just one man's obsession with power. Seventy-one countries had participated in World War II and 60 percent of the casualties had been civilian. By comparison only 5 percent of the deaths in the First World War were civilians. What will happen if there's another great war? It's also mind-numbing to consider not only what the German people had done to their own country but the devastation they brought on the rest of the world. In the final analysis Hitler had operated 20,000 concentration camps all over Europe and executed eleven million men, women, and children six million of whom were Jews. A truly horrific vision to contemplate.

The Nazis had always maintained strong prohibitions against their troops using alcohol and consequently, huge stashes had been hidden all over Berlin. As Stalin's armies marched through the city one by one they were all discovered. This led to a great many celebrations involving large, burly, drunken Russians and non-consenting local woman. It was estimated that as many as 100,000 rapes occurred during the Soviet invasion of Berlin. It is also believed that they directly led to 10,000 deaths and 30,000 thirty suicides. Will the carnage never end?

Germany officially surrendered at 2:41 the morning of May 7. Hitler's depraved work had finally stopped! The United States, Great Britain, Russia and the Free French Provisional government assumed authority over Germany. The separate Potsdam Agreement set up war reparations and territorial boundaries while various other treaties settled other issues. Sadly, many of the countries that had existed in Europe before the war were put under given Stalin's control and wouldn't see their independence again for decades.

In Mid-May a Nazi U-boat was crossing the Atlantic on route to Japan. Besides its unusual destination it had some other odd things onboard; four Japanese passengers, a dissembled jet plane, a guided missile and half a ton of uranium ore—just enough after processing to arm a single atomic bomb. As the ship neared the United States coast, the captain learned of Hitler's death and Germany's surrender. He decided to surface and surrender his ship at the nearest US port Portsmouth, New Hampshire. Everyone on board was taken prisoner and his cargo was seized. Three months later, the confiscated uranium reportedly became part of one of the atomic bombs dropped on Japan.

Heinrich Himmler studied agricultural economics in college but ultimately chose a decidedly different career. Not only did he establish Hitler's one-million-strong Secret Police he also set up and was the commander of all Hitler's concentration camps. Toward the end of April 1945 Himmler also seemed to have realized Germany was going to lose the war. Without the Führer's knowledge he attempted to broker a peace deal with the Allies. When Hitler learned about it and was so furious ordered Himmler's arrest. He managed to avoid capture though and went into hiding. Finally he decided to try for the border but was detained by the British. Though they wouldn't release him they didn't realize who he was. I suppose he felt trapped and eventually he decided to reveal his identity. When he was returned to his cell he swallowed a cyanide pill.

In Holland Dutchman Han van Meegere felt art critics had ruined his painting career by writing that he lacked ability. Furious he devised a unique plan to show them how talented he really was. He began painting original works of art in the style of the Old Dutch masters. He also decided to sign their names, rather than his own. Ultimately he found a ready market for his special paintings by touting them as "recently discovered masterpieces". Art connoisseurs and museum directors snapped them eventually bringing him $11 million. After the war ended, however, one of his "masterpieces" was found in the art collection of Nazi Hermann Goering. Dutch authorities traced the sale of the work to van Meegere and he was arrested for the state crime of selling a Dutch "national treasure" to someone outside the Netherlands. After several weeks in prison, he decided to confess that he'd painted it himself and many others on exhibit in Dutch museums. To his credit, his paintings were so convincing, the authorities refused to believe him. Finally he volunteered to paint one under the watchful eyes of the police. This led to his trial for forgery. During court proceedings the very experts van Meegere had sold his newly "discovered" masterpieces to were subpoenaed to testify that they were forgeries. As none of them wanted to admit they'd been fooled, however, all of them swore they were authentic Dutch masterpieces and Van Meegere was acquitted! That meant that, once again, his ability went unrecognized!

That June, Bill and David resigned their commissions and along with Mary Lou, little Pamela and Jeanne, returned to live at Penterra.

I was overjoyed that the house would be alive again with my sons and their new families. I immediately resigned from the WAVES, as well, though it had been an enlightening and enjoyable experience. Our home was again filled with activity, laughing and conversation, guests and tennis in the afternoon, cocktails and dinner parties. It was wonderful and gave me a new attitude. I felt especially thankful that the boys had come home safely, as many sons and fathers had not. I also greatly enjoyed not hearing so much war news even though fighting continued in the Pacific Theatre.

In the New Mexico desert at the US Air Base at Alamogordo, the Manhattan Project was in full swing. The first US atomic bomb test was July 16 with the force of 20,000 tons of TNT; that was really difficult to actually imagine. It had been twenty-eight months since the project received its first funding and just three months since the discovery of Germany's nuclear research facility. Though the US government would never officially acknowledge Germany's involuntary "contributions" to that successful test after the two atomic bombs were dropped on Japan, the head of the Manhattan Project's research division was heard to remark that they were "made in Germany."

The very day the first bomb was dropped Hiroshima, the United States, Britain and our ally China asked Japan to surrender. The Japanese premier responded by instructing the country's press to ignore the request.

In New York, four million people cheered General Eisenhower in the largest tickertape parade in the city's history.

Meanwhile in Great Britain, a general election had voted the Conservative Party out of office and Winston as a Conservative was out of a job again. He was devastated. Apparently, Clementine tried to console him by saying, "Maybe it's a blessing in disguise." Winston sarcastically replied, "Very well disguised." I think she wanted him to come home and retire. All well and good but many men often lose themselves when they no longer have the job they've spent their whole life perfecting. It did seem ungrateful of the British public after all he'd done for the country, even staying in London during the war and enduring Germany's bombing campaign, but the public can be fickle in elections. His defeat brought the couple to America and they spent a week or so with us. Reg and I greatly enjoyed having them but I don't think it was all that delightful for Winston. Of course, I greatly enjoyed chatting with Clementine in French again and their visit reminded me that we'd known each other thirty years! In spite of some of the frightful things I'd thought Winston had done they seemed less important after so much time had passed.

While they were with us at Penterra there was a terrible accident in New York July 28. A US bomber was flying a routine transport mission over the city and was preparing to land in Newark, New Jersey. When the tower advised the captain the field was enveloped in dense fog, that visibility was zero and he was denied permission to land. He strangely ignored this and continued on to the Chrysler Building where he was to turn left but instead turned right. At 9:30 on a Saturday morning the bomber hit the seventy-ninth floor of the Empire State Building! The impact created a twenty-foot hole in the north side of the building and shot one engine out the south side. It came to a violent rest on the roof of another building a block away and destroyed a penthouse as the other engine and part of the landing gear hurtled down an elevator shaft. Tragically, eleven people in the building were killed, as well as, the pilot and two of the plane's crew. A female elevator operator was also injured and was put in an elevator to take her to the lobby where medical personnel were waiting to take her to the hospital. Unimaginably the cables of the elevator had been weakened by the crash and the poor woman plunged seventy-five floors to the ground but survived! Miraculously she survived! It would be the longest elevator plunge in which someone survived. What a frightening thing to imagine! On the West Coast of the United States ten days after that first atomic bomb test in New Mexico, a cruiser left San Francisco for Tinian Island in the Pacific 1,500 miles from Japan. On board were the disassembled atomic bomb jokingly referred to as "Little Boy." After unloading its cargo the ship proceeded to Guam. En route July 30, a Japanese submarine sighted the vessel and scored two direct hits and she sank in just twelve minutes. The radio operator was able to send out three distress signals before three hundred of his fellow crewmen were sent to the bottom with the ship as nine hundred others were thrown into shark-infested water.

Back at headquarters two men were supposedly monitoring radio communications that night but one was drunk and the other, a captain, saw the three distress calls come in but immediately announced they were just a Japanese trap. Then he headed to his cabin and gave strict orders not to be disturbed. Even after the ship failed to arrive as scheduled no one investigated. Meanwhile, the sailors treading water in the Pacific Ocean watched in horror as their shipmates were being devoured by marauding sharks. After enduring four days of exposure, dehydration, saltwater poisoning, and sharks attacks, a routine patrol spotted the group and a PBY was dispatched to survey the scene. After the pilot witnessed sharks actually attacking the survivors, he violated standing orders and landed to try to save the remaining men. He taxied to the men most in danger and helped as many as he could into the cabin. To save still more he strapped others to the wings and pontoons. With fifty-six additional people weighing down his aircraft he couldn't possibly take off but at least these men were now safe. His plane would never fly again. After all the survivors were finally rescued the huge plane was sunk where it floated. In the end, 583 of the original nine hundred died before they could be airlifted to safety. It was the greatest single loss of life in the history of the navy and the most recorded shark attacks in a single event.

Sometimes the military has strange ways of handling incompetence. Though the two men on duty monitoring the radio that night were reprimanded, the captain of the cruiser was court-marshaled for "failing to adopt an evasive zigzag course" and though the surviving crew members didn't blame the captain, the families of those who died did. They would harass him for the rest of his life. (*The captain killed himself on his front lawn twenty-four years later. When his body was found, he was clutching a toy soldier. After twenty-three more years, he was cleared of all wrongdoing.)

August 6 the United States dropped the first 9,600-pound atomic bomb on the Japanese city of Hiroshima. Within seconds 146,000 people were obliterated. Remarkably, even after seeing all the destruction and death inflicted on the city and his people, the emperor refused to surrender. Three days later the ten-thousand-pound "Fat Boy" was dropped on Nagasaki; fog had saved the people of Kokura, the original target. Even after another 68,000 of his countrymen were killed in seconds, it took six more days for him to surrender; apparently, saving face was a *very* important tradition.

After the first atomic bombs were dropped on Japan one of our top espionage leaders secretly admitted that at that time Germany had the best scientists, mastered the necessary theoretical work, were in possession of the needed materials and had the best chance of producing the first atomic bomb prior to the discovery of Hitler's facility in Haigerloch. That's a really scary thought!

David and Jeanne had their first child, a daughter, the very same day the second atomic bomb was dropped. She was born in the Harkness Pavillion at Columbia Presbyterian Hospital on 168th Street in New York. They chose the name Diana Shipley with her middle name coming from Jeanne's family. As was usual in that day, Jeanne stayed several weeks in the hospital. When they finally came home we had two beautiful granddaughters to admire and showoff. It felt like a family again, even without Reggie and Mummah. Probably because Mary Lou had brought their daughter home to a house without a nurse, she had declined our offer of one for Pamela. Jeanne on the other hand gratefully accepted and seemed delighted with the freedom it afforded her. We were glad to help as it gave us more time to enjoy her company. Because we subscribed to the "children should be seen and not heard" notion still prevalent then none of our grandchildren ate their meals in the dining room but were fed in the kitchen then whisked off to bed early, well before the cocktail hour.

On August 15 Japan finally surrendered and World War II was at last over everywhere. Please, may there never be another. And thank the Lord our two sons had survived it. Gas rationing ended that very day too.

Back in 1940 Himalayan-born John Birch became the first Mandarin- speaking Baptist missionary in China. Later he worked for the OSS and they gave him the rank of an air force lieutenant and during World War II he reported on Japanese activities for the Allies. August 25, 1945 Captain Birch was leading an American, Chinese and Korean party through the jungle in an attempt to reach an Allied POW camp in Japan. When the then twenty-seven-year-old Captain Birch was stopped by Japanese soldiers and they demanded he surrender his revolver, he refused. After a few terse words were exchanged they shot and killed him. He was awarded the Distinguished Service

Medal posthumously. Some years later he oddly became a right-wing conservative hero of some in the United States.

Before the war ended in the Pacific, the OSS had trained the Vietnamese-born Ho Chi Minh in intelligence gathering and, at one point, even saved his life when he contracted malaria. In the aftermath of the war the Japanese surrendered control of Vietnam and it reverted to its former status as a French colony. The French then made the crucial mistake of allowing the Viet Minh Nationalists to "maintain order" and permitted them to keep their weapons. This decision also allowed them to keep the former French leaders of the colony in jail and left the Communist leader Ho Chi Minh free to exert his authority as he pleased. Then the Allies decided to separate Vietnam into north and south in order to better control the occupying Japanese that had remained in the colony. China was given responsibility for the north and Great Britain was to administer the south. Meanwhile in the north, famine in the capital city Hanoi caused vulnerable, hungry peasants to turn to Ho Chi Minh for help. Eventually this dissatisfied group revolted and he took control of Hanoi. Then almost overnight Ho Chi Minh was declaring himself chairman of the provisional government of all Vietnam even though the country was divided. I suppose in an attempt to make everyone happy, the Allies allowed anyone living in either the north or the south to migrate to wherever they wished but after Ho Chi Minh gained control of the north and a million people fled to the south. Alarmed by this exodus he blocked a million others from leaving and his iron rule quickly escalated to crush all opposition. The United States seems to have a long history of enlisting and training allies that turn on us.

On a lighter note, that September Bess Myerson was crowned Miss America. The beautiful twenty-one-year-old Bronx-born Bess had studied piano at New York's High School of Music and Art and decided to enter the contest to further her music education. She would be the first Jewish Miss New York and, subsequently, the first Jew to be crowned Miss America. To me, one's religion didn't seem all that important in a beauty pageant but I think it took a few more years for many Americas to believe that Jews weren't very different from other Americans.

In October the creator of Walt Disney's *Bambi* cartoon character died in Switzerland. I don't think very many people would know he was also the author of a notorious pornographic novel; how novel!

It was around that time that Bill and David began talking about forming a company together. Reg was often there when they were tossing around ideas but for the most part, he kept silent. Leonardo was quite vocal and though he encouraged them he also kept bringing up their lack of experience in business and thought they needed the sort of learning that only comes from starting with in an industry with an entry-level position and gradually moving up. This way one learns every aspect of how a business works and is in a better position to be a productive leader. Privately Leonardo told me Sperry would be the perfect place for them to learn these things but Reg was not offering any job to either of them, even a lower-level one. It did seem strange that a father would be unwilling to give his sons the sort of opportunity a young man without family connections could never have hoped to secure. I guessed he wanted their character to be forged by independent hard work and possible "failure," as his father seemed to have done.

Finally, they decided on starting a business that would use David's somewhat limited abilities in engineering while Bill would be in charge of management. Reg still opted to be completely uninvolved.

As I tried to understand his thinking I was eventually forced to consider another possibility. Reg might have believed that neither Bill nor David was very capable and if he they worked at Sperry, their performances might embarrass him. That seemed unkind but plausible, especially considering what a perfectionist he was. At any rate, the situation was upsetting but seemed out of my hands. A "good" wife in the upper class didn't interfere with things that appeared to be in a father's domain.

But a very disturbing event suddenly cast a decidedly uglier light on Reg's stance. Quite by accident I happened to overhear a conversation between Bill and his father that really startled me. Bill was asking his father if he'd give them a loan to cover their start-up expenses. I will never forget Reg's response. In a very demeaning tone of voice he replied, "I'm not going to invest any money in your little company." He said some other derogatory things about their planned endeavor but I was so shocked I don't want to remember them. They actually seemed mean. As I'd never seen Reg behave this way toward anyone, much less his son, it was actually frightening.

Gimbels began selling America's first ballpoint pens in their New York store that year. They seemed quite expensive at $12.50 each ($164 in 2015 dollars).

A fifty-one-year-old, self-taught electronic wizard was working for Raytheon when he accidentally discovered that microwaves from a radar set had melted a candy bar in his pocket. So what's an inquisitive mind do? Make popcorn and try to fry an egg! The egg exploded but the Radarange was born. Ultimately it would be patented and the microwave oven was born. The story of the inventor was just as remarkable. As a child, he'd never been able to even finish elementary school because he had to go to work to support himself and the aunt with whom he lived. When he was old enough, he joined the navy and taught himself trigonometry, calculus, and physics from the books available in the military library and by the time he was forty-five, he was one of the world's authorities on radar tubes. I just love stories like that! They make you believe that extraordinary things can spring from seemingly ordinary circumstances and highlight how a person's innate ability often manifests itself without external encouragement. Sadly, this also probably means a lot of talented people never discover their abilities.

In early November, the trials of twenty-four Nazis began in Nuremberg, Germany. Considering their eleven million victims that number seemed astonishingly small. Later it would be discovered that many Nazi leaders had managed to escape to South and even North America. Oh, you mean they liked our system of government?

In early December, five bombers left the Naval Air Station in Fort Lauderdale, Florida, on a routine navigation training exercise. The instructor in charge had 2,500 hours of flying experience but he also had an unusual flying record. On several previous missions he'd gotten lost and even been forced to land in the water, twice! That alone should have consigned him to a less tasking desk job. But no, at ten minutes after two in the afternoon he took off with his fourteen students and headed northeast. The weather was clear, and the course was a standard triangular one. The first leg went fine but on the second leg both the instructor's gyrocompass and magnetic compass failed as well as the same instruments in one of his student's planes. Apparently, this served to severely disorient the instructor about his exact location and the landmasses over which the squadron was flying. Suddenly he thought they were over the Florida Keys rather than some islands to the east of Florida. This caused him to believe the mainland was to their east instead of west. His misperception caused him to order all four of the bombers to turn right instead of left. This gross error most probably headed all of them northeast and out over the Atlantic Ocean. When one of the students suggested they should simply fly west but the instructor overruled him. After three hours and fifteen minutes of flying time the group was probably about 230 miles off the east coast of Florida when they ran out of fuel and went down in the heavy seas and high winds prevailing in the area at the time. The five planes would have immediately gone under and no one would have known they were there. Almost four hours later a huge PBM flying boat was launched to search for the squadron and two more seaplanes soon joined it. Two hours and fifteen minutes after the PBM took off two ships in the area reported a huge midair explosion and the disappearance of a radar blip from their tracking screen. The PBM carried such a large supply of fuel it was often referred to as a flying gasoline tank. None of the fourteen men aboard her or the fourteen in the five bombers were ever found. All of this occurred in the infamous Bermuda Triangle where strange navigational anomalies reportedly occur.

Later I heard that a fifteenth airman had been scheduled to fly on the mission but the night before he'd experienced strong premonitions of danger in his sleep. In the morning he asked for and received permission to be absent.

Between 1942 and 1945 the US military lost ninety-five airmen in the Triangle; thirty-one every year! Reg assured me, however, that the area was no more dangerous than a great many other parts of the ocean. It still seemed a little spooky.

In early December a US military plane set a new coast-to-coast flying record of five hours and twenty-seven minutes. Having witnessed the trials of early aviation such an accomplishment seemed astonishing.

Tire rationing ended and the United States officially adopted the Pledge of Allegiance three days before that Christmas.

Between Christmas and New Year's Bill and David's plans for their company really began to take shape. They decided to concentrate on bidding for government contracts that involved products David thought he could engineer for less than their competitors. It actually sounded quite sensible. I was getting really excited even though Leonardo was still actively challenging them at every turn. He kept bringing up adverse situations, hypothetically difficult scenarios and asking questions about production costs, transportation problems and liabilities. In the end, none of these would doom them. Reg either wasn't home when these things were happening or wasn't interested; it was difficult to decide which was worse.

1946

January 1 Japan's emperor defied traditional Japanese custom and publicly declared he was not a god. Though it did sound a little funny to American ears the idea was definitely a widely believed part of Japanese culture and was a stunning announcement from their emperor. He also stated that the Japanese were not superior to all other races and not destined to rule the world, also something quite accepted by the Japanese people.

In early February Operation Deadlight concluded with the disposal of 156 German U-boats. The British were scheduled to sink 116 off the coast of Ireland but fifty-six proved to be in such poor condition that they sank before they could be towed to the designated location. Four others were in East Asia; Japan commandeered three and bought one. Norway was given another and one became a naval museum in, of all places, Chicago. On Valentine's Day 1946, the Electronic Integrator and Computer officially debuted at the University of Pennsylvania; you're forgiven if the name doesn't ring a bell. It will prove to be a very important invention in the coming years though. Project PX under the direction of the US Army, had taken three years and $500,000 ($6 billion in 2013) to invent a machine that could solve the complex numerical problems necessary in the calculation of artillery firing tables. If size was a measure of success, we seemed to have gotten our money's worth; the new machine took up 1,800 square feet and had five million hand-soldered connections. More importantly it was the first computer and would signal the start of a whole new world of possibilities.

In the middle of February a Soviet cipher clerk working at his country's embassy in Canada managed to identify twenty-two Russian spies working in the country. Apparently, he was about to be recalled to Moscow, didn't want to go and thought a few important documents would assure Canada's assistance when he defected. Some of the names on his list were scientists but one was actually a member of parliament!

Bill and David decided their new company would be called Gillmors Inc. and set about looking for a building to house both an office and a warehouse for production and shipping. They also began plotting how to obtain the financing needed to start their new business. It was wonderful to see them working together and acknowledging each other's strengths. Reg's statement to Bill, of course, completely left him out of all the planning and excitement. Sadly, it seemed that's the way he wanted it. As their mother, it also felt distinctly strange and unsettling. Reg could have done so much to help them and his business advice could have been invaluable at such a critical time in the lives of his sons. It felt like he had completely abandoned them.

At the US embassy in Moscow the vice-consul was having some disagreements with President Truman about US policies regarding Russia. The officer, an expert on the Soviet Union with over fifteen years of experience in the field, felt Washington was being naïve about Stalin. To clarify his position he sent a 5,500-word telegram February 22 to the US Secretary of State. In it he advised that there was little reason to cooperate with Russia as Stalin was plotting world domination by violent destabilization. Furthermore, he was promoting chaos in his own country to justify the cruel and oppressive treatment of his countrymen. The lengthy missive had the desired effect, dramatically changed US diplomacy toward the Soviet Union and led to the long-term containment of Russian aggression.

One evening in February I was in the drawing room with Bill and David having a drink. We were chatting about the company's latest news while waiting for Mary Lou and Jeanne to come down for dinner.

Reg was in a meeting and wouldn't be joining us. Suddenly Bill got very quiet, almost as though he had something to tell me but didn't really want to. Finally he said he'd talked to his father about loaning them money to help them start Gillmors, Inc. Then he went on to tell me how disappointed he was with his father's response. He didn't repeat everything I had heard but the message was the same. I tried my best to look surprised but the hurt and confusion in Bill's face was obvious and upset me terribly. I managed to mumble something about "I'm so sorry, maybe you misunderstood him. I'll speak to him," Both boys seemed to know I wouldn't be able to change Reg's mind though. Then Jeanne and Mary Lou appeared and the moment was gone. I will never forget it though.

February 24 Juan Peron was elected president of Argentina. Another despot had taken the reins of his country.

Winston came to the United States in early March to give a speech in Missouri. It would be the first time the phrase "Iron Curtain" was ever used. He said it referred to the divide between the Western powers and those under the control of the Soviet Union. It also marked the beginning of what would come to be known as the Cold War.

That March, the United Nations convened in London for the first time.

Bill and David finally settled on a building in nearby Hicksville as the headquarters for Gillmors, Inc. It had offices in the front and a large attached warehouse with a rail link behind the building.

It was then that I suggested to Mary Lou and Jeanne that we should have some sort of event to celebrate the company's opening. After tossing around some ideas we decided it should be a cocktail party at Penterra. The three of us then spent hours planning everything from the food to the music and, of course, the guest list. What a wonderful time we had. Finally we settled on Friday April 13 for our "launch" party. I know what you're thinking but both Reg and Jeanne's father thought thirteen was a lucky number. In fact, Jeanne said her father had almost every important event in his life happen on that date. When he had asked her mother to marry him he even wanted the wedding on that day but her mother wouldn't hear of it. We also worked endlessly on the guest list, trying to include not only all our friends but anyone we knew that was even remotely connected to engineering. We also chose a lively jazz quartet to play in the living room around the piano. Eventually, we sent out 250 invitations and received over 200 acceptances. It was going to be a very grand celebration and we were so looking forward to our big evening! I remember the three of us even went shopping together to find the perfect outfits. It felt like I now had "two daughters" to replace the camaraderie my sisters and Mummah had enjoyed so much. It was wonderful!

It was even exciting when the boxes of Gillmors' stationary arrived and we first saw the company's name in print. I was so proud of both my sons...and pretended Reg was as well.

By then I was fifty-three and would be fifty-four in just six months. Looking back at the early years of my life time seemed to flow along rather leisurely, punctuated by a few memorable events. As I'd gotten older the scenery of my life seemed to have rolled past with increasing speed, rather like a sled going down a long, icy hill. Before I really noticed, milestones were appearing and were gone before I was even able to remember the details. Then almost without warning the pictures were flying by as if caught in a storm with no time to imprint anything on my soul.

By April the United Nations was temporarily meeting at Hunter College in New York City while a permanent home was being built at the east end of Forty-Third Street. Then suddenly the facilities at Hunter became too small and Sperry's new complex was at the top of the list of larger spaces being considered. Just a week before our Gillmor's party Reg was telling me he had to go to Washington to negotiate a lease for part of the Sperry's headquarters in Lake Success. He told me he would be leaving for Washington on Wednesday but that he'd be back Friday afternoon in time for the party. After he left for work that morning I wasn't expecting him home but he returned before lunch and seemed very upset.

Almost immediately he said he wanted to talk to me in the library so I went in there and sat down. He came in after me and closed the doors; he never closed the doors. I was feeling a little nervous but convinced myself it was something minor. When we were both sitting he told me that Leonardo had given Bill and David $100,000 to start their company. As I knew nothing about this I was quite surprised.

It was a large sum of money and he'd given me no indication that he planned to help them financially. Reg then got a really strange look on his face that I will never forget. He said, "That is quite a lot of money, especially as Leonardo has clearly stated he thought neither of them had enough business experience to start a business or successfully run one." In fact, he went on, it seemed quite unusual that he would give them any money at all. Then he paused and stared at me, like he was waiting for me to say something. When I didn't he asked if I could explain why Leonardo would do that. I kept myself composed and replied that I knew nothing about the gift but thought it was very generous of him. As I spoke a horrifying picture was forming in my mind but I tried to focus the conversation on Leonardo's kindness and draw Reg's attention away from the why of it. After another uncomfortable silence, Reg looked directly at me and said, "Over the years, I have heard rumors about you and Leonardo having had a relationship but I never believed it." Right then I could have died; twenty-four years of fear was taking control of every molecule in my body. He continued, "If what I've heard is true, Leonardo's generosity might be because he thinks David is his son." Somehow I managed to put forth denials but inside I was terrified.

After what seemed like an eternity in silence he looked at his watch, said the car was here and he had to leave. He stood and announced that we'd talk about this later.

No, no, no … I didn't ever want to talk about it again, ever. Then suddenly I was alone, more alone then I'd felt in my entire life. I got a drink then tried to reach Leonardo but was told he was out of town and wouldn't return until Friday. I resolved I just had to decide what to do before then. Bill and David would be coming home and I couldn't face them. I went to my room and closed the door. But the more I thought the more upset and confused I became. I was beside myself with fear for David. I kept going over all the possible scenarios; each seemed more horrible than the one before it. Reg would disown David and he'd lose the only father he'd ever known. My children would be separated. What would become of Bill? Reg would make me leave. Where would I go?

Before long, I felt terrified of making any decision. I thought another drink might steady me enough to see things more clearly.

When the boys came home I told them I wasn't feeling well and not to expect me for dinner. Later the maid knocked on the door and asked if she could bring me something. I immediately thought, *yes, a new life!*

Eventually, it began to look as if there were no good choices; everything I envisioned seemed decidedly terrifying. All avenues pointed to certain heartbreak for my sons and our lives together. I couldn't bear to contemplate any of the paths I could see ahead; all were equally frightening. I had always loved Reg and never meant to hurt him. It had just been a silly Roaring Twenties attempt at independence. I had never wanted a life without him. But I had been unfaithful and he would never accept such a flaw in our marriage, however brief. Even if I confessed and begged to be forgiven it wouldn't change how he felt about David or me. If I denied everything, well I really felt I couldn't do that either. I went round and round grasping at any possible scenario that might make things right or even acceptable; each seemed like a terrible idea. I had another drink. Though it didn't make me feel better it dulled my senses to the catastrophe in front of me. Gradually I came to believe that my twenty-four-year-old secret spelled the ruin of everything I held dear. I had another drink and was overcome by a terrible sadness for David; he had done nothing to deserve this.

Then I happened to look at the clock on the dresser and saw that it was one in the morning. Oh my God, it was Thursday! What was I going to do? Reg would be home tomorrow. I gathered what was left of me and decided if I just got a little rest maybe I would be able to think more clearly. I changed for bed and lay down. I was so upset I couldn't seem to even feel tired. I took a sedative and lay down again. Somehow, I began to believe everything would be fine if I didn't say anything. That was it—no denial, no confession! My life would remain the same as it had always been. Everything would just stand still. I took another pill; maybe it was two. Then I remember feeling very peaceful … about finally having decided … to say nothing, no denial … no confession. A great, calm sense of relief came over me … it was the perfect decision. Everything would be all right.

No one would know anything and David would be safe.

After a little rest I opened my eyes and saw a chair leg directly in front of my face. I vaguely thought I must have fallen but somehow that was fine too … I would just lie there until I felt better.

Then I remember a lovely dream. I was on a ship sailing for England and dear Papa, Mummah and my beautiful sister Margot were standing beside me on the deck. A pleasant breeze was blowing, and I could smell the beautiful sea ... and the ocean was gently rolling by and surrounding us with peace.

CAPTION FOR STATUE
HEKATE

A Roman Empire marble statue carved in 425 B.C. of the Greek goddess Hekate carved in 425 B.C. and given to the Metropolitan Museum of Art in New York in memory of my grandfather Reg. Hecate ruled the Earth, Sea and Sky and her image was often placed at the front entrance to a home to protect the family within from the Evil outside.

The small marble statue of the Greek goddess Hekate dating from the Imperial Roman Period 100-200 AD. The three-sided deity represents the Earth, Sea and Sky and was usually placed at the entrance of a home to protect the family within from Evil. It was bequeathed by Reginald E. Gillmor to the Metropolitan Museum of Art upon his death in 1960.

This book is dedicated to Edwina, the grandmother I never knew, and the seventy-four year old mystery of her death. Her sad and premature departure has finally been resolved.

ABOUT THE AUTHOR

Miss Gillmor graduated with Honors from Parson School of Design after skipping a year and has been an interior designer in New York City and Maryland for decades. She presently lives on the Eastern Shore of Maryland where she also paints still-lifes and does children's portraits. In the past she also enjoyed training and showing dressage horses and fencing. While learning to fly small planes, she also owned and operated a flying school.

She was born in New York City and spent her early years living in Red Spring Colony, Glen Cove, New York. At that time her father was a Navy pilot and her mother a model. The family, along with her younger brother, aunt, uncle and their three children, lived in her grandfather's house "Penterra". Her grandmother also lived there but she died before Miss Gillmor was nine months old. Family life on the estate included a cook, two maids, a gardener, a chauffeur, a butler, a laundress and a nanny; exactly as her father and his brothers had been raised. Adult social life in the house included tennis matches on the "clay" tennis court, swimming and sunbathing on the private beach, a cruise on the family yacht and chauffeured trips to the city and parties. The house was ruled by English customs with dinner at eight in the dining room, served on fine china with monogrammed linens, crystal glasses, silver and fresh flowers. It was always preceded by cocktails with all the women in attendance appearing in long evening attire. These dining rituals did not apply to the children, however. They ate in the kitchen and were hurried off to bed, after a goodnight kiss, by a servant at 6:00.

Eventually, the family's "Gatsby Days" were transformed into a normal middle class life when they moved to a small house in nearby Cold Spring Harbor. The author never thought her early years were any different from the other children she encountered in her new neighborhood or during her years of education at public schools.

9 781649 081841